PORTRAIT OF WIRRAL

Portrait of
WIRRAL

by

KENNETH BURNLEY

ROBERT HALE · LONDON

First published in Great Britain 1981

ISBN 0 7091 9409 9

Robert Hale Limited
Clerkenwell House
Clerkenwell Green
London EC1R 0HT

Photoset in Great Britain by
Rowland Phototypesetting Ltd, Bury St Edmunds
and printed by St Edmundsbury Press, Bury St Edmunds
Bound by Weatherby Woolnough, Northants

CONTENTS

ILLUSTRATIONS

PICTURE CREDITS

The author and publishers thank Mr Ken Thompson for supplying nos 1–8 and 11–36, and Mr John Gittins for nos 9 and 10.

MAP

ACKNOWLEDGEMENTS

Many people, knowingly or unknowingly, contribute to a book of this nature. Librarians, vicars, family, friends, have all helped to make my job a little easier. I would particularly like to thank John Gittins for supplying the photographs of the seals and birds off Hilbre Island; David Smith of the Nature Conservancy Council for information about Reserves in Wirral; and Mr C. A. Humphreys and members of the Wirral Local Studies Group for a mine of useful up-to-date information on many aspects of Wirral's history.

I have consulted many published works, and gratefully acknowledge the use of extracts from the following: *History of the Hundred of Wirral* by William Mortimer (published by E. J. Morten Ltd); *The Verge of Wales* by W. T. Palmer, *Portrait of Cheshire* by David Bethell, *The Wirral Peninsula* by Norman F. Ellison (all published by Robert Hale Ltd); *Companion into Cheshire* by J. H. Ingram (published by Methuen & Co. Ltd); *A Perambulation of the Hundred of Wirral* by H. E. Young (published by Henry Young & Sons Ltd); *The Buildings of England: Cheshire* by N. Pevsner and E. Hubbard (published by Penguin Books Ltd); *The Rise and Progress of Wallasey* by E. C. Woods and P. C. Brown and *North Wirral Coastal Park: The Old Gun Site Picnic Area* (both published by the Department of Leisure Services, Metropolitan Borough of Wirral); *The World Jamboree 1929* (published by the Scout Association); and Woodchurch Parish Church School Play.

Thanks are due also to Mr Ken Thompson, who took the photographs under trying conditions in one of the worst summers of recent years!

To Mum and Dad
for introducing me to the beauty
and interest of Wirral,
and to Gill,
my wife, for sharing it with me

1

INTRODUCING WIRRAL

There's bright sunshine here in Malta, while at home are fog and rain,
With the wet wind on the uplands and the floods down in the plain.
But in spite of winter's weather I would far, far rather be
In the wide, sweet, open country 'twixt the Mersey and the Dee.

Though the woods are bare and leafless and the song-birds all are fled;
Though the flowers in the gardens and the hedgerows all are dead;
And the wet west wind comes sweeping in across the Irish Sea,
To wake the foam on Mersey Bar and flood the Sands o' Dee;

Yet, spite of wintry storm or rain or fog, I love it all,
And long to be on Thurstaston as evening shadows fall;
For no sight is half so beautiful or half so dear to me,
As the stormy, golden sunsets o'er the gleaming Sands o' Dee.

And when the war is over, with what joy shall I return,
To the fields and paths and commons and the woods for which I yearn;
To the moors and the uplands, and the salt kiss of the sea,
In the Hundred of the Wirral 'twixt the Mersey and the Dee.

Frank Jocelyn Priest, Malta, 1915

WHAT is the Wirral Peninsula? To many who work in Liverpool it is merely somewhere to come home to in the evening, somewhere to live, somewhere to shop. To the stranger it is "somewhere in Cheshire – or is it Merseyside now?" To many who live in Liverpool it is somewhere to spend a sunny afternoon.

To me it is standing on Caldy Hill under a clearing sky after a dull, wet day and hoping for a rare glimpse of Snaefell or the Lakeland summits across the wild waters of the Irish Sea. It is the hustle and bustle of Birkenhead Market on a Saturday afternoon, or waiting on Woodside landing stage in the damp gloom of a November morning for a ferry to Liverpool. My Wirral is Burton Marsh on a grey February morning, the Welsh peaks shrouded in mist; or the golden tints of Dibbinsdale woods on a bright October afternoon. It is the springtime greenery of silver birch on Thurstaston Hill, and carpets of daffodils dancing in the April breeze in the woods of Arrowe. Or dark winter days on the Mersey when sea, land, and sky merge to form one grey shroud. And rare days in the depths of winter when snow and ice drape the Dungeon falls and only the song of the robin pierces the silent woods. In my Wirral are breezy cliff-top walks above the wayward Dee, the romance of smugglers still in the air; and the deep cuttings of an old railway, now a country park, rich in wild flowers, birds and animals. My Wirral is to sit on the springy thrift-covered turf of Hilbre Island, the only sound being the call of the curlew and oyster-catcher sounding across the lonely sands of the Dee estuary.

To me and to all those who know and love Wirral it is all of these and so much more. This, perhaps, is the attraction of the piece of land which lies between the Rivers Mersey and Dee. Within its area of a hundred or so square miles are flour mills and oil terminals; seal colonies and salt marshes; housing estates and mansions; shipyards and nature reserves; a colourful history and a wealth of wildlife.

To the outsider, Wirral is generally considered to be a suburb of Liverpool. In fact, many often lump them together as one, and do not realize that 1½ miles of water separate Birkenhead and the rest of Wirral from their bigger neighbour. Until the boundaries were changed in 1974, the whole of the Wirral Peninsula was part of the county of Cheshire. Schoolchildren were often taught that the shape of the peninsula resembled the spout of a teapot, a hen's tail, or a cow's horn. Overnight, Wirral was put into the new county of Merseyside, along with Liverpool and a large slice of Lancashire. A sad change, some would say – a loss of identity for a part of England with its own unique character. Cheshire lost its coastline and its teapot spout when it lost Wirral. But Wirral did not go into Merseyside without a fight from some quarters. South Wirral, including the un-Cheshirelike towns of Ellesmere Port and Neston, remained in Cheshire. So, administratively at least, the peninsula is now divided and even has two postal divisions: Wirral, Merseyside; and South Wirral, Cheshire.

Seven years have passed since reorganization, but still many folk cannot accept that Wirral is part of Merseyside. In name, but not in character, they say. For Merseyside has an image, and that image is not a particularly good one. For the true Wirralian, his home is "over the water" from Liverpool and the rest of Merseyside. Indeed, looking at the map, Wirral is indeed an island from the rest of the county. Yet the majority of Wirral people work in Liverpool and use its shops and cultural facilities. Many were indeed born on the Lancashire side of the Mersey, or come from families who originated in Liverpool. The homes of many Wirral folk are nearer Liverpool city than many Liverpudlians'. Perhaps the relationship is similar to that which exists between Britain and Europe; *in* it but not *of* it. In both cases that narrow channel of water is more than a physical barrier – it is also a psychological barrier.

But what of the name Wirral? Anglo-Saxon records show the peninsula as "Wirheal", a combination of the Anglo-Saxon words *wir* (a myrtle tree) and *heal* (an angle, corner or slope). From this it would appear that bog-myrtle was once plentiful in this area, although it is no longer found today.

The peninsula has often been referred to as "the Hundred of Wirral". A "hundred" was a division of a shire or county, probably instituted by King Alfred, which was itself subdivided into tithings or towns. The origin of the word is uncertain; some say that it was a district able to provide one hundred able-bodied men of war, others that it was an area composed of one hundred families. The title persisted, and was frequently used by writers and historians, until the early years of this century. Alas, it is now simply "Wirral", "The Wirral Peninsula", or, incorrectly, "The Wirral".

The situation of the Wirral Peninsula, enjoying the benefits of a mild climate, easy access to the sea, and seclusion from the more traumatic events of history, has attracted men to make their home here down the ages. We know that Stone Age man lived here, from finds on Thurstaston Hill and elsewhere. During the Bronze Age, and until the time of the Romans, Wirral was occupied by a powerful Celtic tribe known as the Cornovii. The Celts probably gave us place-names such as Liscard, Noctorum and Landican.

The Romans occupied Chester about A.D. 70, and traces of their occupation in Wirral have been found from time to time. In 1834 workmen quarrying on the hill known as the Arno, in Oxton, found a number of small coins bearing the heads of Antoninus and Victorinus. Storeton Quarry may have been used by the Romans, for its stone was used to sculpture monuments, the remains of which have been found and can be seen in Chester Museum. Coins have been found at Neston and at Hooton. The greatest evidence of the Roman occupation in Wirral is, however, the large number of articles found along the shore at Meols, indicating an extensive Roman settlement. It appears that this settlement was connected by road with Chester, some twenty miles away; the route is uncertain, but it probably left Chester by the line of the present Parkgate road as far as Mollington, and then continued past Capenhurst to Ledsham. Its course from Ledsham is less certain, but a road-like surface has been excavated at Street Hey, near Willaston, and there is a lane near Raby which is on the line to Meols. Part of an ancient road, possibly Roman, has also been discovered in Greasby. There may have been another Roman road running from Monks' Ferry, on the Mersey shore, by way of Bridge Street towards Bidston and the coast at Meols. In 1850 a bridge was discovered by workmen converting Wallasey Pool into docks; this appeared to be Roman in origin, and may have been part of this route. The bridge was of solid oak beams supported by stone piers, its ends resting on solid rock at the sides of the creek. The length of the bridge was about one hundred feet. From the depth of the silt burying the bridge (about thirty feet), it must have been buried for centuries.

The Romans left about A.D. 410, and Wirral was occupied

by the Britons, who lived undisturbed for about two hundred years. The Anglo-Saxons under Ethelfrith, the Anglian king of Northumbria, laid waste Chester in A.D. 613 and soon took over most of Wirral, with the exception of Wallasey. The first settlement was probably at Willaston, and from here the early settlers established a branch to the east named Eastham, one to the south named Sutton, and one at Hinderton to the west. Many Wirral villages owe their names to these people, especially those ending in "ham" or "ton", both meaning a home or homestead.

All was peaceful in Wirral for over two hundred years, but in the latter years of the ninth century the Norsemen, the Vikings of the North, invaded our shores. We gain an insight into the character of these wild people, from the Anglo-Saxon Chronicle:

> They reached a waste city in Wirral, which is called Legceaster [Chester]. They besieged the fort from outside for some two days and took all cattle that were without there, and slew the men they were able to intercept without the fort, and burnt all the corn, and with their horses devoured the pasture in the whole neighbourhood.

The Norsemen were apparently attracted to Wirral because of its excellent harbours and proximity to the sea, for there is little evidence of their having occupied the rest of Cheshire. They settled along the Dee side of the peninsula, and along the sea coast, giving their villages names such as West Kirby, Frankby and Irby. They also introduced their own system of local government, and met at Thingwall, an area of high ground in the northern part of the peninsula. At their annual "Thing", or parliament, new laws were made, and other business of the area was transacted. In spite of their ways, it seems that the Norsemen soon settled down and became one people with their English cousins.

The Doomsday survey of 1085–6 shows that Wirral at that time was more densely populated than most other parts of England. Even so, the survey shows only 405 heads of families in the whole of the peninsula. Forty-eight manors were surveyed, with a total value of £51. There was very little woodland: one at Mollington, a large area at Tranmere, and a small one at Prenton. This shortage of timber was soon rectified, for Wirral was afforested from Norman times until the middle of the fourteenth century. At least, plenty of tree cover was provided for the preservation of game. It is most unlikely that the whole of the peninsula was covered with trees:

> Randal de Meschines, fourth Earl of Chester . . . converted Wirral into a forest. It does not follow, as assumed by the few authors who have directed their attention to this Hundred, that tree planting on an extensive scale was then carried out. It is certain that a very large part of the country was wooded from the earliest times, and a Norman forest was little more than a waste or wilderness in which game could flourish undisturbed.

Under an order by Edward III in 1376, Wirral was disafforested. Today the area is short of woodland once again. Roads, housing and neglect have left just a few small areas of woodland; Dutch elm disease has taken its toll of thousands of roadside and hedgerow trees.

Wirral's proximity to Chester had a profound effect on the history of the Dee side of the peninsula during the fourteenth, fifteenth and sixteenth centuries. Hundreds of years before Liverpool's rise to fame as a great port, Chester was providing facilities for trade with Ireland, Spain, and Germany. Seagoing vessels would "lay-to" at the mouth of the Dee, awaiting favourable winds and tides. But the Dee started to silt up from Chester northwards towards the estuary. Harbouring facilities moved to Burton, Neston, Parkgate, Gayton, Dawpool, West Kirby and Hoylake. The Dee side overshadowed the Mersey side of the peninsula for over three hundred years. Adventurous plans were proposed to overcome the silting-up of the estuary. One was put forward in 1857 by Sir John Rennie, who planned to cut a ship canal, 20 feet deep, from a point between Thurstaston and Heswall, to run along the length of Wirral to Chester. This and other schemes came to nothing. Deeside was dying, and Merseyside was being born. Liverpool was growing as a port of international importance, offering good communications by road and canal to the rest of the country, and a safer, more sheltered harbour for shipping.

The growth of Liverpool signalled the start of a new era for Wirral; an era of tremendous growth and rapid change. For as Liverpool grew as a centre of trade and commerce, its merchants and businessmen looked across the Mersey to the sandy shores and green fields of Wirral, and many "crossed over" to make their homes in Birkenhead. Ferries, trains, docks and commerce soon followed. Between 1810 and 1841 the population of Birkenhead leapt from 109 to a staggering 8,000. As the Mersey side of the peninsula became more industrialized, many moved out of the dirt and grime to the greener parts of Wirral. Growth was naturally greatest along the rail routes – the opening of the Hoylake line in 1866 enabled city-weary Liverpool businessmen to live within sight, sound and smell of the sea. This growth has continued to the present day and shows little sign of slowing down. Rural, land-based communities are disappearing under the spreading tide of suburbia. Nine hundred years ago there were about 2,000 people in the whole of Wirral; its population is now approaching half a million.

Two hundred million years ago the area of land we now call Wirral was part of a flat, sandy delta between the Welsh hills on the one side and the Pennines on the other. There was no peninsula as such. Geological pressures in the earth's crust gradually formed the layer of sandstone rock called Triassic sandstone, which was again subjected to stresses which pushed large areas upwards to form rocky outcrops. The outcrops now form two approximately parallel ridges which run down the length of the peninsula from north-west to south-east. Grange and Caldy Hills (256 feet) form the northernmost part of the western ridge, which includes Thurstaston Hill (298 feet), Heswall (359 feet, the highest point in Wirral), ending at Burton (222 feet). The only significant break in this sandstone ridge is between Caldy and Thurstaston Hills. It is thought that the sea once flowed through this valley to Moreton and Bidston Marsh, making an island of this north-western corner of Wirral. In fact Telford and Stephenson, the canal and roadway engineers, produced a scheme in 1825 to project a canal through the valley to Wallasey Pool on the Mersey shore. The Dee outlet would have been at Dawpool, near Thurstaston, thus linking the Mersey with the Dee. However, the silting-up of the Dee estuary, and the opposition of the Liverpool Corporation, who had a monopoly of the Mersey, prevented the scheme from being put into practice.

The sandstone ridge which runs down the eastern side of the peninsula is neither as long nor as continuous as its western counterpart. From New Brighton in the north the ridge rises to 188 feet at Wallasey; between Wallasey and the next high point of Bidston Hill (231 feet) is the valley formed by Wallasey Pool. The ridge continues south from Bidston Hill to Prenton (259 feet) and ends at Storeton Hill (229 feet). Much of this line of hills is now built over, but the Deeside hills are for the most part open, unspoilt heathland where the public are free to roam and enjoy the glorious panoramic views across Wirral and its surroundings.

During the Ice Age, great ice fields descending from the Scottish Highlands, the Lake District, and Northern Ireland pushed along the floor of the Irish Sea and were forced by ice masses from the Welsh hills to travel south-eastwards across Merseyside. The moving ice fields had a dramatic effect on the landscape of the area. They reduced the area of coastal land, which originally extended much further into the Irish Sea, and deposited large amounts of boulder clay, pebbles, mud, sand and other detritus all over the area. The effect of this depositing was to fill in many of the hollows and valleys, changing the landscape from an undulating, hilly area into a relatively flat one.

Since the Ice Age, the greatest natural factors in changing the landscape of Wirral have been coastal erosion and siltation. Until recent times, the flat, low-lying lands of north Wirral were constantly under threat of inundation by the sea, being protected only by a belt of sand dunes. Archaeological finds, together with evidence for the existence of a forest on the coast near Meols, suggest that there was human habitation perhaps extending several miles further beyond the present coastline, where the waters of the Irish Sea now lap. On the other hand Overchurch, several miles inland, literally means "the church on the shore", which suggests that the sea has alternately advanced and receded over the centuries. At Shotwick, ten miles upstream from the mouth of the Dee, sea water came up to the wall at the edge of the churchyard. Now the water is four miles distant, barely visible across the acres of marshland. There is evidence, too, that the Hilbre Islands, a mile off the coast in the Dee estuary, and only accessible at low tide, were once part of the mainland.

Between the sandstone ridges lies an extensive area of gently undulating land, much of it agricultural, but in the northern part, suburban.

There are few rivers in Wirral. The Fender and some smaller, parallel streams such as the Arrowe Brook and Greasby Brook, drain the northern part of the plateau into the River Birket, which itself flows into the Mersey at Wallasey Pool (now part of the dock system). In the south, the Dibbin and the Clatter drain into the Mersey via Bromborough Pool.

Wirral's weather is rarely extreme, neither is it monotonous. It can vary from day to day, from hour to hour, and even from place to place; a bright, sunny day in Hoylake often turns out to be dull and wet in Birkenhead. Although the peninsula is on the same latitude as parts of Siberia and Canada, the prevailing westerly winds, more or less constantly blowing from over the warm Gulf Stream, have a modifying influence on the climate. Mildness is a characteristic of Wirral's weather throughout the year. The growing season for plants is also extended by maritime influences and lasts from mid-March until late November, a fact borne out by the success of the market gardening industry which flourishes along the northern coastal strip. Snow rarely falls, and when it does, lies only for a very short time. The average yearly sunshine for the north Wirral coast is around 1510 hours, which is about 200 hours more than the average for England and Wales as a whole. Wirral is also fortunate in that the mountains of North Wales to the west tend to absorb much of the rain before it reaches these parts. The prevailing westerlies keep the atmosphere relatively free from pollution; some idea of the purity of the air reaching Wirral can be gained by realizing that the wind has just travelled across two and a half thousand miles of ocean!

Whilst Wirral's weather benefits in many ways from its proximity to the sea, not all of the maritime influences are beneficial. The peninsula is exposed to the full force of the wild gales which sweep in from the north-west during the autumn and winter months. Wind speeds of up to 90 m.p.h. are not uncommon during these gales, and many's the time that ships have been blown in from the Irish Sea to be broken to pieces on the Hoyle and Burbo sandbanks. Even in summer, the sea breezes tend to keep temperatures near the coast several degrees lower than those inland. But if the west wind is beneficial to Wirral, the same cannot be said of the east wind. To the east of Wirral lies the industrial heart of England, and the wind blowing from that direction brings with it the smoke and the smells of a thousand industries. On days when the east wind blows, it is often impossible to see across to the opposite banks of the Dee or the Mersey, let alone the prospects of distant hills and mountains normally visible when the atmosphere is purer.

The variety of wildlife found in and around the Wirral Peninsula belies its proximity to a large industrial centre. A wide range of habitats – field and hedgerow, marshland and woodland, coast and estuary, heath and moorland, and of course the suburbs – account for the wealth of plants, birds and animals to be seen in Wirral. The bird life of the coast is of particular interest, the Dee estuary and marshes attracting bird-watchers from far afield to study the great flocks of waders which gather here in their thousands during the autumn and winter. The coast too provides a habitat for several rare plants, one in particular being unique to Wirral.

The peninsula is laced with a network of public footpaths and bridleways almost out of proportion to its area. These give access to fields and woods, cliff-tops and heaths, providing the walker and nature-lover with unlimited opportunities for exploration. The whole of the coastline, from Wallasey to

Burton, is accessible although much of it is man-made, concrete embankment.

Wirral has changed dramatically in the last fifty years; even in the last twenty. Villages are no longer independent communities based on the land. Even outside the built-up areas of Wallasey and Birkenhead, many villages are surrounded by housing estates, and are struggling to maintain their identity. Vast council housing developments such as those on the slopes of the Fender Valley at Ford, Noctorum and Woodchurch cover what was once rolling farmland and woodland. A motorway runs right through the heart of the peninsula. Dutch elm disease has taken its toll of thousands of trees in Wirral, as in the rest of the country; once-shady byways are now open and bare. Large areas of urban Wirral are decaying. Many historically and architecturally interesting buildings have disappeared, bulldozed to fulfil planners' dreams, or left to decay beyond repair through lack of interest. Local authority administration has become faceless and friendless and more bureaucratic since reorganization in 1974.

Not all the change has been for the worse. Many thousands of folk who once lived in dingy back-to-back housing now enjoy the open spaces and clean air of the new suburbs. Heavy industrial traffic has been taken away from narrow roads and village centres never intended for them. Community life in many areas is thriving, as people strive to maintain their identity and spirit of "belonging" in an increasingly impersonal and faceless world. Smokeless zone measures have given large areas of Wirral a cleaner atmosphere than they have had for many years. Two Country Parks, both created since 1968, now provide much-needed recreational space and facilities. Stricter controls over development, adherence to a Green Belt policy, and the creation of Conservation Areas, are all helping to protect our heritage and improve the quality of our environment.

What of the future? Being a peninsula, Wirral has very definite, natural boundaries beyond which it cannot grow. These are rigid limits to growth. The County Plan for Merseyside also specifies limits beyond which Wirral should not step, limits which would maintain and improve the quality of life for Wirral folk. But the limits will need to be jealously guarded, not only by the administrators and planners, but by all those who know and love Wirral.

In the pages of this book I hope to show you the places, people, buildings, and heritage that make the Wirral Peninsula worthy of such concern and attention, seen through the eyes of one who has grown up through these years of change. Some parts of Wirral I love and know well; others, not so well. But to the stranger and visitor to Wirral I hope to convey some of the atmosphere and character of this corner of England; and to the resident I hope to show things which perhaps he or she never knew existed.

2

SEASIDE SUBURBIA

Wallasey – New Brighton

WALLASEY, with its neighbour New Brighton, occupies the north-eastern corner of the peninsula. Seen from any view-point – from the sea, the railway, the motorway, Wallasey just seems to be a ridge covered with drab red-brick, grey-roofed houses. And New Brighton . . . well, everyone knows that this is Merseyside's Blackpool. At least, so they appear to the casual visitor. But let us look a little more closely at these two towns where a large proportion of Wirral people live, work and play.

The Doomsday Book mentions "Walea" (Anglo-Saxon "Waelas-eig"), which literally means "Welshmen's or Stranger's Island". This might seem a little obscure until we remember that the sandstone ridge upon which a large part of Wallasey is built, was almost cut off from the rest of Wirral by the inlet of Wallasey Pool. The Pool is an inlet or creek of the Mersey and, although it does not connect directly with the Irish Sea on the northern coast, it does extend into a low-lying area which was formerly marshland, virtually cutting off Wallasey from the rest of Wirral. The isolated situation of the "peninsula within a peninsula" made it an ideal place of refuge, and we can assume that the early inhabitants of Wirral took advantage of this when defending themselves against the attacks of the invading Saxons. So it became the home of the defeated race of "strangers".

Wallasey's isolation from the rest of Wirral (which was itself relatively unaffected by the mainstream events of British history) tended to make it a closed, insular community, and very little is known about life in the early days of its history.

Wallasey itself is not really a town at all, but an urban area made up of several townships which have grown over the years to render the original communities unidentifiable. Population figures for the combined townships of Liscard, Wallasey and Poulton/Seacombe show 663 people in 1801; the figure had jumped to over 53,000 a century later, reflecting the dramatic change caused by the industrialization of Liverpool and the introduction of efficient, reliable and cheap ferry and railway services to and from the port. The population continued to grow and reached a peak of just over 100,000 in the early 1960s; it has remained fairly stable since then, due in part to the lack of space for further growth, and also to the lack of opportunities in the Merseyside area as a whole. The town was declared a Municipal Borough in 1910, and attained County Borough status three years later. With local government reorganization in 1974, Wallasey became part of the Wirral District Council. Moreton, Leasowe and Saughall Massie, although part of Wallasey for administrative purposes, are now important areas in their own right, and are dealt with elsewhere in this book.

The rapid growth of Wallasey which started in the middle years of the nineteenth century and continued well into the first half of this century is largely responsible for the appearance of the town today. Country lanes, cottages, manor houses and fields were rapidly replaced by "desirable residences" and humbler dwellings, many of which are now nearing the end of their useful days and are giving to many parts of the town a sad air of decay and neglect.

If Wallasey has a centre, then historically speaking Wallasey Village would have greatest claim to this title. Lying at the western foot of the sandstone ridge which forms the backbone of Wallasey, and overlooked by the parish church of St Hilary, this is the oldest inhabited part of the town. Wallasey Village resisted change while its neighbours – Poulton, Liscard and New Brighton – were being developed. The Village remained a village long after the rest of Wallasey had become urbanized. The oldest residents still remember it as a place of neat cottages, small farms, lilac trees and hedgerows. Nothing of this remains. Dual carriageways, shops, houses and petrol stations have completely replaced the rural way of life. The only remnants of this bygone age are the public houses, mostly modern, but whose names tell something of the history of this corner of Wallasey.

The old Cheshire Cheese, demolished in 1885 and replaced by the present building at the foot of the Breck, boasted a room which was used by William of Orange on his way to Hoylake before embarking for Ireland and the Battle of the Boyne. The Black Horse Inn, near the junction with the main road to Moreton and Leasowe, is a reminder of the days when the area was an important horse-racing centre. It is probable that Wallasey had the first racecourse in the country, the first recorded races being in the early years of the seventeenth century. The course, which ran from a point near the present station, along the flat area behind the sand dunes almost as far as Leasowe Castle, was described by William Webb during his seventeenth-century tour through Wirral:

> These fair sands, or plains, upon the shore of the sea, which, for the fitness for such a purpose, allure the gentlemen and others oft to appoint great matches and venture no small sums in trying the swiftness of their horses.

The Wallasey races were evidently popular much further afield; we know that the Duke of Devonshire, the Duke of Monmouth and other well-known figures attended the meetings. Serious racing ended in the early years of the eighteenth century, and the last races were run in the 1790s. Market gardens now occupy the land, and the stables have long been demolished.

The market gardens which replaced the race course provide early, good-quality produce for Merseyside. The soil (a mixture of clay and blown sand), repeated applications of manure, a lot of sunshine, and high hedges between the fields to act as windbreaks, combine to make this one of the most fertile areas in Wirral. Such is the high regard held for this strip of land that, when in 1961 it was proposed to build the new Grammar School on a portion of the gardens, a bitter confrontation began between the planners and the agriculturalists. Notices were erected along the Leasowe Road frontage: "Cabbages or

Buildings?", "Save our Crops", and "Food or Education?" The gardeners won.

Before the days of agricultural mechanization, the market gardens provided employment for large numbers of workers, many of whom lived in a row of nineteen small terraced cottages situated on the site of the present Twenty Row Inn on Leasowe Road. The original inn, the twentieth in the row, was built on bales of straw to prevent it from sinking into the earth, such was the nature of this low-lying land in the days before the embankment was built.

Wallasey's parish church is a prominent landmark on the approach to Wallasey Village from Moreton or Leasowe. It stands alongside a lone tower on one of the highest points in Wallasey. Dedicated to St Hilary, it is one of only eight churches in this country to have this distinction, and has a history dating back to the sixth century. Certainly a church stood on this site at the time of the Norse invasion in the tenth century. Stones have been found which indicate an early Norman building, and an eleventh-century font from this building is now in use at St Luke's Church, Poulton. After the Norman conquest, the church was rebuilt several times. The lone tower dates back to the rebuilding of 1530; the rest of this building was demolished about 1760 and another church reconstructed from the same materials. This church was destroyed by fire in 1857, the legend being that the church fires had been stoked too high after the parishioners had complained of the cold. A lesser-known tradition states that the tower of the church was for years the hidden storehouse of contraband goods, and that the night it was burned the high, blue blaze of burning brandy could be seen for miles along the Welsh coast! The present building was built between 1858 and 1859 from stone dug from the quarries at Stroude's Corner, Rake Lane (now bowling greens). The church's colourful history is preserved in a local saying that it is "thrice burnt, twice been a church without a tower, and once a tower without a church"!

The churchyard surrounding St Hilary's commands an open, extensive view of the north Wirral plain, now largely covered by housing, but with patches of green where there are golf courses and playing fields. But, as in so many parts of Wirral, the sea predominates. The gravestones around the churchyard tell many stories of local people lost at sea. "Died on the passage out to Australia 1889", "Lost in hurricane 1889", "Drowned whilst bathing 1887" and "Sailed from Liverpool to Bombay 1866 – not been heard of since".

The ridge on which St Hilary's Church stands is known as the Breck, and stretches from the sandhills by the coast to Poulton in the south. "Breck" is a corruption of "Brake" and denotes an area of natural scrub and heathland. Now almost completely engulfed by houses, it is difficult to imagine that this was open, wild, common land until the turn of the century. The few remaining open areas have been ravaged by generations of children's feet, the grass and vegetation now struggling to survive. The sandstone outcrops, characteristic of this and much of Wirral's higher land, have been worn smooth and daubed with memorials to present-day heroes: "Liverpool are ace" and "Joey rules".

The largest mill in Wirral stood proud and high on this exposed, windy common for over a hundred years. Built in 1765, it worked for the local community in competition with its rivals at Poulton, Liscard and Bidston (Bidston Mill can still be seen from here, perched high on Bidston Hill), until it was demolished in 1887. The old, rough track which served the mill can still be traced, now overgrown with brambles, cutting up the side of the hill off St Hilary's Brow.

One of the oldest buildings in Wallasey nestles into the slopes of the Breck on the main road to Poulton. Built in 1799, this tiny sandstone cottage set in an old-fashioned flower garden once housed fifty pupils in the early days of what was to become Wallasey Grammar School. It is known that Wallasey had a school as early as 1595, when the parish register of St Hilary's for that year records the death of Randulph Geest, "Schoolmaister at Walezie". Modern advocates of small classes in spacious surroundings would shudder to hear that at one time this building housed eighty-three children of mixed ages and sex, under the supervision and instruction of one man!

The growth of Wallasey's population forced the school to

move to new buildings in St George's Road in 1864, and again to Withen's Lane, Liscard, in 1876. This building was replaced in 1911 by buildings which befitted a grammar school of national distinction, an oasis of learning and study in a fine setting of spacious grounds off Withen's Lane. These outstanding buildings are now used by a local school. However, teaching methods and learning needs do change, and the Grammar School moved out of Withen's Lane in 1967 to the present buildings at Leasowe.

Prior to the move to Leasowe, there were strong fears that the change would not be a purely physical one. The school which for so long had been part of Wallasey was moving to new buildings on a post-war council estate on the outskirts of the town. Coinciding with the move was the reorganization of secondary education in Wirral, which effectively removed grammar-school status from the school. That the school would change was inevitable. Shortly after the move to Leasowe, the late Maurice Eggleshaw in his *History of Wallasey Grammar School* wrote: "The School is a very different place from what it was as little as ten years ago, but it has, at least, suffered less than some schools of similar standing which have lost their identity completely."

On a recent visit to the school, I too was aware of the changes that had taken place since my own schooldays, nearly twenty years ago. But I was also aware that the school still has an identity. Although set in pleasant modern buildings with up-to-date facilities for learning in many varied subjects, the school still had that indefinable quality which shows that it is aware of all that has gone before, and knows how precious that is.

Almost opposite the old Grammar School building in Breck Road a public footpath sign points to Bidston, 1½ miles away across Bidston Moss. This ancient right of way was once the only safe route across the low-lying marsh to Bidston. Until the construction of the M53 motorway, and the industrial and residential development around Bidston, this was a much-loved walk for families going for picnics on Bidston Hill. The walk is no longer pleasant, passing under flyovers, alongside rubbish tips, a railway line and a steel mill. The Moss has, though, always been a haven for wild flowers, and despite the disturbance the keen-eyed nature lover will find here marsh and spotted orchids; heron too are regularly seen along the River Birket.

Further along the road to Poulton, where the Mersey Tunnel approach road (formerly the Seacombe-Bidston railway) passes through a cutting beneath the road, stands the Boode Memorial. Margaret Boode, "the kind old lady of Leasowe Castle", was killed near this spot in 1826 when she was thrown from her horse in a carriage accident. To understand this dedication we must first look back to the days when the coastline of Wallasey and north Wirral was notorious for shipwrecks. Boats entering and leaving Liverpool were often caught in severe gales and blown directly on to the sea-facing coast. Not all wrecks were due to natural elements. Professional wreckers who made a living from the cargoes washed ashore would erect false beacons and lure unsuspecting boats on to the treacherous sands. The survivors would be mercilessly robbed and left on the sands, often dead or badly wounded. The Royal Commission in 1839 reported that

> on the Cheshire coast not far from Liverpool, they will rob those who have escaped the perils of the sea and come safe on shore and will mutilate dead bodies, for the sake of rings and personal ornaments.

Margaret Boode became a friend of the shipwrecked and turned Leasowe Castle into a receiving house for survivors. Her fame as the sailors' friend spread far and wide, and seamen from all parts of the world came to know and respect her name. The Memorial stands above the busy twentieth-century motorway as a reminder of the kindness of that lady in those wild, wrecking days.

Poulton – "the town on the Pool" – is one of Wallasey's townships which is no longer recognizable as such. Travelling along Poulton Road from Wallasey Village, the modern traveller may be forgiven for not noticing any distinction between this part of Wallasey and the rest. Fifty years ago this would not have been so. Poulton then was a place of splendid trees, fields and manor houses. It boasted its own mill. W. Mortimer wrote in 1847:

> Poulton, which lays a mile up Wallasey Pool, from its situation in a small cove interspersed with flourishing trees, and the rural simplicity of its houses, forms a pleasing contrast with the activity and bustle displayed at the ferries, and the bleak and dreary country of the adjacent townships.

Life still had its problems, however. Several streams (one of which followed the course of the present Mill Lane) flowed into the Pool, and local people were in the habit of using the streams as sewers. When the Pool was converted into docks, the cleansing action of the tide was restricted, and the Pool became "a cesspool which engenders malaria, and will in the coming hot season be a fruitful source of fever and disease to a neighbourhood already notorious for its unhealthiness".

Poulton has always been an important point for travellers crossing Wallasey Pool to Birkenhead. A ferry crossed near to the present Duke Street Bridge, and a ford or causeway of large sandstone slabs enabled pedestrians to cross at the head of the Pool. The "Penny Bridge" takes its name from the toll which was charged in 1896, replacing the "Halfpenny Bridge" of 1843.

Like so much of Wallasey, Poulton is now a sprawl of houses and shops, its Pool-side area grim and dirty, a ribbon of docks, warehouses, storage tanks and derelict quaysides.

The adjoining township of Seacombe is also down-at-heel, although regeneration of some of the riverside areas is starting to improve the environment. Seacombe ("the combe by the sea") in 1850 was "a country village consisting of one main street, two or three cross streets, an outlying terrace or two, a few scattered houses and a district bordering on the Pool given up to various industries. Beyond were stretches of corn and pasture land, lanes and dells". It was shortly after this, due no doubt to the influx of population created by the ferry service to Liverpool, that the character of Seacombe changed completely. Some idea of the area's character can be gained by the fact that, before the houses were built, Bidston Hill could be seen away across the fields.

To most Merseysiders, Seacombe is synonymous with "the Ferry". There has been a service from this part of the Wirral coast since the middle of the seventeenth century at least. In the 1920s, the Seacombe Ferry carried nearly 32 million passengers each year. With the opening of the Mersey road tunnel, and improved rail services under the river, the number of passengers has steadily declined. Now, the future of the service is in jeopardy. But the ten-minute trip across the Mersey to Liverpool is world-famous, immortalized in song during the "Mersey Beat" boom of the early 1960s. On summer weekends hundreds still enjoy this trip. Come with me on a week-day morning on the "Ferry 'cross the Mersey".

Hurry through the turnstiles, the boat is already in! It ties up at a floating landing-stage connected to the land by the pedestrian tunnel down which we are now scurrying. We are lucky today – it is low tide. Downhill all the way to the landing-stage (but remember that it will be a steep climb up on the Liverpool side!) The wind often howls through these tunnels, but not today. Over the gangway, on to the boat. The service now has only four operational ferry boats; several have recently been sold as part of the rationalization efforts to reduce costs. On the boat, we have a choice of where to sit – warm and snug inside, or on top deck, exposed to the invigorating Mersey air. Let us go atop, as there is so much to see from there.

As we pass an open doorway leading down to the bowels of the boat, a blast of hot, oily-smelling air reaches us from the engine room. On the top deck, we are just in time to see the ferry hands raise the gangway and cast off the ropes from the capstans. The engines rumble, the water foams, and the boat turns towards Liverpool. As the boat pulls away from Seacombe, we can clearly see the floating landing stage, with its great buffer tyres chained around the edge. The Wallasey promenade, stretching away into the distance towards New Brighton, contrasts with the line of docks bordering the river in the opposite direction. Towards the estuary the river broadens out with clear, bright horizons towards Liverpool

Bay. Followed by its entourage of gulls, the boat is now in mid-river and the famous Liverpool waterfront, dominated by the Liver Building, is rapidly approached. Gone are the ocean-going liners which used to berth here; only the Isle of Man boat ready to sail. The appearance of the waterfront has changed in other ways too. Decades of grime have been removed from Liverpool's waterfront buildings to reveal their natural, light colours.

The engines die down and the deck hands wait ready with their ropes as the boat is skilfully manoeuvred into position alongside the landing stage. Today the operation is accomplished in seconds; in stormy conditions, it can take many minutes to secure the boat to the capstans. Down the gangway, and our journey is over; one of the most interesting short trips in the country.

What is the future of the ferries? Well, the service to New Brighton was discontinued in 1971, leaving only the Seacombe and Woodside ferries. Declining cross-river commuter traffic has put these two services in jeopardy. Perhaps, like steam trains, the future of the ferries lies in pleasure trips. Already, weekend and evening leisure and educational cruises are becoming popular.

Seacombe was a thriving shipbuilding centre in the middle years of the last century. Born with the development of the docks in Wallasey Pool and Birkenhead, Seacombe shipbuilders built many fine craft, among them the famous *Sunbeam*. This yacht, built for Lord Brassey, Lord of the Admiralty, was used by him to visit many overseas countries. A model of the *Sunbeam* is housed in Wallasey's Central Library.

"The Potter of Seacombe", John Goodwin, in the mid-1800s set up a pottery which was to produce plates and stoneware which are now collectors' items. Claimed to be the best built and equipped pottery in England at the time, it produced colourful pieces and provided much-needed employment in Wallasey for many years.

Opposite the Ferry entrance, near the beginning of Birkenhead Road, stands the Marine Hotel. Now several hundred yards inland from the river, old photographs show water lapping right up to its frontage. The land between the Hotel and the Ferry buildings was made up in the last century, and buses now park where once the Mersey flowed.

Another link with the river is St Paul's Church. This has long been known as the "Sailors' Church" as mariners on the Mersey hailed its tall spire (now no more) as a landmark. Near the church, the derelict land surrounded by modern housing is the site of the old Seacombe station. A regular service ran via Bidston to West Kirby, whence a through coach to London Euston could be obtained. The route of the old railway is now part of the M53 motorway, and the second Mersey Tunnel (Kingsway) was opened in 1971, burrowing under the river from the old railway cutting.

From the Ferry at Seacombe a promenade runs along the coast as far as Hoylake, a distance of about eight miles, continuous except for a short break at Leasowe Bay. Most of this promenade is closed to traffic, making it a fine walk for viewing the River Mersey and Liverpool Bay, with on the one hand buildings and urban life and on the other the sea and shore with its shipping and bird life. The river frontage was open to the shore until the first stretch of promenade was built in the 1890s. Maintenance of Wirral's coastline is a heavy item of expenditure, and each winter takes its toll of damage to the promenade and embankment, the coast being exposed to the full fury of wind and waves.

The shore from Seacombe to New Brighton was famous for its expanse of clean sand which attracted trippers in their thousands. Photographs taken during the early years of this century show them tightly packed together on the sands, reminiscent of Mediterranean holiday scenes. There was little room to move. Gradually the sands disappeared and the beach got dirtier. The trippers came no more. But now the sands are improving, the shore is becoming cleaner as industry on the Mersey declines and stricter controls on pollution take effect.

A short distance along the promenade from Seacombe, Wallasey's Town Hall stands proudly overlooking the Mersey. Often called the "back-to-front town hall", it was built to face the river, with its fine steps leading down to the promenade and its back facing Brighton Street, the main thoroughfare. So the visitor to the Town Hall on business misses its grandeur on entering, whilst the river tripper and promenader obtain by far the best view! Many ask why the Town Hall was built so far from Wallasey's centre (if indeed Wallasey has a centre). It was erected in the early years of this century on a site exactly midway between the ferries of Seacombe and Egremont, at that time Wallasey's main inlets and outlets. So it stands today, a fine building inside and out, but tucked away in a run-down, hard-to-get-at part of town.

Seacombe's neighbour Egremont, a mile away along the riverside, also had its ferry. Built in 1828 by Captain John Askew (whose house "Egremont" he named after his birthplace in Cumbria), it boasted the longest pier on the Mersey. Along this pier day-trippers tramped in their thousands to bathe on the shore around Egremont, and bowler-hatted businessmen marched for the boat to and from their offices in Liverpool. The pier was rammed in 1932 by a drifting oil tanker, and again in 1941 by a coaster. The damage resulted in the pier being scrapped in 1946, and with it the end of the ferry service. All that remain are the foundations of the "Beehive" (a glass-sided public shelter), some dilapidated ferry buildings, and a public house bearing the name of the Ferry. The esplanade at the side of the old Ferry building is Wallasey's "Speakers' Corner".

Further along the promenade from the old Egremont Ferry stood, until 1974, a notorious Wallasey building known far and wide as "Mother Redcap's". Built about 1595, the building owed its name to its proprietor in the days when it was a public house-cum-café. Mother Redcap's was closely associated with the smuggling which was prevalent in the area during the eighteenth and nineteenth centuries. Its isolated position on the banks of the Mersey, backed by open moorland, its hidden cellars, its several caves connecting (supposedly) with various parts of Wallasey, and the compliance of old Mother Redcap made it a favourite haunt of smugglers involved in the wrecking along the Wirral coast. The building was turned into a private residence in 1888, but later became a café again. During the 1960s Mother Redcap's was left to rot away, open to the elements and modern-day "wreckers". By the early 1970s little was left of the building. The remains were demolished in 1974.

Inland from Egremont Ferry, Church Street leads to St John's Church. "Externally this is without question the finest church in Wallasey" reported Pevsner and Hubbard in their survey of Cheshire's buildings in 1971. And indeed it does look different, if nothing else. Grecian in design, and capable of seating up to 2,000 people, it was built in 1832 and apparently harmonized well with the neighbouring properties in Church Street. John Goodwin, the Seacombe potter, is buried in the churchyard.

St John's Church is backed by the open spaces of Central Park, a small oasis of much-needed greenery in a densely populated part of Wirral. Originally part of the gardens surrounding the house of Liverpool merchant and shipowner John Tobin, the land was purchased by the Council in 1889, together with the house and associated buildings. Known as Liscard Hall, this fine building was built about 1830 and, as it stands on relatively high ground, commanded good views of the surrounding district. It is said that Lady Tobin kept a telescope in an upper room of the Hall so that she could see her husband arrive safely from the ferry crossing in stormy weather! Liscard Hall is now a college building.

The modern centre of Liscard ("the fort on the height") is indisputably its twentieth-century shopping centre, no different from any other precinct in the land, but struggling to attract customers in the face of strong competition (and better parking facilities) from its rival in Birkenhead. Liscard's importance as a shopping centre is nothing new. Brown and Woods wrote: "Liscard was also the main shopping centre up to about 1880. Ladies in carriages and pairs came daily from the surrounding large houses, and as many as thirty or forty could be seen at one time shopping."

Liscard a hundred years ago had trees and lanes, picturesque cottages and imposing residences. Today there are few buildings worthy of mention. The Boot Inn on Wallasey Road, with its half-timbered work, attracts the eye; in the lounge a large black boot in a glass case reminds the visitor of the origin of its name, with the legend inscribed alongside. Along Seaview Road towards New Brighton, nondescript suburban sideroads with the names "Turret" and "Castle" immortalize an odd, supposedly haunted house known as Liscard Castle, which stood on this site in the last century. Built to look like a castle, this large residence had legendary links with nearby Captain's Pit, an old water-filled quarry now used as a recreation area. A young sea-captain's wife living at the Castle drowned herself in the Pit after hearing news of her husband's drowning at sea, and her ghost supposedly walked in the rooms of the Castle. A workman, after supervising the blocking up of some old passages in the basement of the Castle apparently heard a loud knocking and, thinking that someone had been accidentally walled up, enquired further. No one answered, but the knocking continued, whereupon he was overcome with fear and ran out as fast as he could!

It is difficult to say where Wallasey ends and New Brighton begins, although the planning authorities have tried to define the boundaries with place-signs at various points along the main routes. In fact, most of New Brighton's hinterland is indistinguishable in character from the rest of Wallasey; road upon road, street upon street of late nineteenth and early twentieth-century housing. But, nearing the coast, the quality of the light changes, that indefinable quality which indicates the nearness of the sea. And suddenly, after the claustrophobia of inner Wallasey's urbanity, the sky meets the sea, horizons are wide, and the air has a tang to it.

These very qualities brought about the development of New Brighton in the 1830s. Originally an area of grassy, windswept moorland leading down to the wave-beaten shore dunes, its potential as a "Watering Place" was noticed by Liverpool merchant James Atherton. He bought 170 acres of the sandy heathland and built "villas" in spacious grounds, each with an uninterrupted view of the sea and estuary. His prospectus for the estate makes the properties seem very desirable indeed:

> New Brighton is situated at the Rock Point, three miles distant from Liverpool, and from its elevated situation commands from all points the most interesting and extensive

> views. The Welsh Mountains, the Orme's Heads and the Isle of Man are all distinctly visible. . . .
>
> As a Bathing Place it has peculiar advantages, not only from its being the nearest point to the open Sea, but it also possesses the most beautiful Beach, the Sands are hard and clean, free from Mud, Gravel, or Quicksands, they are many miles in extent and cannot be equalled for the purpose of Exercise, whether in Carriages, on foot, or on Horseback.
>
> New Brighton also possesses a more interesting Sea view than any other Watering place can boast, being constantly enlivened by the passing of vessels to and from the rich and flourishing Port of Liverpool, in many instances approaching so near as to admit of persons on the shore conversing with those on board.
>
> Among its other advantages may be enumerated the salubrity of the Air, the certain supply of purest Spring Water, the aspect of all the Rooms fronting the sea, enjoying the refreshing breeze, and sheltered from the oppressive heat of the afternoon's sun, while its proximity to Liverpool, together with the certainty and safety of Steam Navigation must tend to render New Brighton a most agreeable and desirable place of resort to the Nobility and Gentry of all the neighbouring Counties.

Mortimer, writing at the time of the erection of the villas, states: "The building of these ornamental residences continues, and the young colony of New Brighton promises to be, at no distant day, one of the most fashionable watering places in this part of the kingdom." His prophecy came true. For over one hundred years New Brighton prospered. Every summer brought crowded beaches, many folk coming from the mill-towns of industrial Lancashire and the Midlands for a taste of the seaside. The ferries were crowded with trippers from Liverpool. Theatres played to full houses, entertaining the crowds with famous names from showbusiness. The water was "as clean as the Mediterranean". There were oyster stalls, minstrels on the beach, and bathing machines. These were indeed New Brighton's golden days. Right up to the late

1950s the people came. But the waters lapping New Brighton's beaches were getting dirtier; the sand was disappearing and being replaced by mud; and the trippers came fewer and fewer. The last twenty years have seen the resort at its lowest ebb. Guest houses have closed and the resort has had a general air of decay about it. Time and again the local authority have come up with plans for rejuvenating New Brighton, to no avail. But the tide is turning. The water and sands are becoming cleaner. The cost of travel has forced many families to look nearer home for their weekend outings. Once again it is becoming increasingly difficult to find parking space on a sunny summer's afternoon.

Many of the attractions which made New Brighton popular have disappeared. The resort's slender steel-lattice tower, 621 feet high and taller than Blackpool's, was called Merseyside's answer to the Eiffel in Paris. It was built in the late 1890s by a group of businessmen who thought they could make a neat fortune from the venture. It was widely acclaimed as one of the wonders of modern design and steel erection, and was opened with great fanfares of publicity. At the tower's base was a splendid theatre and ballroom, surrounded by extensive pleasure grounds. For many years it was one of the north-west's greatest attractions. Trippers queued for a ride to the top, or to see spectacular entertainments, circuses, Wild West shows (complete with real Cowboys and Indians) and concerts. Then came the First World War, the tower was neglected and had to be demolished shortly after. The grand red-brick buildings and pleasure grounds remained to dominate this corner of New Brighton until they were destroyed by fire in 1969. The site has remained empty since. Much has been planned for this potentially grand site overlooking the estuary – luxury housing development, pleasure grounds, public open space – but as I write it still stands sad and derelict, its future uncertain.

A short distance along the promenade from the Tower grounds, towards Egremont, stands a small piece of Wallasey's history largely unnoticed by those who pass by. Just beyond Vale Park, Wallasey's Magazines (or Liscard Battery) were housed on this site overlooking the river, chosen because of its remoteness at the time (about 1755). The Magazines were used to store all gunpowder and shot from the sailing ships entering the Mersey for their stay in the Port of Liverpool. Mortimer, writing in 1847, described the Magazines:

> They consist of separate chambers perfectly detached from each other, the intervening space being filled with earth, and the whole enclosed with a strong wall; this is again belted with a thick plantation, and the whole surrounded with a lofty wall, so that all chance of communication is prevented.

This strict security evidently paid off, for only one explosion is recorded, when in 1763 the West Indian brig *Charlotte* blew up killing all the crew except for one man. It is thought that the loose powder lying around after loading was accidentally ignited when a boy on deck struck a light.

As the area became built up in the middle of the nineteenth century, public concern over the presence of such large quantities of gunpowder increased, and the store was transferred about 1851 to floating hulks anchored lower down the river.

The Magazines remain empty, forgotten, hidden beneath the cellars of Emmanuel Church Vicarage. This building, formerly the barracks of the adjoining battery, is connected with the cottages across the road by an underground passage, now blocked up. The walls and gateway of the battery, built in 1858, survive, dark-red sandstone and castellated towers lending a military air to the area. The cottages opposite the battery, which may date back to the seventeenth century, are said to have been fishermen's cottages, and it is likely that they were used by senior officers of the battery. The Magazines' watchman used to live in the nearby Round House, now a private dwelling. The Magazine Hotel ("The Mags") is one of Wallasey's oldest inns, built in 1759 for the sailors who had time to fill whilst waiting for powder to be loaded on to their boats. The charm of this historic corner of Wallasey is irresistible, a community within a community, isolated from the urban scene surrounding it on three sides.

New Brighton's pier was demolished in 1973, the ferry service having ceased in 1971 because of siltation in the Mersey estuary. Like all good piers, the one at New Brighton had its attractions: bright lights, dancing, puppet shows. A one-legged diver plunged into the river once every hour during the summer days of long ago. In its latter years the pier struggled hard to pay its way. Finally, the sea, the very reason for its existence, was to be the cause of its demise. After a hundred years standing in the briny waters of the Mersey, its supports rotted away and it was declared unsafe. The pier's end did not come without a strong and determined fight from those who saw its demise as yet another nail in New Brighton's coffin. But no one was prepared to pay the vast sum necessary to keep the pier alive, and the demolition men moved in. Now this corner of the peninsula where the Mersey meets the sea seems empty and bare; yet (dare I say it?) better without the pier.

Almost opposite the former entrance to the pier, Victoria Road climbs away inland. Derelict shops, "For Sale" boards, peeling paintwork, bingo halls and amusement arcades make this a place to avoid if you want fresh air, open spaces and the sea.

The three-mile walk along New Brighton's promenade to Harrison Drive is a delight at any time of the year, but particularly so when the tide is high and when a vigorous wind is blowing in from the north-west. On such days the horizons are far and wide, we will have only the seabirds for company, and we will have to dodge the waves breaking over the sea wall.

Fort Perch Rock Battery, the red sandstone building standing in the mouth of the Mersey, is the fort that never was. Nicknamed the "little Gibraltar of the Mersey", it was built between 1826 and 1829 to protect the Port of Liverpool. The idea of having some sort of protection for Liverpool was born some years earlier during the Napoleonic Wars. The Fort was built upon outcrops of sandstone originally known as Black Rock, where Wirral's wreckers and smugglers used to lure ships aground. Here was erected a "perch" or navigational aid for boats entering the Mersey; but this was swept away by storms so often that something far more substantial was needed. Built to withstand the tremendous impact of high seas, the Fort was constructed of Runcorn stone and could accommodate one hundred men with officers' quarters, kitchens, storerooms and eighteen guns. But for all this, it is said that the Fort only ever used its guns twice: at the beginning of the First World War when a warning shot was fired across the bows of a Norwegian ship; and again at the start of the Second World War when a fishing smack tried to enter the Port through the wrong channel. During the last war the Fort was camouflaged as a tea garden complete with painted lawns and paths, and a TEAS sign across the roof.

The War Office sold the Fort in 1958 and it became a pleasure centre until 1975 when it was abandoned after a series of severe storms. The present owner bought the Fort in 1976 and, with the help of the Manpower Services Commission, has started to restore it to something like its original condition. This has not been an easy task; much of the Fort has been altered over the years, and tons of sand have covered much of the original parade ground. Restoring the red sandstone has involved a lot of searching to obtain suitable replacement stone – some of which has come from Woolton Jail, old churches, Liverpool Cathedral, and Bebington Station. The owner has kindly opened the Fort to the public, and as well as the structure itself, visitors can view craft shops and a museum of aircraft wrecks.

To stand atop this rock-like fort on a wild, windy day with the grey waters of the Irish Sea foaming all around, is to experience a sense of isolation that belies the proximity of the funfairs and bingo halls.

New Brighton lighthouse stands alongside the Fort, sharing the same outcrop of sandstone. Built in 1827–30 at a cost of £27,500, it is 90 feet high and is constructed of Anglesey granite. The stone blocks are dovetailed into each other and covered with Puzellani, a volcanic material which eventually sets rock-hard. The first 35 feet of its height consist of solid rock built to withstand the constant battering of the sea.

In the latter years of the nineteenth century, facing the lighthouse and Fort, stood a building which locals were glad to see demolished. The "Ham and Egg Parade", also known as "Teapot Row" and "Aquarium Parade", was a terrace of tawdry eating-houses, shooting galleries and fortune-tellers' parlours which stretched from the corner of Victoria Road to the site of the Floral Pavilion Theatre. The Ham and Egg Parade was described at the time as "the favourite resort of the Liverpool and Lancashire trippers and roughs. Here are stationed the eating house and refreshment room keepers, whose constant solicitations to dine early and often are such a nuisance". The Parade attracted pickpockets and street hawkers. It was notable for rowdyism unknown in other parts of the town, and outbreaks of trouble there often brought trippers before the local magistrates. When the decision to knock the Parade down was taken in 1906, the *Wallasey News* commented: "The passing of the Parade has been regretted by none."

Victoria Gardens, complete with Pavilion (now the Floral Pavilion), and bandstand, replaced the Ham and Egg Parade, and were built about the same time as this stretch of promenade, in 1913. Until the advent of the cinema, this corner of Wirral was rich in theatres providing local audiences with the top names in live entertainment. Sybil Thorndike, Richard Tauber, Tommy Handley and Gracie Fields came to the Tivoli, the Palace and the Winter Gardens. More recently, the Tower Theatre enjoyed regular visits by the Beatles and other famous names of the "Beat Boom" of the 1960s. All of these theatres have gone, leaving only the Floral Pavilion. The modern exterior of the Pavilion belies the true age of the structure, which was built some seventy years ago, and of which the original wrought-iron entrance porch still remains. The theatre is still a popular venue for summer entertainment programmes and local amateur productions.

For those who enjoy entertainment of a different nature, the stretch of the Marine Parade from here to the Swimming Pool provides everything in the way of indoor and outdoor amusements. The pool occupies a large site overlooking the sands. Built in 1934, it was for many years one of the largest and finest open-air pools in the world, with accommodation for 3,000 bathers and 30,000 spectators. The seemingly long hot summers of the thirties drew tremendous crowds to the pool, but now it struggles to pay its way.

Beyond the pool, the promenade stretches away into the distance, several miles of land reclaimed from the sea and made up to present a solid face to the waters of the Irish Sea; looking inland from here, the original coastline can be made out, a line of bramble-covered cliffs and dunes straddled by houses and flats at first but soon opening out. In the cliffs opposite the swimming pool, several outcrops of brightly coloured sandstone stand out against the green backcloth. These rocks – the Red Noses and Yellow Noses – were one of the big attractions of old New Brighton. Originally overlooking the shore, they were a favourite venue for picnickers, and youngsters would clamber over them, hiding in the nooks and crannies. They contain caves (now blocked up) reputed to have been used by smugglers, and it is said that passages from here linked up with old Mother Redcap's at Egremont and with St Hilary's Church at Wallasey Village.

I have been inside one of these caves, and it was a fascinating experience. Access was via a trapdoor in the garden of one of the private homes above the "Noses". A flight of stone steps led into the dark bowels of the earth. Along a narrow passage and into a large "hall" with smaller, inaccessible passages leading off at all angles. Close examination of the soft sandstone walls revealed inscribed dates as far back as the seventeenth century. Who carved them? Shipwrecked sailors hiding from the hands of the murderous wreckers? Men and boys fleeing from the Press Gangs of the eighteenth century? Who knows? These caves must have been used by Wirral folk for thousands of years before their entrances were filled in by development. Now only the occasional visitor seeks out the nooks and crannies eroded by centuries of tidal action.

Back on the promenade towards Harrison Drive, there is much bird life to be seen on the sands below a receding tide. As well as the masses of gulls, many waders – oyster-catcher, knot, dunlin, redshank and the occasional cormorant and curlew – are to be seen scavenging in the mud and sand. In the spring and autumn flocks of waders are a spectacular sight winging their way along the coast to the estuaries, their forlorn cries echoing across the wet sand.

The roadway along this section of the promenade is occasionally used at weekends for motor-cycle racing, its wide carriageway and roundabouts being particularly suitable for this "sport". Towards the end of the promenade, modern housing development has taken a sizeable chunk of the open land alongside the sand dunes which form an almost continuous chain between New Brighton and Leasowe.

And so we end our look at Wallasey and New Brighton almost where we started out, on the outskirts of Wallasey Village. Woods and Brown in 1929 published a book *The Rise and Progress of Wallasey*, which has become indispensable to anyone interested in the history and development of the town. Their title was chosen in days of optimism, days when Wallasey had much to look forward to. Wallasey has risen. It has progressed. But, alas, in the eyes of many the town is falling and regressing.

Wallasey and New Brighton have much to offer both visitor and resident alike. It has a coastline full of variety and interest. It has open spaces, entertainments, excellent shopping facilities. It has a unique and colourful history, evident to those who take the trouble to search it out. Yet it is up to the individuals who make up the town to strive to prevent Wallasey's downhill slide.

3

THE NORTH WIRRAL COAST

Leasowe – Moreton – Saughall Massie – Meols

THERE must be few places in this land of ours where it is possible to walk along a stretch of coastline between two estuaries in a matter of hours. Two estuaries as different as those of the Dee and the Mersey; the one broad, bright and sandy, with a backcloth of green hills and misty mountains; the other narrow and murky, backed by a man-made skyline of cranes and docks. And all the while to have on the one side the briny waters of the Irish Sea and on the other Wirral's coastal plain with its towns and villages.

Wirral's northern coast is entirely man-made, presenting a sloping concrete face to the pounding sea. It has not always been so. Although protected by sand dunes between Harrison Drive and Leasowe, the low-lying land between the coast and the higher ground of Bidston and Upton was constantly under threat of flooding. The very place-names Moreton ("the town on the mere") and Overchurch ("the church on the shore") show that encroachment by the sea as much as two miles inland was probably a common occurrence. The Mersey Docks and Harbour Board in 1813 made the following report to the "Proprietors of lands under the level of high water mark in several townships contiguous to Wallasey, Leasowe":

> If means be not taken to prevent it the sea will quickly render useless the greater portion of the lands under its level, and will eventually effect a junction with Wallasey Pool . . . it appears that between 1771 and 1813, 95 yards of the line of coast had, opposite the Leasowe lighthouse advanced inwards 90 yards and a little further westwards 120 yards.

The possibility of the sea breaking through to Wallasey Pool worried Liverpool Corporation, who feared that the Rock Channel, the main waterway through the Mersey to Liverpool, would lose its depth of water.

Remains of a forest, together with evidence of a settlement found on the shore off Meols (of which more later), point to the peninsula having been much longer than at present, and this has been borne out by the early charts which show the Burbo and Hoyle sandbanks as part of the peninsula.

One of the first attempts to erect a barrier to the sea was a sloping wall built about 1794. This was repeatedly eroded and torn down by the sea, and it became clear that a substantial, permanent barrier was necessary. As the result of an Act of Parliament, work was begun on a concrete embankment in 1829, incorporating stone from the Breck quarry at Wallasey. This embankment sloped gently towards the sea, with a steeper slope on the landward side. Over thirty feet high, it withstood the merciless waves of the Irish Sea until quite recently. Increasing maintenance and repairs during the last twenty years or so resulted in reconstruction being necessary and, as I write, this is almost complete. The work, a miracle of construction engineering made doubly difficult by the atrocious conditions, has replaced much of the original embankment and provides the walker with an attractive walkway along its entire length. Only those who have experienced the power and fury of a 33-foot tide running before a force 9 gale can appreciate the necessity for such a sturdy construction. A breach under such conditions could flood over fifty thousand homes in north Wirral.

In 1978, during the embankment's reconstruction, a passer-by noticed an old bucket apparently full of rubbish among the excavations. Further examination of the bucket's contents revealed a hoard of everyday articles from 1897, accompanied by the following note: "To the finder, greetings. We, the undersigned do hereby most solemnly vow and declare that we are this day permitted by the grace of God to commit to the keeping of this concrete block, the enclosed articles of every-day use, signed G. Cecil Kenyon C.E. resident engineer; George Beed; William E. Ewing; Thomas Hopkins." It bore the date 18th September 1897. Amongst the articles were several magazines and periodicals, a Wallasey Ferry ticket from Liverpool to Seacombe, a box of matches, a tin of Capstan Navy Cut tobacco, and a programme for the Wirral and Birkenhead Agricultural Society's 55th Annual Show.

One hundred and fifty years ago this stretch of coast was renowned for its wreckers; robbers and smugglers who would lure the Liverpool-bound vessels on to the sandbanks using decoy lights and flares. Once ashore, the wreckers showed no mercy towards the unfortunate crew and passengers; if their lives were spared, their cargoes and belongings were not. But not all wrecking was deliberate; winter storms claimed many ships, and local people were quick to arrive on the scene to salvage what they could. Henry Aspinall, of Birkenhead, wrote this vivid description of a severe storm in 1839:

> On 6th January 1839, the day was fine; a fair wind blew for outward-bound ships. Many left the Mersey under sail, among them the St Andrew, the Lockwoods, and the Pennsylvania, first-class packet ships, loaded with valuable cargoes and emigrants together with a few saloon passengers for New York. On the morning of the 7th, the barometer fell to a very low point. The vessels had almost reached Holyhead, when suddenly the wind changed to the north-west and blew a hurricane. The three vessels at once put back for the Mersey, the only shelter in such a gale. Unfortunately the wind veered dead north-west, and took the three vessels on to the Burbo and West Hoyle Banks. The sea rose to a fearful height, and the vessels settled in the sand until they were literally smashed to pieces. No boats could live. The moment they reached the water they were swamped and all on board were washed away. Many were drowned and washed ashore at Leasowe, Hoylake, and the neighbouring coast. Such a sight I never saw before or since, nor should I like to. The scene deeply impressed. The beach was covered with wreckage and dead bodies. I vividly recall the latter . . . it was, indeed, a most pitiful sight. To this day, in old Hoylake cottages, may be seen cupboards, doors, satinwood fittings, and glass and ebony door

handles, washed up and appropriated by the finders – sad relics of a catastrophe which caused a great sensation in the district.

The coast from Harrison Drive to Meols, together with its immediate hinterland of sand dunes and rough common land, has recently been suggested for designation as the North Wirral Coastal Park. To quote the official literature: "It was felt that the North Wirral Coast and foreshore offered a unique opportunity for the development of a Coastal Country Park which would, eventually, combine a wide range of active and passive recreation facilities to meet both local and sub-regional leisure requirements." It has also been suggested that the Coastal Park could eventually link up with the Wirral Country Park to form an almost continuous walk through a large slice of Wirral.

The first part of the scheme to have received official designation and publicity is the Old Gun Site picnic area. This former anti-aircraft gun emplacement is sandwiched between two golf courses, and is approached from both south and east along ancient, dusty, potholed lanes. Green Lane was at one time the only route to the parish of Leasowe, and replaces an even older route from Wallasey. Telegraph Lane, off the busy Leasowe Road, is probably the oldest track to the shore. Conservation measures have been taken to protect the remaining sand dunes, and to encourage the establishment of plants and shrubs. Few species can survive in these exposed, sandy, wind-swept conditions, but coastal plants such as marram grass, burnet rose and lady's bedstraw can be found in the more sheltered parts. Erosion of the dunes through wind-blow and over-use has been a serious problem, but it is hoped that conservation management will encourage sand-anchoring plants and grasses to grow and stabilize the dunes.

A short distance from the Gun Site, along the embankment and across the sands of Liverpool Bay, lies Leasowe Castle. Do not go to Leasowe Castle expecting to see a fortress on a hill, surmounted by tall towers and surrounded by a moat. Castellations and turrets it *has* got, but there the likeness ends. Built in 1593 as "New Hall" by Ferdinando, fifth Earl of Derby, the

Fort Perch Battery and Lighthouse, New Brighton

The Town Hall, Wallasey

The Old Schoolhouse, Breck Road, Wallasey

Moreton Cross

Leasowe Castle

Leasowe Lighthouse

Ivy Cottage, Saughall Massie

The Dee Estuary from Caldy Hill

Oyster-catchers on Hilbre Island

Grey seals off Hilbre Island

Thor's Stone, Thurstaston Hill

castle has had a colourful history during its existence. Its original purpose is uncertain; the popular theory that Ferdinando used it as a grandstand for viewing the racing on the "leasowes" can probably be discounted, as it would appear that the racecourse was too far away to make this a worthwhile proposition. Ormerod is probably nearer the truth: "Whatever the ostensible reason for the creation of a structure so substantial that sea air and the storms of over three centuries, in an exposed situation, have failed to affect it, it is more likely that it originated in a desire on the part of the builder to be prepared for any eventuality which the disturbed times in which he lived rendered probable." A stone bearing the date 1593 and the "three legs" emblem of the Isle of Man (the Earls of Derby being Kings of Man from 1407 to 1735) has been removed from the castle and is on display at the Williamson Museum and Art Gallery in Birkenhead.

The castle's present unplanned, sprawling appearance is the result of the work of its several owners who have added extra towers, wings, turrets and outbuildings. Towards the end of the seventeenth century the castle became derelict and acquired the name "Mockbeggar Hall", a name given to any deserted or lonely building. Memories of this era of the castle's history are still perpetuated in the "Mockbeggar Wharf", the name given to the sands along the shore opposite the castle. After having been used as a farmhouse for a period, the Egerton's of Oulton occupied the building and probably gave it its present name.

The castle was sold in 1786 to a Robert Harrison, and again in 1802 to Margaret Boode, daughter of the Rector of Liverpool, and friend of the shipwrecked. As we have seen, in Chapter 2, Mrs Boode was tragically killed in an accident in Wallasey in 1826, and the castle passed into the care of her son-in-law, Sir Edward Cust. After unsuccessfully running the castle as an hotel, Sir Edward resided there off and on until his death in 1878. During his period of ownership, Sir Edward transformed the castle from a building into a home. He built the perimeter wall and entrance, panelled the dining-room with wood from the original Star Chamber at Westminster, and fitted out the library with oak timbers from the submerged forest at Meols. He was probably responsible for "Canute's Chair", a huge oak seat which stood on the sea wall above high-water mark. The chair, which bore the inscription "Sea come not hither nor wet the sole of my foot", disappeared some twenty years ago.

After the death of Sir Edward Cust, the property was owned by several other members of the Cust family, until it became the Leasowe Castle Hotel in 1891. It was bought by the Trustees of the Railway Convalescent Homes in 1910 and, except for a short time during the First World War when it was used to accommodate German prisoners, was occupied by retired railwaymen right up to 1970.

As I write, the castle stands empty, derelict, as it did 300 years ago – a twentieth-century Mockbeggar. Only security guards walk the rooms where shipwrecked sailors were comforted. It is the castle nobody wants. Wirral Borough Council, the owners, have made ambitious plans for its future; these have been scrapped, and the castle is up for sale yet again. What does the future hold for this fascinating piece of Wirral's – no, England's – history? I recently visited the castle to try to capture something of its past – and perhaps to glimpse its possibilities for the future.

As I turned into the driveway a watery November sun bravely tried to penetrate the veil of grey cloud, and a biting easterly wind cut across the waste flats of the foreshore. The colourless afternoon gave the grey stone walls of the castle a cheerless appearance. Away from the busy Leasowe Road, it was like stepping into another world; the weather-worn stone dogs keeping watch over the main gateway eyed me curiously as I passed into the castle grounds.

The immediate surroundings of the castle are very bare, only a few hardy shrubs being able to survive the merciless winds and sandy soils of these parts. From the main driveway, the castle appears a hotchpotch of additions and extensions, the black and white timbering contrasting sharply with the sturdy grey stone of the main structure. The drive curves gently to the right of the castle, the main doorway being sensibly placed in the lee of the prevailing westerly winds. A massive stone lion keeps watch over the main doorway, which leads into the entrance hall. My first impression on entering this lofty hall was that of age and decay (an impression justified by my subsequent wanderings). Tiles were loose on the floor, and paint was peeling from the walls. And yet, as I stood alone within these cold stone walls, I felt a sense of grandeur. A fine stone and iron staircase takes pride of place in the entrance hall. This is the renowned "Battle Staircase", so called because of the hand-painted nameplates of famous British battles set into the wrought-iron rails. Erected by Sir Edward Cust, the hand-rails also show the dates of the battles, the sovereign reigning at the time, and the generals in command of the troops. I noticed that, regrettably, some of the nameplates were missing, apparently removed by visitors.

My guide suddenly appeared from one of the many doorways leading off the entrance hall. We wandered down a long, dusky corridor and peeped into side rooms: kitchens, laundry rooms, showers, all once busy during the castle's occupation as a convalescent home, but now quiet and empty. A spacious snooker room complete with table waited expectantly for the next pair of players to chalk their cues. Was I imagining it, or did I hear the click of cue against ball, ball against ball? Echoes of games past, perhaps?

Doorways led to stairs; here there were bedrooms looking out across the grey waters of the Irish Sea and across the dreary Moreton plain to the Welsh hills. Everywhere the damp had penetrated; and indeed, workmen were busy making good rotting timbers where the weather had got in. A bright nursery room resounded no more to the sounds of children playing. My guide showed me an escape route hidden behind a false bookcase, a hiding place behind a huge mirror on the landing, and grim spiral stone stairways thick with cobwebs and leading down into the bowels of the castle.

The daylight was beginning to fade as we neared the end of our tour; the cold which had permeated the thick stone walls had found its way into the depths of my being; and I found myself eagerly anticipating my own cosy room and fire awaiting me at home. But my guide had more in store for me yet. Like all good hosts, she had left the best till the last. Unlocking a sturdy door, we entered what must surely be the most attractive room in the castle. The "Star Chamber" was originally a dining-room and was fitted out by Sir Edward Cust with the original panelling from the Star Chamber in the Old Exchequer Buildings at Westminster. The light oak panelling in the walls sets off the exquisite ceiling of gilded stars on a pale background. Four old tapestries depicting the four seasons complete the magical effect of this room; it is sad that the original furniture is no longer here to complement these fine decorations. As I was leaving, the setting sun cast a rich, rosy glow across the room and the panelling seemed to be reflecting the flames from the roaring fires which surely burnt in the great hearth over the centuries.

Before leaving the castle, I looked up to the alabaster bas-relief on the landing, which depicts Wirral as it was in the days when "From Birkinheven unto Hilbree a squirrel might leape from tree to tree". I pictured the castle, a haven for the shipwrecked, its rooms warm with life, a place of comfort on the deserted, wild, unfriendly Wirral coast.

Will these rooms and corridors ever again hear the cosy chat of people relaxing after a day's work? Will fires ever again flicker in the cold hearths? Will children ever again run up and down its staircases, discover its secret passages, run across its lawns? Will the laundry and shower rooms ever again run with condensation? The castle would make a fine hostel, school, nursing-home, museum, leisure centre. Its possibilities are endless. Or will it continue to decay – cold, silent, with only the ghosts of times past to walk its rooms and corridors?

Inland from Leasowe Castle, there is little to interest us. Acres of post-war housing cover the low-lying land of the north Wirral plain, with only the playing-fields of Cadbury's extensive factory providing any relief before the outer housing of Moreton is encountered. The Henry Meoles School (formerly Wallasey Gramar School) squats on the marshy perimeter of the housing estate, looking out across a dreary landscape towards the slopes of Bidston Hill and more housing in the Fender Valley. Yet here is the setting for a Wirral "first". On Leasowe Road is the first building in the world to be heated entirely by solar energy. St George's School was built in 1961 to the designs of Emslie Morgan, a "genius" who spent a lifetime looking into ways of harnessing the sun's rays. His research resulted in the "Solar School", a matchbox-like building with, on one side a drab, windowless façade and on the other 10,000 square feet of glass, a giant solar wall. The wall is built of glass leaves two feet apart. These draw the ultra-violet rays from sunshine and bounce them around the walls of the classrooms. The walls become warm and heat the air. Hardly any warmth escapes through the school's massively thick roof and walls covered with slabs of plastic foam. On the coldest days it is always 60 degrees Fahrenheit inside, and in summer the school is cooler than its more conventional neighbours, for panels inside the glass wall can be turned to deflect heat or absorb it. It need hardly be said that, despite the uniqueness of the building at the time of its erection, it was left to foreign designers to take up the invention and use it on a world-wide scale.

My earliest memories of this world are of Moreton. I shall be forever thankful to my parents for moving from the cobblestones and grime of Seacombe to the fresh air, green fields and open spaces of the "West end" of Wallasey. Thirty years ago we were pioneers in what was to become not just a satellite of Wallasey, but almost a new town, a community with its own identity, and a community with its own problems. Wirral has seen many changes of recent years, but probably nowhere has seen such radical change as Moreton. Ellison wrote in 1955: "Moreton is so obviously brand-new that we will not stop there longer than we must. . . ." A lot of that newness has worn off in the years since that was written; thousands of families during that time have contributed to give Moreton a sense of community, that undefinable quality so important today.

Mortimer, writing in 1847, said this of Moreton: "It is situated in a dreary flat, close to the shores of the sea, with roads excessively bad . . . it is, in every point of view, an extremely poor village, and the greater part of the township is below the level of the sea at high water." With a population of about 350, Moreton in those days was, like most other communities, isolated and insular. Its inhabitants lived under constant threat of inundation by the sea; and its low-lying land made farming difficult. Even the coming of the railway in 1866 did not attract the Liverpool merchants and businessmen as much as other parts of Wirral.

It was not until shortly after the First World War that Moreton began to change. Homeless families came and erected makeshift shacks and chalets in the muddy fields. More than 2,000 asbestos and corrugated iron dwellings, without water or sanitation, became homes for the homeless, and gave the area nicknames such as "Shanty Town" and "Moreton in the Mud". Conditions were appalling; money was scarce, facilities were few. But in spite of the hardships (or because of them?) the bungalow-dwellers were a friendly, close-knit group of people. A contemporary writer recorded:

> Till pretty recently, Moreton was no more than a tranquil group of old Wirral homesteads, but just at present its name is associated with contention by reason of a number of camp dwellers, whose wholesome aspiration for liberty and love of nature is not uncharacteristic of the soil. You catch something of the new atmosphere on stepping down towards the village. Almost the first house you come to is called "Jocular Cottage" and the next is dubbed "Rainfall Villa". There is such a merry-and-bright-don't-care-if-it-snows-air about the choice of titles.

However, when Moreton was incorporated into the Borough of Wallasey in 1928, one of the Council's first jobs was to do something about its notorious West End. An embarrassment to the borough, the dwellings were cleared away and replaced by permanent housing. With the construction of sewers and drains, and the widening of the River Birket and the Arrowe Brook, Moreton gradually became "civilized", although it is only in recent times that it has lost its "Moreton in the Mud" image.

Moreton's population in 1921 was 4,000; by the mid-seventies it had risen to 24,000, and it is still growing. Building activity (mainly residential) has been such that the only remaining open land lies between the railway line and the coast;

southwards Moreton's housing merges indistinguishably with Upton's, and to the west the fields up to the Meols boundary are rapidly disappearing under yet more houses.

Although still linked with Wallasey for administrative purposes, few Moretonians would claim to have any affinity with their bigger neighbour. Moreton's residents most definitely live in "Moreton, Wirral"; not "Moreton, Wallasey" – such is the feeling of identity for this new town which emerged from the marshes. For new it certainly is; the interested enquirer must search out Moreton's links with the past, for there are few enough remaining.

Moreton's focal point, the Cross, is the meeting point of four busy roads. Shops border three sides of Moreton Cross, but on the fourth side an imposing inn, the Coach and Horses, dominates the scene. There has been an inn of the same name on this site since the seventeenth century when, like its neighbour the Plough, it was a favourite venue for visitors to the Leasowe Races. The present building was built in 1928 and, with its sandstone walls, half timbering and mock turrets, is known far and wide as "The Cathedral", such is its grandeur.

Moreton's oldest building lies tucked away behind the Coach and Horses in Barnston Lane. Old Hall Farm bears a name-plate inscribed DMW 1719 and was probably built by Daniel Wilson, one of the sons of Robert Wilson of Bidston Hall. There is little in the external appearance of the building to suggest its age; its blue paintwork and white rendering attract scarcely a second glance from passers-by. And its farming days are well and truly over.

Most of Moreton's shops are modern, many of the smaller family concerns having been ousted by the supermarket giants. However, on the south-east corner of the Cross is a group of shop buildings which tell an interesting story. Set in the brickwork above the shop-fronts is a series of plaques inscribed with the names "The Golden Valley", "Spring Gate", "Sweet Cecil" and others. Each is the name of a famous Grand National racehorse of a bygone age. And why here? Well, they were placed here as a tribute to local jockey F. ("Tich") Mason, a well-known Moreton personality who rode each of these horses in the Grand National during his career as a jockey. One of the horses, Kirkland, he rode to victory in 1905.

Christ Church, on the Upton road just beyond the Cross, was built in 1863 to designs by John Cunningham, who also designed neighbouring Upton Church. Its insignificant spire is only offset by the church's situation on a slight eminence, and there is nothing of interest in the church itself.

A long, wide, straight road leads from the Cross northwards to the shore. Between here and Meols is a wide tract of "Common" land, dominated by the disused lighthouse; springy, wind-swept turf, the embankment providing little shelter from the persistent winds blowing off the sea. Designated a Site of Special Scientific Interest, here is the home of the rabbit and hare; skylarks nest in the clumps of turf; and rare plants such as yellow button (the only occurrence in Britain) grow in the sheltered, boggy ditches. Sun-seeking humanity takes over on sunny afternoons, but their occupation is brief. Come here mid-week when the tide is high and the wind is fresh. Stand on the ridge of the embankment and look out to sea. Turn around and look to inland Wirral; and be thankful for the sturdiness of the tons of concrete beneath your feet protecting homes, shops and factories from the cruel waters of the Irish Sea.

History was made here during the summer of 1962, another Wirral "first". The world's first scheduled hovercraft service operated between here and Rhyl (on the North Wales coast) for eight weeks during that summer. Having paid their fare (£1 single, £2 return) passengers were whisked across the sands of the Dee estuary in 25 minutes, a journey which usually takes an hour and a half by road. Whether this trial service was successful or not can only be judged by the fact that it never operated again after that summer! At the time, it seemed that the slightest adverse weather conditions affected the craft, and more often than not it failed to run. For all that, it was an exciting experiment which provided much-needed experience of operating a hovercraft under harsh maritime conditions.

The lighthouse at Moreton (known far and wide as Leasowe Lighthouse) stands back from the embankment, uncared for and unused, a sad state of affairs for what is probably the oldest lighthouse site in the country. Do not be misled by the date stone set in the wall above the door; that was taken from the original lighthouse, built in 1763. The initials MWG are those of the Mayor of Liverpool at that time, a William Gregson.

Two lighthouses were erected on this coast in 1763: a "lower light" on the shore and an "upper light" on the site of the present building, the theory being that an approaching ship's master had only to line up the two lights to achieve a safe entrance into the Rock Channel and the Port of Liverpool. Unfortunately, as might have been expected, the lower light was soon troubled by encroachment of the sea, and so the upper light became the new lower light. A new upper light was built on Bidston Hill, three miles distant, in 1771 (not the present lighthouse on the hill). The existing building at Moreton was built in 1824 on the site of the original beacon, and continued to send its beam out into Liverpool Bay until 1908. The last keeper of the light (a woman, even in those unemancipated days!) continued to run the building as a tea house for summer visitors, but when it was put up for sale in 1929, no one wanted to buy. Wallasey Corporation bought the lighthouse in 1930, and it has remained closed ever since. Ambitious plans have been put forward for its inclusion in the proposed North Wirral Coastal Park as a museum or recreation centre. Hopes were raised in 1973 when it was given a coat of white paint – but nothing further has been done since. The briny winds have turned its once-white exterior a dirty grey, and it now looks worse than ever. It is said that the lighthouse's foundations are of cotton taken from a wrecked cargo ship, this being an ideal material to settle into the soft sand, but there is little basis for this belief. I expect little remains of the building's seven floors, or the cast-iron staircase winding up to the lighthouse space, 101 feet above ground. Only dust and cobwebs. . . .

Back on the embankment, workmen recently unearthed a nineteenth-century fishing smack, the *Emblematic*, which had been embedded in the sea wall. Ellison wrote of this in 1955:

> Evidence of the great storm that raged in October 1889 may be seen in the wooden timbers of the Hoylake fishing smack

Emblematic still embedded in the embankment itself. She was so securely wedged into a gap torn by the sea that to remove her and repair the damage would have cost the unfortunate owner, James Eccles, more than she was worth; so she was buried in stones and cement where she lay, leaving some of the woodwork visible to this day.

There seems to be some dispute over the date of the storm which wrecked the *Emblematic*; some authorities say January 1883 is more likely. However that may be, when the boat was unearthed it was found to be in a fairly good state of preservation, but it unfortunately sank at its moorings and defied all attempts at salvage.

A little way along the coast in the direction of Meols, Carr Lane provides an opportunity to head inland again. The word "Carr" means "marsh", an apt description of the land hereabouts. The lane forms the westernmost boundary of Moreton, and although it starts off in fields and market gardens, it ends in a brand-new housing estate on the main Moreton-Hoylake road. On the other side of the road, a direction sign points to Saughall Massie, our next stopping-place.

Mortimer, writing in 1847, said of Saughall Massie: "It is in every respect, if possible, worse than the adjacent township of Moreton", despite Webb's earlier description of the place as "a very gallant lordship". I wonder what the two historians would say of it today? Perhaps something along the lines of "a carefully preserved eighteenth-century village encircled by twentieth-century housing". The remarkable thing about Saughall Massie is that, despite the encroachment of the houses, the village has an undeniable "country atmosphere" about it. The farms still farm, and the people who live here still work, to a degree, on the land.

The name Saughall Massie is probably derived from "the hall or slope of willows" and the name of an influential Wirral family of the Middle Ages, the Massies. Although the Massies are no longer, there *are* willow trees in abundance along the banks of the Arrowe Brook which runs through the village. While its neighbour, Moreton, expanded into a town, Saughall Massie remained unchanged and unnoticed for decades. No main roads pass through, neither is there a railway station within walking distance. One of the first hints that things might change came in the 1960s with the straightening and widening of the main lane into the village. The completion of the North Wirral Sewer Outfall in 1971 opened the gates for numerous planning applications, many of which had been held up for lack of drainage facilities. With the bulldozers came the realization that Wirral could lose yet another piece of its precious heritage, and so the then Wallasey Corporation declared Saughall Massie and its immediate surroundings a Conservation Area. This did not mean conservation regardless, for so often this means stagnation; but each planning application was to be looked at according to its merits and faults. And, as can be seen from the village today, new buildings *have* been put up – some people would even say that they are more attractive (and certainly more habitable) than their older neighbours.

It is worth while looking at the buildings in Saughall Massie; there are several fine house plates, the histories of which have been studied and well documented by Woods and Brown in *The Rise and Progress of Wallasey*. On the northern outskirts of the village, almost opposite Garden Hey Road, Diamond Farm dates back to 1728; alongside the farmhouse a small enclosure is a mass of daffodils and tulips in spring. A little further on, the farmhouse at Poplar Farm has a plate inscribed IJP 1714; the letters SX were added at a later date. On the corner of Saughall Road and the Upton road stands the White House which, although bearing a stone dated 1323, is a 1951 reconstruction of the original building. On the opposite corner, Ivy Cottage with its thatched roof and ivy-covered walls dates back to 1690. Prospect Farm, an attractive group of buildings in red sandstone, faces Ivy Farm. Saughall Massie's Hotel, the Saughall, contrasts sharply with these fine old buildings. There has been an inn on the site since 1561, and parts of the present buildings are eighteenth century. Most of the hotel, though, is modern and without character.

Will Saughall Massie survive as a living, working community, carrying on the village traditions passed down through the generations? Or will the farm owners give way to outside pressures and sell their properties for conversion to high-priced des. res. and craft shops? That, of course, depends upon the people who live and work in Saughall Massie.

A narrow, winding country lane (threatened with "improvements") leads out of Saughall Massie in the direction of West Kirby, but half a mile out of Saughall Massie, at Three Lanes End, a lane leads to the coast of Meols. This lane is possibly part of an ancient highway used by the Romans. It is known that a Roman road left Chester in this direction, and traces of such a route have been found in various parts of Wirral. The road here is on the line of the Roman road and ends at Meols, a coastal area with strong Roman links.

The interest of Meols (pronounced Mells) is mainly historical, for the place today is residential, with a little market gardening clinging precariously along its Moreton boundary. Indeed, but for its legendary associations with submerged forests and ancient civilizations washed away by the sea, Meols would probably have lost its identity entirely and became part of the urban belt of Hoylake and West Kirby.

The name Meols is derived from the old Norse word meaning "sand dunes". The dunes have gone, blown flat and replaced by more effective (if less attractive) twentieth-century coastal defences. The present site of Meols is probably the last in a series of different sites dating back over 1,700 years. For along this stretch of coast, below the high-water mark, have been found literally thousands of objects – coins, brooches, spurs, buckles, keys, and human and animal remains – which span a period of history from prehistoric times to the eighteenth century.

It is thought that the original settlements were on a high, sandy promontory which projected well out into the sea (the area marked "Dove Point" on the maps). This would have given its inhabitants an excellent look-out along the coast in both directions. The Reverend A. Hume, in his detailed account of the finds on the Meols shore, *Ancient Meols*, writes:

> It is probable that this position was occupied as an outpost by the Romans, not only for the purpose of embarking and

> disembarking with greater facility on their sea journeys, but as a permanent outwork and place of observation.

Maps of the sixteenth and seventeenth centuries show Meols as an important seaport town.

However, tidal erosion constantly forced the settlements to move further inland; between 1750 and 1828 over 200 yards of land were removed by the action of the sea. About 1828, when Telford was surveying the area in connection with his proposed canal between the Mersey and the Dee, workmen uncovered a number of human skeletons, neatly laid out in rows, about 150 yards below the flow of the tide. An ancient well or spring of fresh water, rising far within the area covered by the tide, was known to exist during the last century. It is believed to have been used by keepers of the shore lighthouse at Leasowe, and was covered by a brick archway. Foundations of ancient British wattle-and-daub huts, with clay floors and posts resting on stone bases, were exposed by the spring tides of 1891. The huts were arranged in the form of an irregular village street, and human footprints and cartwheel tracks were also uncovered.

But undoubtedly Meols' greatest claim to fame was its "submerged forest", which covered a large area along this coast. As recently as 1947 the shore at Meols was described thus:

> At low tide the trunks, stumps, and roots of a vast number of trees are clearly visible, stretching for a distance of a couple of miles along the shore. Oak, birch, and conifers are the principal remains; some of the trunks are of considerable size.

However, less than ten years later, there was little to show that it ever existed. In the days of the "forest" the shore was a mass of black turf bog and rotting vegetation (the word "Dove" means "black" – Dove Point). Locals would carry away cartloads of the rotting trunks, for it made excellent firewood. Door handles and trinkets were carved from the harder stumps. A room at Leasowe Castle was panelled with wood from the shore. This must have been a forest in the real sense, for the bones of many animals have been found here. And seventy years ago, after a fierce storm which had exposed the hard, black clay, a number of hoof prints of the wild ox and other forest animals were discovered.

Walking across the flat expanse of sand today, the imagination runs riot. How many tales of human joy and tragedy lie beneath these wet, shifting sands? How many battles fought? Are there more treasures, hidden for ever beneath tons of mud and sand? Or will the wind and tides yet reveal relics of a bygone age to the curious gaze of twentieth-century man?

4

SAND, SEA AND SUNSETS

Hoylake – West Kirby – Caldy

How can I convey to you, within a few pages, the many delights of this corner of the Wirral Peninsula? They draw me back from my wanderings like an irresistible magnet. My work takes me far afield to many lovely places in this country, yet it is always with a deep feeling of thankfulness that I return to West Kirby.

THESE words, written just twenty years ago by local historian and naturalist the late Norman Ellison (about whom more later), sum up the problem facing any writer dealing with this north-western tip of the peninsula. The twin townships – some would say "resorts" – of Hoylake and West Kirby do indeed boast many delights, and there can be few places in England with such a variety of scenery matched with a rich and fascinating history. A list of the area's attractions reads like an extract from a guide-book: sailing, fishing, walking, championship golf, birdwatching, panoramic views of mountain and estuary, magnificent sunsets. It is hardly surprising that Hoylake and West Kirby have become one of the most sought-after residential areas in the north-west.

As we have seen in the previous chapter, this corner of Wirral has had a long and varied history of human occupation. However, in the days when neighbouring Meols was an important Roman outpost, Hoylake as such did not exist. A deep channel or "lake", protected from the full ravages of the Irish Sea by a great sandbank, had probably been used as a safe anchorage by generations of mariners and fishermen. The earliest mention of this "lake" dates from the reign of King John, when it was known as "Heye-pol"; in those days it extended several miles along the coast from Hilbre to Dove Point at Meols, and even at low tide had a depth of 15 to 20 feet of water. The lake's name underwent many changes over the years, eventually being applied to the village itself as it grew up to serve the shipping using the anchorage. The present name "Hoylake" is little more than a century old; the existence of the "Hoyle" sandbank is a present-day reminder of the town's former name.

In the days when the Hoyle Lake was a deep-water anchorage, it was much used by armies passing to and from Ireland. During the Tyrone rebellion, 4,000 foot soldiers and 200 horses sailed from here for Ireland, and in 1689 Duke Schomberg, King William's general, assembled an army of 10,000 here for an attack on King James's forces which still held out in Ireland. Men-of-war and transports were anchored in deep water, and nearly 10,000 men, including at least one brigade of Dutch troops, were taken across the Irish Sea.

The following spring, transports were still voyaging to Ireland – 400 recruits and the Nassau and Brandenburg regiments on one occasion, and a regular stream of foot and horse troops in April and May. King William III came in the following month to join the great army which had assembled in camp along the flats by the shore. The road known today as "King's Gap" is named as the point where the Royal escort with the monarch went down to the ships, accompanied by some 10,000 men. What a sight that must have been for the handful of local fishermen and farmworkers! This massive exercise culminated in the Battle of the Boyne, when William III fought and defeated James II in a decisive victory.

For all its importance as an embarkation point, there was no accommodation for travellers during those early days; in fact there were only two houses at Hoylake, and travellers had to stay at West Kirby, or even Chester, until a ship was available. It was not until 1792 that the first hotel was built, by Sir John Stanley. His intention was not, however, to accommodate travellers and seafarers (for by this time the lake had begun to silt up) but to attract folk to the pleasures of sea-bathing. A letter which appeared in the *Gentleman's Magazine* in 1796 extolled the benefits to be enjoyed at Hoylake:

> I am writing to you from the extreme point of the Hundred of Wirral in Cheshire, near the broad estuary of the Dee, and only seven miles from the confluence of the more commercial waters of the Mersey with the ocean. The Hoyle sand breaks the force of the waves, so as to render the High Lake a safe road for vessels of any size in the roughest weather. Although, at the first glance, we appear shut out from the rest of the world, a very short time conveys us to Parkgate (the station of the Dublin packets), across the water into Wales, into the bustle of Liverpool, or the less busy capital of this county. The coast of Flintshire displays itself with great beauty on the other side of the Dee; whilst the rugged mountains of Wales form the boundary of the prospect towards the south-west. The Dee affords abundance of fine salmon, cockles, shrimps, soles; and various kinds of flat fish are taken on the sandbanks and in the lake. Every vessel that comes into or goes out of the Dee or Mersey is distinctly seen hence; and the lake is frequently enlivened by brigs and schooners beating to windward. It is well calculated for the inhabitants of the central counties, who, at no great distance from their own house, will here find genteel society, good accommodation at reasonable prices, and one of the most commodious bathing-places in the island.

And so, as the boats left Hoylake with the silting up of the anchorage and the growth of Liverpool, the village became first a watering-place and then a resort. Before the coming of the railway in 1866, Hoylake was little more than a fishing village, with few houses apart from the fishermen's dwellings. A row of cottages and small villas on the sea front constituted the residential part of the village, where the "holidaymakers" had their lodgings.

Hoylake had its own racecourse between 1840 and 1876; it was said that the Hoylake turf was "the finest in the world on which to gallop a horse". Village sports were regularly held too, the donkey and pony races proving particularly popular. But the sport which was to establish the name of Hoylake both nationally and internationally was golf. Founded in 1869 by a handful of local enthusiasts, the Liverpool Golf Club grew to become the Royal Liverpool Golf Club, and is today recognized as one of the finest golf courses in the country.

Hoylake today is a residential area rather than a seaside resort. Holidaymakers still come – but in their hundreds, not thousands. Any fine summer's day will see plenty of day trippers strolling along the promenade or sitting on the sands. But enough – let us take a stroll around Hoylake and see for ourselves what kind of a place this is.

Hoylake is one of the few seaside towns fortunate enough to have had its railway line built well away from the sea front, giving unrestricted access to the beach. There is little of interest in the town itself, which occupies a ribbon of land along the West Kirby road between the railway and the shore; the railway has proved an effective limit to growth inland. Along the main shopping thoroughfare, every other shop seems to deal in antiques, a fairly recent trend.

The town boasts two parish churches – Holy Trinity in Trinity Road, built in 1833 by Sir James Picton of Liverpool, and St Hildeburgh in Stanley Road, built 1897–9. Both are good, but neither is outstanding. Possibly of greater interest is the octagonal brick tower of a lighthouse in, of all places, a garden in Valentia Road. This was the upper light of a pair erected about 1761 and rebuilt in the 1860s to guide shipping into the Hoyle Lake anchorage. This was, incidentally, the first light in the world to be fitted with paraboloidal mirrors. Near here, the Green Lodge Hotel dates back to about 1750, when it was constructed as a shooting box for the Stanleys; portions of the original walls still remain.

Hoylake's promenade starts at Meols and follows the coast for two miles, finishing at King's Gap. Good, clean sands, wide sea views, and something of interest at every step make this a fine walk at any time. Ellison wrote: "Here you will find no Fun Fair or Pleasure Beach; no souvenir kiosks or questionable postcards; no bathing belles competing for some title and substantial prize money; no fake-auctions to trap the unwary; no touting; no blaring loudspeakers." Walk from east to west and you will have the hills and mountains of Snowdonia forming a fitting backcloth to the waters and sands of the Dee estuary. In the opposite direction the cranes and waterside buildings of Liverpool's dockland form a backcloth of a different kind. Cast your eyes seawards, to the sandy ridge of Hoyle Bank, its sands high and dry at low tide; and think about recent scatter-brained proposals to build an airport for Merseyside out there on those wind-swept, watery flats!

The promenade ends at King's Gap. At high water the way to West Kirby is inland via Meols Drive, where grand detached residences skirt the links of the Royal Liverpool Golf Club. But of far greater interest, tide permitting, is the trek along the sands to the north-west tip of the Wirral Peninsula at Red Rocks, and thence by the dunes to West Kirby. Waders and gulls feeding on the wet sands are an ever-present source of delight. At Red Rocks the sandstone headland makes an ideal point for viewing the flocks of waders winging their way along the coast. Here too is an area of brackish marsh of particular interest to nature lovers. The Red Rocks Nature Reserve is managed by the Cheshire Conservation Trust and, as well as supporting many interesting plants, the marsh attracts many migrant birds on passage in spring and autumn. These include large flocks of siskin, brambling and snow bunting, and hundreds of redwing and fieldfare. Occasional rarities attract bird-watchers from far afield – a total of 216 species of birds has been recorded at Red Rocks over the years. The Reserve supports what is probably the last remaining colony of natterjack toads in Wirral. This colony is the most southerly on the west coast, and is one of Britain's rarest amphibians – easily recognizable by the yellow stripe down its back and its loud nocturnal croaking. Many interesting coastal and marsh-loving plants grow here too; but access to the Reserve is restricted to permit-holders only.

The Hilbre Islands appear tantalizingly close from here; but, although barely a mile distant, treacherous mudflats and deep gullies can easily trap the unwary. Do not be tempted to cross to the islands from here; the safest route is from West Kirby, as we shall see later.

On this tip of Wirral the horizons are clear and wide; sky and sea predominate in a scene which is never the same for two consecutive hours. The estuary is constantly changing as tide, sun and clouds interact on this vast tract of wilderness. This sense of spaciousness is not lost as we leave the open sea and head towards West Kirby. Sand dunes skirt the golf course along this stretch, providing welcome relief from the man-made sea defences of much of the Wirral coastline. Clumps of spartina grass on the beach hereabouts add strength to Ellison's prophecy twenty-five years ago that people living then would one day see the marsh stretching up the coast almost to West Kirby. Attempts have been made (mechanically and chemically) to eradicate the grass, but to no effect.

Large coal deposits were once thought to lie beneath these sandhills:

> Hugh Williams was a man of enterprise. He built several houses at Hoylake; and believed the celebrated Mostyn coal deposits extended under the Dee into the Wirral Peninsula, more especially beneath the sandhills at Hoylake. Consequently, he employed a number of men in boring operations, and spent a large sum of money, until he was wearied with the perpetual drain upon his resources. It was reported that the men employed were so well satisfied with the work, that they made up their minds Mr Williams should not cease the operations without a struggle on their part. They therefore passed small pieces of coal and slack down the bore-holes, so that when the boring tools were drawn up from time to time there was every indication of a good deposit of coal. At last, Hugh Williams discovered the deception and dismissed the men.

The peace and quiet of this walk around the coast from Hoylake is in stark contrast to the hustle and bustle of West Kirby. On most fine days the beach here is crowded, the ice-cream shops are busy, and the promenade is lined with cars. On not quite so fine days the shopping area and leisure centre come into their own. For West Kirby has developed from a small fishing and farming village into a large residential town in little more than a hundred years. The reasons are easy to see. A mild climate, the town being protected from the biting easterly winds by a range of low hills; a pleasant situation at the mouth of a beautiful estuary; and good communications with Chester, Birkenhead and Liverpool.

The original Kirkby ("West" was added to distinguish the place from Kirkby-in-Walea – Wallasey) is half a mile from the modern town centre, in what is now called old West Kirby, near the parish church. Norse settlers landing in Wirral from Ireland in the tenth century were quick to spot the advantages of the site, and established a small community. They built a church which they dedicated to St Bridget, a dedication still held by the present church.

During the sixteenth century West Kirby rivalled its sister Kirkby in Wallasey for its lawlessness, and gained a similar reputation for wrecking and smuggling. A large floating population of travellers, and even armies, awaiting a favourable wind to leave for Ireland, added to the confusion. Sir Henry Bunbury, writing to Queen Elizabeth's Council about this time, reported an abnormal number of alehouses:

> Men of all ranks, nobles and others, flock hither, whom it is impossible to restrain their pleasures, and passengers for Ireland sometimes wait a quarter of a year together for a wind, so that if the alehouses were twice as numerous as they are, they would not be too many, for passengers are occasionally obliged to go to the country house for lodging.

The curate of West Kirby church at that time took advantage of the shortage of accommodation by turning the over-large rectory into an inn, thus adding a sizeable amount to his income! He was brought before the bishop and eventually dismissed from the Church.

West Kirby's importance as a port during this period is often overshadowed by Hoylake. And yet a fair amount of trade was carried on from West Kirby, which had a fleet of twelve ships. Trading lists show imports of live animals – otters and horses – and many kinds of animal skins. As Liverpool grew, so West Kirby declined as a port, and all was quiet for several hundred years. Charles Dawson Brown, a West Kirby man born in 1830, has given us a fascinating glimpse into life in this part of Wirral 150 years ago:

> The roads, not only in the parish, but the Hundred of Wirral generally, were deplorably bad. . . . Farmers took their produce to market in waggons to Woodside and Seacombe . . . the nearest post office was at Neston, later at Upton . . . there was only one newspaper subscribed for in the parish, and that was jointly by the curate and two farmers. It was a weekly one, and came a little irregularly. There was quite a belief in ghosts . . . there was a ghost in the narrow part of the lane between West Kirby and Caldy.

Mortimer, who was something of a prophet of his time, said in 1847 that "the extension of the public works in Birkenhead and Seacombe will drive many to seek the seclusion in these parts [that is, West Kirby], which these townships no longer afford". And so, with the coming of the railway twenty years later, West Kirby, like Hoylake, changed from a small fishing and agricultural community to a prosperous commuters' town and seaside resort.

From Dee Lane, the mile-long promenade skirts the shore, with a glorious panorama of the Welsh hills across the estuary. Nearer at hand, the marine lake is often the scene for summer sailing events, and during the winter months a variety of duck make the lake their home.

At the end of the promenade, the road turns inland to old West Kirby. A recent report, which designated the old village as a conservation area, gave its reasons thus: "With few exceptions, the buildings and landscape in the area have a harmony of scale, form, and materials which are in delicate balance. The fields around the village form an integral part of the village structure and vary from grazing land to fairly dense woodland and include the site of the original pond." The parish church and a picturesque thatched cottage, "The Nook", were listed as being of historical and architectural interest. The popular Ring o' Bells Inn and seventeenth-century Manor Farm combine with winding lanes, red sandstone walls, small fields and cottages to form a very attractive whole which is certainly worth conserving.

The focal point of the old village, St Bridget's Church, has a history dating back to the time of the Norsemen, although the oldest surviving part of the present building is probably late Norman about 1150. The church was rebuilt about 1230, and the chancel rebuilt about a hundred years later. Various additions and alterations, including the reconstruction of the tower, took place over the next 500 years. In the eighteenth century the interior was gutted and the building reduced to the simplicity of a "meeting house". Several restorations have since taken place, the latest being 1869–70. The alterations made over the centuries have left little of interest today. On the south wall of the tower can be seen the incised lines of an old scratch-dial. The east window has some fine stone tracery, one of only two such examples in the country. On the south wall of the chancel is a tablet to the memory of one Jan van Zoelen, dated 1689. It is said, without substantiation, that van Zoelen was with Schomberg's army encamped at Hoylake and Meols, but died before the voyage to Ireland. Whoever he was, he must have been a man of some standing for a memorial to have been erected in his name. The church owns a copy of the renowned "Breeches Bible", printed at Geneva in 1560 and donated by the late Norman Ellison.

Away from the church, in an old schoolroom, is the little-known Charles Dawson Brown Museum; a single room chock-a-block with relics going back almost a thousand years, and all local in origin. Here are things to stir the imagination – items preserved from the days when the Vikings ruled the Wirral coasts. Who was the Viking leader whose "hogback" gravecover gathers dust at one end of the room? What did the first West Kirby church look like – can we visualize it from the few dusty remains gathered here? And there are fascinating items from more recent times – an Elizabethan bench-end, a nineteenth-century water bucket, and a tithe board recording tithes payable in West Kirby in 1712. How I wish every parish church had such a museum!

On hot summer days when the beach at West Kirby is crowded, when the promenade is thick with cars and pedestrians, I like to take to the hills behind the town. Here, I know, I will find peace and quietness. Although little more than 250 feet at their highest, they offer spectacular views of the Dee estuary and the surrounding country. Wild areas of heath and open moor broken by smaller patches of birch wood, intersected by countless paths and tracks, offer unlimited scope to the walker.

Start just outside the town at the war memorial on Grange Hill, where there is a far-reaching view across the north Wirral plain to Wallasey, and across Liverpool Bay to Southport and Formby. At your feet the purple heather and golden gorse give way to the red-brick houses at West Kirby. The town's "suburbs" of Newton and Larton meet the green fields and hedgerows where, on another day, there are field paths to explore. Down there are farms such as China Farm, dated 1753, so called because of the large china plate set into the front wall of the farmhouse. Or Oldfield Manor Farm, early or mid seventeenth century, an attractive red sandstone building with mullioned and transomed windows, hidden in a crescent of a lane.

When you have had your fill of Grange Hill, cross the busy A540 and head in the direction of the beacon. This tall (60 feet) stone column surmounted by a large ball is a well-known Wirral landmark, and is often called the Mariners' Beacon. A windmill originally occupied this site, and was a valuable landmark for sailors "frequenting the River Mersey and its vicinity". In 1839 the mill was destroyed during a gale and, as a result of a petition, the present beacon was erected as a replacement. The beacon stands in a piece of heathland known as Liberty Park, a name supposedly derived from the fact that ratepayers formerly possessed the right to quarry stone there for house repairs. Paths wander in all directions, but keep to the ridge and you soon come upon a view-finder set at the highest point along here.

This is, without doubt, the finest view-point in Wirral. Ellison's description cannot be bettered:

> On a clear day the view on every side is far-reaching: Blackpool Tower and Black Combe, the nearest Lakeland mountain, to the north (perhaps five times in my life I have seen from here the central heights of Lakeland – Scafell, Great End, Bowfell, Helvellyn, etc); the Snowdon range, the Llandudno Ormes and Anglesey are silhouetted against the

western sky; perhaps twice in a lifetime the summit of Snaefell in the Isle of Man appears just above the north-western horizon. The silver stretch of the Dee lies at our feet, the Hilbre Isles and the placid waters of the marine lake are in the foreground. Turn round and the view embraces the flat plain of north Wirral, with the steep ridge of Wallasey and the Mersey beyond; to the south-east the country is well wooded up to the wide expanse of Thurstaston Common.

Come here as the sun is setting on a summer's evening and be prepared for an experience beyond description. The hills on the far side of the estuary darken as the sun sinks low in the sky. The colours are reflected in the waters, or on the wet sands, of the estuary. All is quiet, save for the call of the curlew or oyster-catcher far away by the Dee. It said that Turner, the immortal landscape painter, came here to put the effects on to canvas. If he did, which is doubtful, it is unlikely that he could have recorded such beauty in mere painters' colours.

This is Caldy Hill, over a hundred acres of untamed heath-land where the public can roam at will. Bird-lovers will find a variety of birds in the rich habitats the hill provides. Tits and warblers, finches and buntings on the more open parts; woodpeckers, jays, tree-creepers and owls in the wooded areas. And always the chance of spotting a rare visitor blown off course by freak winds. The gorse here is often in flower all the year round; what a joy it is to see the sunshine-yellow blossoms on a cold, dreary December day. Heather, bilberry, and the delicate tracery of silver birch all add to the beauty of Caldy Hill.

On the landward side of the Hill is West Kirby's Grammar School, Calday Grange. The school was founded in 1636 by William Glegg, who considered "how very Godly, virtuous and necessary it is to provide that youth should be brought up in virtue, learning, good order and obedience".

Also on this side of Caldy Hill is Stapledon Wood, a fine stretch of mature woodland with many noble beech trees, given in memory of William Olaf Stapledon who died in 1950. This gifted writer and lover of this corner of Wirral gave this and other land in the area for public use. But for the generosity of Stapledon, Paton and others like them, these open spaces would now be covered by detached villas like those already creeping up its lower slopes.

Fleck Lane is an old bridle path which cuts across Caldy Hill to the village of Caldy itself. Caldy, often described as the prettiest village in Wirral (and probably the most photographed), was, 150 years ago, "one of the worst in the neighbourhood, consisting of a few fishermen's huts and small cottages". A far cry from Edward Hubbard's much-quoted description of Caldy just ten years ago: "By reason of its prosperous commuter country Cheshire is something of a Surrey of the north, but Surrey has nothing to compare with this."

Caldy was mentioned in the Doomsday Book as Calders, and subsequently passed through the hands of substantial Wirral families – the Thurstastons, the Heselwells and the Whitmores. The village owes its present appearance to a Manchester man, R. W. Barton, who in 1832 bought the township and set about renovating and rebuilding the properties on the estate. The Barton family built the manor (although seventeenth-century parts were probably incorporated into the design) and the church (built originally as a school).

The character of the village is almost entirely due to the blend of mellowed local red sandstone and black and white timbering set among mature trees along a narrow, twisting road. The village shop – selling antiques now – was originally an inn. Legend has it that during the construction of the West Kirby to Hooton railway in 1884 (now the Wirral Country Park) the landlord of the Hop Inn made a small fortune by rolling barrels of beer down to the bridge on the labourers' pay-day! Well-kept seventeenth-century buildings in the centre of the village hide the modern (but sympathetic) development immediately behind. Away from the village, large, individual, architect-designed residences set in ample grounds off curving tree-lined roads complete Caldy's "perfection".

Caldy Beach is just a short walk from the village. Here are

fine sands, good bathing and, in the late evening, a sense of peace and solitude rarely found today.

I started this chapter with the words written by Norman F. Ellison. Ellison was born in Lancashire, but moved to Wirral while still a boy. His love of the peninsula, its wildlife, its people, its nooks and crannies, found an outlet in his writing and broadcasting. Known as "Nomad", he brought the enchantment of river and stream, hedgerow and field, tree and flower, bird and beast, to listeners of *Children's Hour*. He put into print his experiences as a travelling observer of nature in the "Nomad" books. He wrote magazine articles on subjects as diverse as Colorado beetles and Celtic crosses. His book *The Wirral Peninsula* has been a rich source of information, interest and pleasure to many for a quarter of a century. He it was who inspired to no small degree my own love of Wirral. His death in 1976 has left Wirral a poorer place.

Ellison lived for much of his life in the corner of Wirral which I have been describing in this chapter. Let the last words be his:

> My home is on the fringe of Caldy Hill, and I ask for nothing more satisfying than a stroll before breakfast on a sunny spring morning, beneath silver birches wearing their delicate new greenery, or a brisker walk when a harvest moon is flooding the channels of the Dee with light, and borne on the still air there comes the murmur of countless sea-birds seeking their supper at the edge of the ebbing tide.

5

SANCTUARY IN THE SEA

The Dee Estuary and the Hilbre Islands

THE Wirral Peninsula is situated between two major rivers. To the east the Mersey, which rises in the distant Pennines as a pure, sparkling stream, but during its course through industrial Lancashire becomes increasingly polluted until, by the time it flows through the narrow channel twixt the ports of Birkenhead and Liverpool, it is virtually an open sewer. The Dee, on the other hand, rises in the Welsh uplands and, twisting its way across open moorland and wooded valleys, makes its way through the city of Chester and across the broad sands between Wales and Wirral, to empty its untainted waters into the Irish Sea.

If the two rivers are so different, then so too are their estuaries. That of the Mersey is narrow, barely a mile across, its banks lined with the cranes and wharves of Liverpool's dockland. The estuary of the Dee is wide, five miles from Red Rocks on the Wirral side to Point of Air on the Welsh side; its backcloth the hills and peaks of North Wales, its sands and channels the haunt of birds and seals.

Here is a "surviving wilderness", a sanctuary for wildlife of every description, where the only sounds are the lonely cries of curlew and oyster-catcher, the moaning of the seals and the rushing of the tide. A beautiful area at all times of the year: in summer, when the setting sun casts rainbow colours across the ebbing waters; or in winter, when the wind churns the waters of the estuary into a foaming, churning cauldron. And always, the mysterious hills and mountains are an ever-changing backcloth to the waters and sands of the estuary; sometimes dark and brooding under a glowering November sky; often a green patchwork of fields and hedgerows in summer; and occasionally capped with snow on a January day.

The peace and solitude to be found in the estuary belies its history. For this was the gateway to Chester for over 1,700 years, a period which began with the Romans and their troopships, and ended with the seventeenth-century traders desperately trying to keep alive the anchorages along Wirral's Deeside in competition with burgeoning Liverpool. The ghost-quays of Dawpool, Gayton and Neston still stand as reminders of those long-forgotten trading days when ships from the Baltic, Ireland, France, Spain, Portugal, and the Low Countries plied these waters.

The trading ships left, and the Dee with its estuary was left to the local fishermen and the sea birds. Even the twentieth century has had little impact. Fortunately so, for the Dee estuary is now officially recognized as being of international importance for the wading birds which winter here in their tens of thousands. Each autumn, about three million waders leave their breeding grounds in the Arctic to spend the winter on the estuaries of Europe and north-west Africa; of these, some 150,000 come to the Dee, making it one of the four most important sites in Britain.

The birds are attracted by the fifty or so square miles of sand and mud which are exposed at low tide, and which harbour an abundance of marine life. Some forty thousand dunlin and knot, often to be seen in flocks of ten thousand or more, feed in the mudflats of the estuary during a typical winter. Oystercatchers, whose total numbers often exceed twenty thousand, sit out the high tide in the fields of Wirral, often many miles inland, and return to their favourite mudflat haunts as the tide recedes. Redshank, turnstone, curlew, purple sandpiper all winter here in large numbers.

The concentration of winter birds in the estuary is not generally noticeable at low tide; but as the water rises, so the birds are forced off the mud and sand to the rocks, islets and the margins of the estuary. As the feeding grounds are covered by the tide, so flock after flock rises, performing mass aerobatics, their colours alternating black and white against the sea and sky. Suddenly the birds, as if with a single corporate eye, will spot a suitable patch of sand or rock and drop to the ground with one accord.

During spring and autumn, huge numbers of passing migrants use the estuary to feed and rest during their long flights between Africa and the Arctic. In spring ringed plover, sanderling and dunlin pause here briefly *en route* to Greenland where they breed during the short Arctic summer. During autumn the estuary is a global cross-roads; returning spring migrants feed alongside oyster-catchers from Scotland, bar-tailed godwits from Russia, and knot from the Arctic.

The summer months are the quietest for bird life, although the arrival of the terns in the spring – sandwich, common, Arctic and little – makes up for the reduced numbers of wading birds.

The estuary's greatest attraction, the Hilbre Islands, are situated right at the mouth of the estuary, where the waters of the Dee meet the Irish Sea. Here is a group of islands, accessible on foot twice a day, with a charm and fascination found nowhere on the mainland. On these islands it is possible to experience that sense of isolation and remoteness rarely found in modern living; especially so close to a large centre of population.

The Hilbre Islands are about a mile and a half off the north-western tip of the peninsula, and consist of Hilbre itself (12 acres), Middle Hilbre (3 acres), and Little Eye (½ acre). The two larger islands are only a few hundred yards apart; but Little Eye is almost a mile from the main pair. All three are connected by a strip of sandstone reef intersected by countless channels and rock pools.

It seems certain that the islands were originally much larger than their present size, and possibly joined together as one. It is known, for example, that in the middle of the sixteenth century some 4,000 foot and horse troops camped here on their way to Ireland – an impossibility today. Early maps of Cheshire show the Hilbre group as a single island; and it seems likely that the islands were at one time part of the mainland. Geologically speaking, such rapid changes in so short a time span would seem unlikely unless seen against the nature of the rock and the local climatic conditions. Hilbre, like so much of

Wirral, is made up of the red-yellow Bunter sandstone; an extremely soft, crumbly stone which simply cannot stand up to the ferocious battering so common a feature of these western coasts. In fact, it is likely that, but for the extensive work carried out to reinforce the seaward-facing cliffs of the main island, it would have been almost cut in two by now.

There is much to see on the Hilbre Islands; but first a short account of their fascinating past. In spite of their apparent remoteness, man has used the islands since very early times. Various finds indicate the presence of Stone Age and Bronze Age man. The Romans, too, used the islands; shards of third- and fourth-century pottery were found here in 1926. During the seventh century Hilbre was the home of one Hildeburgh, who chose this barren place to live out a solitary life of penance and prayer. The island owes its name to this good lady who was remembered long after her death. It seems likely that she became an almost legendary figure, for a shrine or chapel dedicated to St Hildeburgh was set up, and this became known as the Chapel of St Mary. Brownbill suggests that a small religious house had been founded on Hilbre, possibly before the Norsemen settled in the district in or about 905. Although this is not mentioned in the Doomsday Book, mention *is* made of the two churches of Chircheb (West Kirby): "One in the town and the other on an island in the sea near thereto." Before 1081 these churches belonged to the monks of St Evroul in Normandy, who later gave them to the Benedictine monks of St Werburgh's Abbey, Chester.

The monks of St Werburgh's established on Hilbre a small cell dedicated to the Virgin Mary. The island became a popular place for pilgrims during the thirteenth and fourteenth centuries; Holinshed, the famous chronicler of the time, remarked: "And thither went a sort of superstitious fools, in pilgrimage to our Lady of Hilbree, by whose offerings the monks there were cherished and maintained." No traces of the cell have been found, although a red sandstone cross said to be from the early church was found on the island in 1853. A 40-foot well, cut through the solid rock and commonly thought to have been sunk by the monks, is more likely to have been made in the nineteenth century.

The monks lived out their lonely life on Hilbre until the middle of the sixteenth century. What an isolated existence it must have been for the two monks who "did their turn" here. Small wonder that legends have been woven around them. The sands between Hilbre and the North Wales coast are often referred to as the "Constable's Sands". About the year 1101 Richard, Earl of Chester, was on a peaceful pilgrimage to St Winifred's Shrine at Holywell when he was ambushed by "Wicked Welshmen". Richard sent word to his constable, William Fitz-Nigel of Halton, to raise a great army to meet him at Basingwerk. The constable and his men rode fast to Hilbre, hoping to find barques to take them across the estuary to Wales, but all the boats were out. Remembering the monks on the island, Fitz-Nigel asked them to pray to St Werburgh on behalf of his master, promising them a substantial gift on his way home. Instantly the deep waters of the estuary parted, and the constable and his men crossed over a bank of dry sand to the Welsh shore where he rescued the earl and returned safely to Chester.

The last monk left the island about 1550, probably because Hilbre was becoming less of a sanctuary. In fact, by this time it had become a busy place as a shipping centre for vessels sailing to and from the port of Chester. The following extract from the Chester Customs Accounts for the year 1566 gives some indication of the volume of traffic trading between here and Ireland:

27th March "George of Hilbre" (12 tons) owned by Thomas Mowely of Hilbre, to Dublin with 6 tons coal from Chester.

7th October "John of Hilbre" (16 tons) owned by Richard Rathbone to Dublin with small wares – £4.

8th October "Jesus of Hilbre" (14 tons) owned by Thomas Queyntrie to Dublin, 2 pieces of Yorkshire Kersey, 1 piece of yellow western Kersey, ½ piece of western Kersey.

17th October "Bride of Hilbre" (24 tons) owned by Thomas Queyntrie, to Dublin, 10 tons of coal.

27th March (1567) "Ellen of Hilbre" (12 tons) owned by Richard Rathbone of Hilbre to Dublin, 6 tons of coal.

Inwards to Chester

2nd April "Sunday of Hilbre" (3 tons) owned by William Ratclyff, Kersey and 1 case white wooden cups value £8, 2 cases hops, ½ case aniseed, ½ case castle soap, 5 cases of trenchers of the common sort.

6th April "Katherine of Hilbre" (16 tons) owned by John Androwe of West Kirby.

"Nicholas of Hilbre" (16 tons) owned by Thomas Ratclyff of Dublin, 3 cases of sheep fells, 4 cases of Brockfells.

18th April "Eagle of Hilbre" (10 tons) owned by Richard Little from Dublin, 2 cases Brockfells, 1½ cases Checkers (cloth with a check pattern).

Such was the traffic that a Custom House was established to deal with "great smuggling which went on in the old days, when the ships stole quietly up the Dee and hid a cargo of contraband, to be removed when an opportunity occurred". The importance of Hilbre as a port continued to grow in the days of Queen Elizabeth and Cromwell, the Irish wars requiring regular despatches of troops and stores.

It is, perhaps, difficult to imagine the island being put to any kind of industrial or commercial use; but in 1692 a small works was set up to refine rock salt, brought from the great salt mines of Cheshire, into white granulated salt. Likewise there was a beer-house on the island at the height of its days as an anchorage; but when the sea traffic deserted the Dee for the port of Liverpool, the inn shut down for lack of custom. Part of the inn is now incorporated into the Custodian's residence.

The Hilbre Islands were bought by the Trustees of the Liverpool Docks (the Mersey Docks and Harbour Board) in 1856, who in turn sold them to Hoylake U.D.C. in 1945 for £2,500. During local government reorganization in 1974,

Hilbre came into the possession of Wirral Borough Council.

The importance of these small islands to geologists, bird-watchers, nature lovers, or those who simply want to "get away from it all" for a while, has been recognized in their designation as a "Site of Special Scientific Interest" by the Nature Conservancy Council; Wirral Borough Council has also declared the area a Statutory Local Nature Reserve.

Join me, then, on a visit across the Sands of Dee and we shall see if we can capture that special flavour only to be found in this wilderness of sky, sand and sea. But first, a word or two of warning. Near though the islands appear from the mainland, do not be tempted to cross straight across the sands towards the main island; deep channels and treacherous mudbanks not visible from the shore make this a dangerous crossing. There is only one safe way: from the slipway at the bottom of Dee Lane at West Kirby, head towards the left-hand side of the Little Eye (the first of the three islands in the group). Once at the Little Eye, keep to the seaward side of the islands until Hilbre itself is reached. The state of the tide must be heeded before crossing. It is usually possible to walk across to Hilbre three hours after high tide; the return trip should be made at least three hours before the next high tide. Visitors wishing to remain on the islands over a high tide should leave the mainland at least three hours before high water. Obviously, weather conditions and other variables affect the height and time of the tides, and extreme care must be taken in planning before crossing.

Likewise, the weather in the estuary can change in a matter of minutes; fog and rain can suddenly descend to reduce visibility to yards – a compass is essential if the weather seems at all unstable. Appropriate clothing is important – including Wellington boots to protect feet from glass, shells etc. And don't forget the permit which is necessary if you wish to visit the main island.

For our visit, I have chosen a day in mid-October – heavy overnight rain has been blown away across inland Britain by a fresh westerly breeze – the sky is clearing, and a fine day is promised. We are early today – high water is mid-morning, and we want to stay on the islands over the high tide;

moreover, there will probably be fewer people about at this hour.

From the slipway at West Kirby, the sea is nowhere to be seen; and yet as we tramp across the damp sands, we know that within a couple of hours, the water will be several feet deep where we now tread. This thought makes us quicken our footsteps as we make for the Little Eye. Already, the sights, sounds and cares of land are far behind us; the sun is sending its warm rays down on the estuary; and there is a sense of excitement and anticipation in our hearts. On the far side of the estuary, the green hills of Wales beckon as if to say "Come on over, we are not so far away"; but we know that there are five or six miles of deep channels and mudflats twixt here and the safety of the Welsh coast.

There are few signs of birds hereabouts; the sand has dried out, and there is little to attract them. However, as we reach the higher land around the Little Eye, we can make out the water's edge in the distance and, parallel with it, a narrow black band of birds. And across the sands come the faint sounds of the waves and chatter of thousands of sea birds feeding at the edge of the incoming tide.

Around the Little Eye we change direction as we head for the two main islands; yet we are still only halfway to our destination. But this is certainly the most interesting part of the walk. Although it is many hours since the tide receded, this rocky plateau linking the islands is interlaced with channels and rock pools. Here are starfish, sea anemones, crabs, shells and seaweed. Here we may see a lone curlew or oyster-catcher poking about amongst the seaweed for some tasty morsel.

Interesting though this stretch is, we have not the time just now to linger; the tide is making fast and the sea is no respecter of persons. There will be a time a-plenty on the return trek – what's more, the tide will have left countless creatures high and dry for our perusal.

We soon reach Middle Hilbre, just three acres of springy turf and bracken. This island presents a virtually sheer cliff-face to the sea on all sides. Having no building of any description, not even a shelter, and with its turf ablaze with thrift in summer, it is, to my mind, the best of the group on which to sit out a high tide. It is small enough to wander around on without that "hemmed in" feeling one gets on the Little Eye. From the cliff-top we get a fine view of the seal colony hauled out half a mile away on the West Hoyle Bank. Although only a mass of black specks to the naked eye, binoculars reveal large numbers of seals splashing about in the water which is now covering the sand. These are grey seals, and their numbers here have increased steadily over the past fifty years, from a dozen or so in the 1930s to their present population of over 150. Highest numbers are in the spring and summer, and during high water they will swim quite close in to the islands. Their antics are amusing to watch, for they will dive in one place, to emerge minutes later hundreds of yards away. But best of all is their eerie "song", described by Ellison as reminiscent of "the deep, contented mooing of cows, interrupted by the howling of several dogs".

On the seaward side of Middle Hilbre is a tall, narrow cave known as the Devil's Hole and said to have been used by smugglers. A walk around the base of these rocky cliffs can be fascinating; the geologist is in his element examining the layers of sandstone and pebbles; and the nature lover examining the cracks and crevices for marine life – sea-slaters, barnacles, molluscs and crabs.

But our goal today is the main island where, while the tide is up, we can explore its twelve acres at our leisure. It is but a few minutes to Hilbre from here, but we must hurry, for already the sea is lapping the seaweed-draped rocks on Hilbre's seaward side. Through the gate, up the slipway, and at last we are on Hilbre Island. Having reached our goal, we feel a unique sense of achievement at having beaten the tide!

On the left of the main path across the island is a small freshwater pond, apparently artificial, its purpose unknown. The uncommon two-flowered narcissus grows here, and hereabouts too may be found the Duke of Argyll's Tea Plant, the dried leaves of which when infused make a drinkable tea. The four wooden buildings on the landward side of Hilbre were originally boathouses, but have been converted into holiday homes. Further north is a stone building erected in 1856 as a buoy store, but now too converted into houses. The next building is the Keeper's residence, originally part of the Seagull beer-house and extended in 1841 when the telegraph station was built.

It is only as we reach the highest point of the island, by the coastguard look-out, that we see that Hilbre really *is* an island – for the tide has now completely encircled us, and there is no turning back! Continuing northwards, we pass the reinforced sheer cliff-face of a small bay and, at the most northerly point on the island, the remains of a lifeboat station. From here the rippling waters of the Irish Sea stretch away before us in every direction; a hundred yards offshore a seal shows its head briefly but quickly disappears again. The quietness is broken only by the lapping of the waves against the rocks, the cry of the redshank and, in the far distance, the gentle throb-throb of a small fishing boat going out on the tide.

All the time we have been on Hilbre, flocks of birds have been winging across the estuary, twisting and turning with one accord and landing on every patch of vacant space. Obviously, few birds will settle on or about the islands while there are people about, but if bird-watchers keep out of sight, flocks will settle on the rocky ledges around the islands. In fact, on Lion Rock, to the east of Hilbre, birds have been known to pack so tightly together that dunlin roosted on the backs of sleeping knot! To view the birds from close up, some kind of hide is virtually essential. A permanent observatory has been set up on the island, recording to date some 230 species. Small wonder, then, that Hilbre has been visited by such eminent people as H.R.H. the Duke of Edinburgh and Eric Hosking, the famous bird photographer. It is not for me to detail the birds to be seen here – others have done a far better job than I could ever do – but suffice to say that the variety of bird life at any time of the year is a constant source of wonder and delight to all who come here.

Our time on Hilbre is nearly up, for the tide is receding and the sand is once again being revealed. But before we go, let us scramble down the slippery rocks below the pond to the Lady's Cave. This dark, dank cave has, not surprisingly, had legendary tales woven about it. Ellison's version is as good as any:

> On a ledge in this cave one of the Benedictines stationed on the island found a dying maiden cast up by the sea. Before she died the monk learned her story. She was the only daughter of the Custodian of Shotwick Castle and against her father's wish had fallen in love with one of his esquires. As fathers did some six hundred years ago, he ordered her to marry the man of his choice, a Welsh knight. Now you have two versions from which to choose. One states that the angry father packed her off in a boat to wed Llewellyn, the Welsh chieftain; the boat was lost on the passage and the unfortunate maiden was washed ashore and died. The other version is rather different, and this shall be my choice. One day, while off the Point of Air, sailing to meet the Welshman, her father told her that the esquire she loved was dead, hoping that she would then agree to his plans. The maiden, stricken by the sudden news, fainted and fell overboard, leaving the father crying out in despair that the story was not true. The tide left her high and dry in the cave but, broken-hearted, she died in the presence of the monk.

And, as we sit here, watching the tide ebb across the sands of Dee, shut out from the sun, we can picture the sad scene in all its detail.

On the homeward trek across the wet sands, we feel a little sad to be leaving this sanctuary in the sea. The turnstones are busily searching the rock-pools for titbits; a lonely curlew wings its way across the estuary, its "cor-lee" echoing across the mudflats; the seals are once more basking in the sun on their sandbank. And as we approach the West Kirby beach, the picnickers and shoppers seem oblivious to the different world we have just left. Back on land, the traffic still roars, life goes on. But we will be back – perhaps on a wet and windy day in December, when the storm-clouds gather about the Welsh peaks and hailstones bounce off the sands. Or on a crisp morning in January when icicles drape the frost-shrouded rocks around Lady's Cave.

The Dee estuary has many moods, many faces. And yet there has been talk of putting a motorway and a barrage across these wild, lonely expanses of sand, sea and marsh, to speed traffic across to North Wales, and to give the thirsty north-west the water it is said to need. Such schemes would provide facilities for power boating, water-skiing and a dozen other water sports, say the planners. Perhaps, but what about the hundred thousand birds who travel vast distances each year to make this their winter home? Or the colony of seals whose home is the lonely sandbank? Or the glorious mosaic of sunshine and cloud playing across the dappled blue waters? Or those people who just want somewhere where they can be away from the rush, noise and fumes of motor car and lorry, away from the shops, roads and houses, alone with the sand, the sea and the birds – people who, like the Benedictine monks a thousand years ago, just wanted a bit of peace and quiet?

6

HIGH LANDS AND LEGENDS

Thurstaston – Frankby – Greasby – Irby – Heswall – Pensby – Thingwall – Barnston

THE stretch of beach between Caldy and Thurstaston makes a fine walk at any time of the year; a mile and a half of good sand with something of interest at every step. Come along here on a receding tide in autumn and you will be accompanied by flocks of waders – oyster-catchers, knot, dunlin – who turn, scream and settle in the mud at the water's edge. The cliffs here are 60 feet high and are regarded as one of the most spectacular relics of the Ice Age in Britain. The boulder clay of which they are composed contains debris brought down from the north by the ice sheet. On a recent visit the exceptionally high autumn tide had washed away a layer of clay to reveal rocks, stones, shells and minerals from places 500 miles from here – from Scotland, Ireland and the Lake District. Many of the larger boulders are scattered about the shore and their smooth, grey, rounded appearance contrasts sharply with the long rectangular slabs of local red sandstone lying parallel with the shore, embedded in the sand. These are obviously hand-made and are all that remain of the old port of Dawpool. This was once a busy place for shipping; at least sufficiently busy to necessitate the employment of two Customs officers during the eighteenth century.

Dean Swift landed at Dawpool from Dublin in 1707, and again two years later set sail from here for Ireland. The Dee had been gradually silting up towards the estuary for over a hundred years, and it became Dawpool's turn to share some of the traffic which had abandoned the ports of Parkgate and Neston. But, like these anchorages, Dawpool too had to be abandoned; only the stones of the quayside remain, washed twice a day by the waters of the Irish Sea.

It was from here that in 1825 Telford, the great roadway engineer, planned to cut a canal through the valley between the hills of Caldy and Thurstaston to Wallasey Pool, thus uniting the two rivers Mersey and Dee. Sir John Rennie too, had visions of a canal from hereabouts running along the length of the Wirral Peninsula to Chester. Fortunately these plans came to nought, for Liverpool by that time had eclipsed all possible contenders; I say "fortunately", for if these schemes had come to anything, this lovely part of Wirral might now be another Ellesmere Port or Birkenhead.

The cottages on the shore at the foot of the cliffs here are known locally as "Shore Cottages", but their precise history is obscure. It is thought that they were originally houses for the Customs officers of Dawpool, or perhaps coastguards' cottages. Certainly their situation is unique; set in the sand just above high-water mark, they are virtually cut off from civilization. The small dell behind the cottages has a rich variety of bird and plant life, and the nature lover will find much of interest. A path goes through the dell to the Thurstaston Visitor Centre of the Wirral Country Park, where it is often possible to obtain refreshments – very welcome after the tramp along the beach, especially on a winter's day!

A long, straight road cuts inland across the fields to the village of Thurstaston (note the traces of the original road in the fields on the side midway along this road). Thurstaston is not so much a village as a cluster of red stone buildings grouped around a grassy area which could pass as an unkempt village green. Beazley, in his highly detailed description of the parish in 1924, wrote: "Thurstaston is undoubtedly a parish as happy as it is beautiful; it has no history, and indeed it almost seems at times as if a conspiracy had existed to stop us from learning anything about it." I feel the parish today would be a little happier and a lot more beautiful if traffic for the Country Park Visitor Centre did not have to pass through its heart.

This is one of the only Wirral villages with fewer inhabitants now than a century or two ago. Its inhabitants of those days apparently made a living from the activities of the neighbouring "port" of Dawpool, as well as from fishing and agriculture. The parish registers record a variety of maritime occupations – fishermen, ships' carpenters and mariners – as well as the more usual farmers, labourers and the like.

Dominating the village is the parish church of St Bartholomew. The present church is the third to occupy a site in the village. The first, probably erected in the twelfth century, stood until 1820, and was replaced by a plain stone building in 1824. The tower of the second church still stands in the churchyard, its stonework recently renovated; the rest of the building was pulled down in 1886. The plaque in the north wall of the tower records the names of the churchwardens at the time of its erection. The present church was built in 1886 and, with its exotic interior ornamented with marble and alabaster, is surely one of the finest nineteenth-century churches in Wirral. In the graveyard and on the lych-gate are inscriptions commemorating the Ismay family, famous steamship owners, and responsible in the nineteenth century for diverting the course of the railway and the main high road away from their property in order to preserve its solitude.

Next to the church is Thurstaston Hall, a fine, mellow old building rich in lore and legend. Like so many of Wirral's old halls, this has been altered and extended over the years so that today it appears a pleasing hotch-potch of building styles and materials. The oldest part is the west wing, fourteenth or fifteenth century; the central part was built about 1680, and the east wing about 1835. But the Hall's history may very well go back to the eleventh century when Hugh Lupus, Earl of Chester, granted the Manor of Thurstaston to his friend and general-in-chief Robert de Rodelent. Hugh – nicknamed "the Wolf" – was a ruthless leader who was committed to a vigorous campaign of warfare against the Welsh. The Welsh came to hate this marauder and gave him other, not-so-nice, names – Hugh the Gross and Hugh the Fat. His statue remains to this day in Thurstaston Hall, a reminder that Wirral's proximity to the Welsh border often involved its people in bloody skirmishes between the two countries.

If the exterior of the Hall seems disjointed, the interior is even more so. Here is one recent description:

> I cannot remember an interior which intrigued me more . . . a maze of passages, with steps and short staircases in the most unlikely places, for there are two floors at the front of the house and three at the back. The massive oak entrance doors open into a large and lofty oak-panelled hall with a beautifully carved oak Tudor mantelpiece above a large fireplace. It is quite impossible to describe all the delightful rooms of this venerable house: each possesses its own individuality, from the completely oak-panelled Gun Room with leaded window-panes of 1680, to the Arch-Room with the rough original beams of the 1350 hall and now used as a bedroom. The best bedroom of the 1680 period is completely panelled in oak and has the original uneven oak floor.

No account of Thurstaston Hall would be complete without mention of the ghost which is supposed to haunt one of the bedrooms. The noted portrait painter Reginald Easton was staying at the Hall as a guest when he awoke during the night to see an elderly woman standing at the foot of the bed, wringing her hands and looking downwards at the floor as if searching for something. Easton spoke to the woman but, on hearing his voice, she vanished. The following night, sketch-book at the ready, Easton eagerly awaited the phantom's return. Sure enough she reappeared and the artist was able to sketch her. On examination, the drawing bore a close resemblance to a portrait of a former owner of the Hall who was said to have murdered the rightful heir – a young boy – to gain possession of the place for herself. Her crime was not discovered until she confessed on her deathbed; the phantom appeared in the room in which the murder had taken place. The interesting thing is that the sketch was very similar to a portrait of the murderess which had at one time hung in the Hall, but which Mr Easton had never seen.

In 1971 workmen digging up the road near Dawpool Farm in the village discovered what is thought to be an old smuggler's tunnel. The tunnel is carved out of the sandstone and seems to run in the direction of Thurstaston Hall. Legend has it that it used to emerge a mile and a half away at the old port of Dawpool, and that it was used by smugglers to avoid the Customs officers.

Thurstaston, though, is synonymous in most people's minds with the hill behind the village. Put on your walking shoes and join me on a bright spring morning for a walk over the hill. Fleecy white clouds scud across a blue sky, and the footpaths beckon. There will be few people about today; we will probably have the hill to ourselves. Not so on a warm Sunday afternoon; every family on Merseyside seems to be here then. This popularity is causing concern amongst conservationists: footpaths across the hill seem to be wider and dustier each year; fires devastate large areas during dry spells; and the presence of large numbers of people is certainly driving away the wildlife. And yet this is an open space for public use, bought (with amazing foresight) by Birkenhead Town Council as long ago as 1879, "having regard to the health, comfort, and convenience of the inhabitants of the Borough of Birkenhead, and the benefit of the neighbourhood". Today, as we walk through the heather and gorse, we are indeed grateful to those whose vision so many years ago has safeguarded this and other parts of Wirral for the enjoyment of this and future generations.

There are many paths and tracks over Thurstaston Hill. It is not strenuous walking, but full of interest, particularly as most paths lead up to the summit with its spectacular view – a surprise view, particularly if approached from the east. For the prospect changes from one of heath and woodland to a panoramic, far-reaching vista of sea, sky and mountain. The summit view-finder, erected in 1942 in memory of Andrew Blair (founder of Liverpool and District Ramblers' Federation, and whose little footpath guides did so much to awaken the urban dwellers on Merseyside to the beauty around them), stands at the highest point (255 feet) and gives details of landmarks and distances. Immediately below are the fields and woods around the church and village of Thurstaston. The fields sweep down to the Dee (with the water reflecting the sparkling blue and white of the sky today) and the eye follows the estuary out to the wide, grey waters of the Irish Sea. Today is so clear that the hills on the Welsh side beckon to be touched;

the monument on the summit of Moel Fammau is clearly visible; and in the far distance, the Snowdon range shimmers in the haze some forty miles away.

Northwards Caldy Hill is clothed in fresh greenery and the north Wirral and Lancashire coast are easily traced. Beyond, the fells of the Lake District are a smudge on the horizon. Turn eastwards, and what a contrast! The woods and fields of rural Wirral give way to the houses, factories and urban life of Birkenhead and Liverpool. The large grey-and-red complex of buildings rearing up out of the trees in the middle distance is the new hospital at Arrowe Park. Beyond is the unmistakable Liverpool skyline, dominated by the two cathedrals and St John's Beacon. Today the Pennine range is just visible on the far horizon. Southwards lie the hills, woods and fields of mid-Wirral.

What a tonic these wide horizons are; but let us take one of the many tracks back down the landward side of the hill and take a look at something to stir the imagination. Set in a hollow here is the legendary "Thor's Stone", a large, rectangular rock of sandstone, some 50 feet long, 30 feet wide, and 25 feet high. Its surface is covered with irregularities, crevices and projections, enabling the nimble feet of the young to climb to the flattish top. Indeed, the stone is so well used that the soft sandstone is rapidly crumbling away under the constant wear and tear. Its soft texture has enabled generations to carve their initials into the surface; there is now barely a square inch left untouched. It seems that the desire to "graffitize" public property is no new thing; a hundred years ago, a visitor to Thor's Stone commented that "the flat portion of the summit and parts of the sides are covered with the initials and graffiti of successive generations of visitors".

Romantic tales have been woven around this isolated slab of stone. Some say that it was used by the Danes as a sacrificial altar in honour of their god Thor (it has even been suggested that the name Thurstaston is derived from "Thor's Stone Town", but however romantic this notion it seems probable that the correct derivation is the "tun" or farmstead of one Thorstein). Has sacrificial blood ever trickled down the sides of Thor's Stone? Is its present blood-red colour due to the staining of hundreds of sacrifices? It seems unlikely: this great slab was left when the better-quality stone surrounding it was quarried and taken away for local walls and buildings. But the fiction, as usual, is far more interesting than the truth, and will probably continue to be told to future generations. There is no trace now of the Fairy Well which used to be near the Stone; yet local people still vaguely remember young children taking flowers to the well.

From here we may take one of many tracks through the heather. And, as we walk, keep a look out for the wildlife of Thurstaston. For this heath has now been designated a "Site of Special Scientific Interest" and is also the site for a proposed Local Nature Reserve. The reasons are easy to see. Being a typical lowland heath, there is a varying range of habitats for plant and bird life. All three species of heather cover the drier slopes of the heath: ling, bell heather, and cross-leaved heath or bog heather. Growing amongst the heather, bilberry plants provide fruit for many birds in summer. Damper hollows provide a suitable habitat for common cotton-grass, sundew, mosses and other moisture-loving plants. Bird-lovers are not disappointed either. Tree-creepers, goldcrest, all three kinds of woodpecker, tawny owl, jay, tits, nuthatches and warblers can all be seen, and north-westerly gales occasionally bring in rare birds blown off course. This mixture of woodland and open heath is undoubtedly one of the attractions of Thurstaston Hill. And always, there is the tang of sea air to remind us of the proximity of the coast.

From Thurstaston Common most footpaths lead to Royden Park, an area of wooded knolls, reedy meres surrounded by rhododendron bushes, and open grassy spaces where the public can roam at will. Set upon a hill here is Hill Bark, "one of the most notable Victorian essays in half-timbered design anywhere in the country". This magnificent house was, believe it or not, originally built several miles away on Bidston Hill in 1891 but Sir Ernest Royden had it taken down and re-erected here in 1929. In case you think this was a rather drastic and eccentric action, compare the present setting of Hill Bark, with its fields and woods rolling away to the Dee and the Welsh hills beyond, with the view from its original site – an urban panorama of the roofs, motorways and pylons of Birkenhead's outer suburbs.

On Sir Ernest's death in 1960, Hill Bark was bought by Hoylake U.D.C. who converted it into a home for the elderly. Take advantage, if you can, of visiting the house on one of its rare Open Days, for there is much worthy of inspection. Part of the exterior design is based on Little Moreton Hall near Congleton in Cheshire, yet few know of this fine example of pseudo-Elizabethan architecture.

The architect of Hill Bark, Edward Ould (whose partner, incidentally, had designed the previous building on this site), said of the house:

> No style of building will harmonize so quickly and so completely with its surroundings . . . and none continue to live on such terms of good fellowship with other materials, whether rosy brickwork, grey lichen-covered masonry, or pearly flag-slates, which last it loves most of all. And then it is hard to say which season of the year most becomes it. In its cap of virgin snow, in its gorgeous garb of Virginia Creeper or in its purple veil of Wisteria it is equally bewitching. At noon-day it throws the broadest shadows, and at eve (as no other building can) it gathers on its snowy breast the rose of sunset, and responds to the silver magic of the moon.

On Sunday afternoons the woods on the edge of the estate echo to the sound of narrow gauge steam trains on the miniature railway, but at other times this is one of the most peaceful parts of inland Wirral, where the only company is the red squirrel and kingfisher.

Royden Park and Hill Bark are on the edge of Frankby, known best of all for its vast cemetery laid out in the grounds of Frankby Hall. The Hall, with its castellated walls and turrets, was built in 1846 as the home of Sir Thomas Royden, and occupies a commanding site overlooking the village and a good part of the surrounding countryside. The Hall, with the estate of sixty-one acres, was bought in the mid-1930s by Wallasey Corporation and is now a chapel for the cemetery. The village of Frankby is one of those places which cannot make up its mind as to its identity. It has a village stores, a village green, a pub and a church – but the pub and church are each half a mile out of the village in opposite directions! Although there are farms in the heart of the village, its rurality is somewhat undermined by the busy main road which runs right through. And, inevitably, modern housing creeps ever nearer to the village, although a recently confirmed Conservation Area tag may prevent the worst from happening.

The origin of the village's name is uncertain: some say it is from the old English name for a Frenchman, "Franca", therefore "Frenchman's Farm"; others that it is from an old Danish name "Frankï" – "Franki's Farmstead". The church, on the Greasby road, is nineteenth century, of red sandstone, and has little of interest apart from some fine stained-glass windows portraying Adam and Eve, Abel and Enoch, and Abraham and Moses. The village itself has some well-preserved seventeenth- and eighteenth-century buildings; Tudor Cottage dates back to 1676 and was formerly part of an old inn. The old post office (dated 1740), Yew Tree Farm, and several other old buildings in The Nook together make a fine group around the Green. The pub, the Farmer's Arms, is near the entrance to Royden Park, and is one of the few remaining unmodernized pubs in Wirral. It is at least two hundred years old; but regrettably the old village smithy was demolished a few years ago to make room for more cars – such is the popularity of a "country inn"!

Rubbing shoulders with Frankby is Greasby, the "fortified house with a pit or trench". Mortimer said this of Greasby just over a hundred years ago: "Inconveniently situated, at some distance from the ferries, in a remarkably poor and cold country . . . the land is in general inferior, the rocks in many parts rising to the surface." Estate agents today describe it otherwise: "Conveniently situated near open countryside, with easy access to motorways for Liverpool and Chester." For Greasby is house builders' country. The "inferior land" is apparently perfectly suitable for new housing estates, which are springing up in almost every available space.

Like many other Wirral villages, Greasby's growth from a small agricultural community to a suburban area has been relatively recent. At the turn of the century its population was only 290, it had few shops, and the nearest post office and railway station were at Upton, 1½ miles away. The late 1940s and 1950s saw the first sizeable developments and, as I write, the fields of Homestead Farm alongside the footpath to Saughall Massie are being churned up for more houses. This land is part of 200 acres which, in the 1960s, was allocated for development in the MALTS Plan (Merseyside Area Land and Transportation Study), which suggested that the area would need to accommodate another 28,000 people up to the turn of the century. However, it appears that this forecast grossly over-estimated the growth in population, and the plans for Greasby and the surrounding areas are being reviewed in the light of recent downward population trends.

For all its new houses, Greasby still retains a semi-rural atmosphere. A by-pass takes much through traffic away from the village, where there are several buildings of interest. Greasby Old Hall, near the old crossroads, is probably the oldest building in the village. Although the main part is sixteenth century, it has an interesting fifteenth-century porch with alms holes and a studded oak door. Inside the house there is a "priest's hole" and, in the cellar, a natural spring which is said never to have dried up. There are, too, some fine old oak ceiling beams, and an immense chimney breast which rises from the cellar and goes up through the centre of the building. At the back of the Hall is a large well, a pump and the remains of an old cheese press.

Manor Farm, built in 1680, has been a bank and a restaurant; it stands in a commanding position at the brow of the hill in the centre of the village. Greasby library was, in the nineteenth century, a smallpox isolation hospital, a reminder of the days when this and other infectious diseases were common in Wirral. Just outside the library, notice the old milestone inscribed "Woodside Ferry 6m". This dates back to about 1860 and originally stood in the centre of the village.

Greasby has no parish church of its own; it shares Frankby's. But the village does have two inns. The Red Cat replaced an older pub, the New Inn, and the pub's large car park occupies the site of the old cattle market. The Coach and Horses, near the old crossroads by the Irby road, is mid-nineteenth century, but much of the fabric has been modernized.

Alongside the Coach and Horses an iron cross bearing the initials of John Shaw of Arrowe, the Lord of the Manor in 1862, stands rusting and neglected. This replaced an ancient stone cross which stood on the village green. The cross was known as a "living cross", and labourers requiring work would gather at the cross once a year, in the spring, to be taken on by local farmers for the following year.

Although Greasby is changing – perhaps *because* Greasby is changing – there are folk who are very much concerned about the area's past. Even as I write, plans are afoot to clear and restore the site of the old village pump at the corner of Pump Lane, a corner of Greasby overgrown and neglected for nearly fifty years. Although the original pump has disappeared, it is hoped to obtain a replacement which will prove a focal point for the scheme.

From the Coach and Horses Inn, Mill Lane climbs steadily out of Greasby to higher ground on the way to Irby, leaving the houses and shops behind. This is Irby Mill Hill, a lovely stretch of countryside with far-reaching views in all directions – northwards and a surprise glimpse of the sea, and eastwards across the fields to the woods of Arrowe. From Irby Mill Hill there are field-paths and woodland ways rich in wild flowers and bird life, leading across Irby Heath to the higher Deeside land of Thurstaston and Caldy, or inland to the mid-Wirral byways. Irby Hill's splendid isolated setting was used to advantage last century when a lepers' home was established here.

At the crossroads the once-popular Lumsdens Café has given way to a new pub; many regret the change, but the old café buildings had been derelict for many years and were an eyesore and blot on the landscape. Fortunately the brewers have erected a building which complements its surroundings, the new extensions harmonizing well with the original sandstone house. The mill from which the area takes its name stood behind the café building, and replaced an even earlier one a few hundred yards nearer to Irby village. The later mill was probably the last peg mill in Wirral to survive, and was pulled down in 1898. Accounts of the demolition of the mill make interesting reading. The three men who offered to knock it down tried to do so by knocking out the bricks from around its base. This was usually done by supporting the structure with wood and setting fire to the wooden supports, enabling the men to get clear of the building in time. However, this was not done with the Irby mill; the men knocked the bricks away one by one, the mill gave an ominous creak, and the men ran for their lives! The miller, who was watching the operation, described the men's escape as "marvellous"!

From the crossroads, there is a choice of ways to Irby village, all of them attractive. The main road continues uphill past Irby Hill Farm (where the first group of Irby Methodists met for worship before their chapel was built opposite the farm) and the National Trust land of Irby Common. For the walker, little-known, ancient byways provide longer, but finer, ways to Irby. A sandy path opposite Irby Mill Farm (dated 1694) goes through the old Irby Hill quarry (from which the stone for many local buildings was obtained), and down to the Greasby Brook, which it follows to the outskirts of Irby village. Another track, Sandy Lane, leads uphill from the road opposite the Cricket Club, past some cottages and along an ancient bridleway to come out a short distance from Irby on the Thurstaston road. This was presumably the original route to the mill at Irby used by the inhabitants of Thurstaston.

Limbo Lane (so called because it skirts the Irby/Arrowe boundary) starts near Redstones Farm on Arrowebrook Lane as a wide, grassy "green lane" but soon narrows to a twisting footpath through field and woodland, emerging after a mile or so at the Irby-Thingwall road. Almost directly opposite is Harrock Wood, another National Trust property, given in 1927 by Mr J. Brocklebank. Here a small brook runs through a wooded valley, its banks decked in spring with bluebells and celandine, and where owl, woodpecker, jay and other woodland birds ring out their song. The wood is small, but the path continues across open fields just quarter of a mile from Irby village.

A hundred years ago Irby was paid the following compliments: "a very pretty village", "the village has a more respectable appearance than others in the vicinity" and "quiet and quaint". Irby today is still a pleasant enough place. Gone are most of the "picturesque old farmhouses" and "the highest ash-trees in this part of Cheshire". But its situation, fairly high and with a good view of the Welsh hills, makes up for what it lacks today in "prettiness". Some of the old buildings remain. Irby Farm, near the crossroads, is a large brick and stone building, dated 1613. The home of the Ball family for many generations, it has been altered and extended over the years, as evidenced by the name-plates dotted about the outside walls. Almost opposite Irby Farm an insignificant-looking building, which now houses Irby Club, was originally a farmhouse called The Rookery. The Anchor Inn was originally a seventeenth-century cottage, but it has been greatly altered so that very little of the original remains. The interior patternwork of cast iron came from St Mary's Church, Birkenhead. The inn's name is not pretentious; a field-path right alongside is on an almost direct line with Dawpool, from which much of the inn's custom came in the days when boats tied up at that anchorage.

Irby's finest building is undoubtedly the Hall. Here is a remnant of the days when the Manor of "Erby in Wirhale" was given to the abbot and convent of St Werburgh by a foundation charter in 1093. On this site stood the ancient manor house, "one of the four principal establishments that were required to be at all times large enough and kept in sufficient order and repair to receive the abbot and his retinue when they held their courts in Wilaveston or Wirral". The manor house was subject to attacks from raiding bands of Welshmen from across the Dee, and the remains of a moat and earth banks are still visible around part of the perimeter of the Hall's grounds.

The present Hall is seventeenth century and was at one time the home of a branch of the Gleggs, an important Wirral family. The building was originally completely half-timbered until its reconstruction in 1888, but now the ground floor is of local red stone. On the north and south walls are massive buttressed chimney breasts which give an appearance of strength and solidity. The rear of Irby Hall looks out across the Dee towards Wales; no more marauding Welshmen come scrambling up the slope to attack the manor of Irby. The only attacks these days are from the builders, ever ready to grab a suitable-looking piece of land, especially in the green fields of places like Irby. No moats or fortifications will stand up to such attacks; but may Irby Hall and its surroundings long remain untouched by the hand of progress.

"Heswall is an intriguing place, with much to offer to those who seek a permanent home, to the businessman contemplating widening his activities, or to the visitor seeking relaxation from the everyday cares of life." So ran the opening paragraphs in a Heswall guide-book of not so long ago. The weary motorist rushing along the busy A540 from Chester to West Kirby or Hoylake, would hardly describe Heswall as "intriguing" – just another congested bottleneck to negotiate on the homeward trek. But there is more to Heswall than just a busy high street. Search out the quiet backwaters and you will find narrow sandstone-walled lanes terraced above the Dee, and rugged gorse-covered tracts of open land commanding fine views across to the hills of North Wales. You will never be far from houses – luxury developments of "executive residences" have sprung up in Heswall as in so many other parts of Wirral – but they seem as natural a part of the local scene as the gorse and the sandstone.

The known history of Heswall starts with the Doomsday Book in which the place is mentioned as "Eswelle"; early medieval deeds refer to Haselwell or Haselwall. By the seventeenth century the district appears to have become comparatively cultivated and, although there was some fishing and seafaring, remained primarily an agricultural area up to the early part of the present century. A hundred years ago Heswall was a village of some 700 people with the houses clustered around the church; the only main road ran through Gayton and what is now called the Lower Village. The coming of the railway in 1887 and the construction of the higher road were catalysts for development, although ten years earlier Thomas Helsby referred to Heswall as "having become a favourite place of resort in the summer by the residents of Liverpool and

Birkenhead". Heswall today is unashamedly commuter land, with only small pockets of farmland to break the ranks of "des. res." which almost reach the banks of the Dee. It is a pleasant area, though, and one that has attracted many people to make their home here above the Dee.

The Wirral Peninsula reaches its highest point, 350 feet, at Heswall. Its elevation is not immediately apparent today – modern buildings tend to obscure the natural contours of the area. But 120 years ago Heswall was "a picturesque village on the banks of the Dee, and the hills were unenclosed land over which the visitor could roam at his sweet will amidst a wreath of heather and gorse, and the picturesque cottages situated on the sides of its steep hills ended in the village".

The oldest part of Heswall is this Lower Village, with the parish church of St Peter as its focal point. This part of Heswall is in stark contrast to the busy shopping centre of the Upper Village. It is a Conservation Area and, to show that conservation is not a static process, the seventeenth-century smithy's workshop has recently been lovingly restored as a pottery and gift shop. Folklore has it that William III had his horse shod here before he embarked for Ireland at Hoylake.

The oldest part of the church, which stands on a fine commanding site overlooking the Dee, is the fourteenth-century tower, the rest of the building having been rebuilt in 1739 and again in 1879 after a great thunderbolt burst over it during Evensong, killing the organist and the boy who was blowing the bellows. Although seemingly far removed from the mainstream of national and international affairs, the church has played its part in the history of England. On the occasion of Queen Caroline's triumphant return to England in 1820 against the wishes of her husband, King George IV, the Heswall bells were rung out in defiance of all authority, and beacons blazed by the rocky lych-gate all through the night. Caroline, it seems, had a special place in the hearts of Heswall folk. Not so the King; for on his Coronation Day the following year, the Heswall ringers had to be bribed to produce a peal!

Byways lead from the church down to the shore where there

is still enough sand to picnic on, although it can only be a matter of time before the relentless marsh engulfs this too. Small boats bob up and down in the tidal channels where the heron stands proud and motionless. Northwards, sandy tracks wander across the Dales, a small but fine tract of bracken, gorse and heather, to Oldfield. Now a farmhouse, Oldfield Hall was built in 1604 for Sir Rowland Stanley of Hooton, one of the most famous Cheshire knights of Queen Elizabeth's time. Oldfield is the last outpost of Heswall's suburbs, for beyond fields and hedgerows sweep down to the edge of the Dee estuary. A fine, airy field-path cuts across to Thurstaston village from Oldfield, a nice enough walk in itself, but, even better, giving access to the Dungeons. Dungeon is a local name for a dell, and here a brook tumbles over rocks and stones and over a small waterfall before meandering through meadows to join the Dee. Bluebells and violets carpet the woodland floor in spring, while out on the open heath gorse and bracken provide cover for foxes. The Dungeon is a Scheduled Site of Special Scientific Interest, and there is something to see here at any time of the year. Like many other places along the Wirral coast, the Dungeon is reputed to have been the haunt of smugglers, its rocky clefts providing ideal hiding-places for the vagabonds.

During his wanderings through Wirral at the turn of the century, Harold Young encountered a farm labourer near here whose remarks give us a fascinating glimpse into rural life in Wirral eighty years ago:

> I had some talk with a farm labourer close to Heswall, and was informed that in this neighbourhood land commanded a rent of two pounds to the acre, and that his weekly wages were 20s including a nice cottage, to which was attached a good and well-cultivated garden. Once he had worked for some builders in the neighbourhood, and for a short period had earned as much as 30s per week, and that was the most money he had ever earned at one time. He had brought up a family, and had placed them out in the world in better positions than he enjoys himself, and had no wish to leave the country for the town, although employment had several

times been offered him in Liverpool at much higher wages than he received in Heswall; but, all things considered, he appeared to be as well off as he would have been in Liverpool if receiving 28s per week.

Heswall's tide of housing has spread eastwards across the peninsula to embrace the former township of Pensby, now unrecognizable as a village but in 1840 "situated in a moorish flat with 31 inhabitants occupying the two or three farmhouses of which the village is composed".

Sandwiched between the houses of Pensby and the fields of Landican is the area called Thingwall. Nothing remains today to show that here was one of the oldest settlements in Wirral. Hereabouts was the meeting-place of the "Thing" or parliament of the ninth-century Danish or Norse settlers, which met once or twice each year to formulate and review matters of law. Wirral shares its Thingwall with such places as Tynwald in the Isle of Man and Dingwall in Scotland, similarly named places of Norse origin. The exact site of the meeting-place is uncertain, but general opinion is that it may have been on or near Cross Hill, an elevated site alongside the main Chester road.

Mortimer, writing in 1847, is somewhat scathing in his description of Thingwall: "There is nothing in Thingwall, which stands high and is almost destitute of trees, deserving the least notice. The land is in general very inferior." Today there are trees, houses and fields – in fact all the trappings of outer suburbia. The place commands a sweeping view across inland Wirral to the eastern hill-ridge, with the tops of the taller Liverpool buildings just peeping over the top.

There used to be a windmill in Higher Thingwall, near the junction of the Barnston and Pensby roads, and was one of the most conspicuous landmarks in Wirral. It was run by the Capper family for over 250 years along with the adjoining Mill Inn. Both buildings have long been demolished, and houses now cover the site.

A busy road speeds traffic through Thingwall, but a narrow, sandy track, the original highway, makes a far more enjoyable way for the walker. Near the start of the lane is an old manor house, built about 1776 and until recently used as a farmhouse but now restored for use as a private dwelling. The path climbs gently to Cross Hill, near the entrance to Barnston Dale. The artificial-looking mound on the other side of the road here is a sunken reservoir built about 1915 to receive water piped from the Alwen Reservoir in North Wales. The smooth, green turf hides the details of what was probably a unique construction for a covered reservoir. It is a concrete, brick and steel structure, hexagonal in plan, 32 feet deep, 5 feet of which are below ground level. The roof is formed of 217 concrete domes, each of which is 30 feet in diameter and supported on concrete groins carried by 432 concrete block pillars.

Barnston is one of the few truly rural villages left in Wirral. Mentioned in Doomsday as Bernestone, the group of buildings constituting the village stand together at the junction of the Chester and Storeton roads. The combination of church, school, vicarage, coach-house, inn and village shop set in a landscape of fine trees and open fields belies the unseen sprawl of outer Heswall not so far away across the fields.

Christ Church was built in 1870, but in spite of its attractive setting, contains little of interest. Barnston had an old hall, but nothing remains today. The area's greatest attraction, however, is surely its dale, a deep, wooded valley where a brook meanders through meadows of bluebell, buttercup and bracken – "a Surrey in miniature" as one writer described it.

Barnston Towers (or, correctly, Barnston Tower, since one of the towers has been demolished) is a "folly" on the road out of Barnston towards Gayton. It is a circular tower, complete with castellations, dating back to 1852 – an oddity in this landscape of luxury executive-style dwellings.

Barnston stands at the gateway to rural Wirral – an undulating, fertile land of meadows and woods, farms and hedgerows, footpaths and meres – a microcosm of rural England itself but with an added dimension – the quality of light and the tang in the breeze which only coastal areas possess. And as we pass through Barnston the road, like so many in Wirral, swings back to the coast – to Gayton, on the banks of the Dee.

7

PORTS OF THE PAST

Gayton – Parkgate – Neston

GAYTON today wears an air of peace and self-assurance which belies its turbulent past; read the words of this piece of verse written some 180 years ago:

Up rose the sun, the sky was clear,
And gently ebbed the Dee;
The winds of heaven were fast asleep,
Though Gayton all was glee.

The lads of Wirral came in crowds,
The nymphlets neat and trim;
To stay at home on such a day
Is very near a sin.

And love, who never missed a Wake,
Brought quivers filled with darts;
He'd much to do on all such days,
And wound a world of hearts.

And Cambria's youth from Edwin's shores,
An annual voyage take,
What lass would stay on that side of Dee,
When Love's at Gayton Wake?

Youth, manhood, age, even childhood came,
To share this jocund day;
The hedges shone with gaudy shops,
And Gayton all was gay.

Dwarfs, giants, players, learned pig
With other creatures odd.

The Dee brought cargoes rich
And with them Mary Dodd.

When Mary first approached the place,
To get on shore was trying,
That she was there, on every voice,
Through all the Wake was flying.

A crowd collected – bought her cakes,
And gazed till they were weary,
And they who'd of the mammoth read,
Concluded it was Mary.

From Hoylake Hall to Gayton came
Fine ladies – gentlemen;
They come, my friends to look at you
And you may look at them.

The day wax'd short – the Wake grew thin,
Some sail'd adown the Dee,
Whilst others tugg'd against the tide,
And row'd to Hilburee.

This description in verse (can we call it poetry?) of the annual Wake at Gayton is by Richard Llwyd, a Welsh poet. More than anything else, perhaps, the poem gives us some idea of the importance of Gayton in times past. We can picture the scene: a fine day dawns, lads and lasses, ladies and gentlemen, young and old, converge on Gayton from all corners of Wirral. The ferry brings more merry-makers from North Wales across the placid waters of the Dee. As the visitors arrive, the side-shows spring into life with all kinds of wonderful entertainments. There is a man who eats glass bottles and stones; a dancing-bear; human oddities of all kinds – giants and dwarfs, fat ladies and thin men. The place resounds to the playing of pipers and fiddlers. Dancing-booths are set up. There are races and competitions for the more energetic: ducking for apples in a barrel of ale; a sack-jumping match; catching a pig by its tail; grinning through a horse collar; races for everyone – men, women, children, dogs and ponies.

The arrival of Mary Dodd, a huge fat woman from Chester, is obviously something of a highlight in the proceedings, but whether for her own sake or for her cakes is not known! The afternoon wears on, the sun sinks behind the Welsh hills; lovers arm in arm leave to walk the field-paths home. The Dee is specked with small boats rowing their tired but happy passengers across to the Welsh side. The Wake is over for another year.

But for how many more years did the Wakes continue? This is not known – but probably into the early years of the nineteenth century. The passing of this annual, harmless reverie surely left Wirral a poorer place – and Gayton passed into relative insignificance.

Surprisingly, perhaps, the name Gayton has its roots not in the gay *bonhomie* of the place, but in its position as "the farmstead on the gate or road" – that is, the main road along the Dee side from Chester to West Kirby. This is still true today, for at Gayton roundabout the incoming traveller from Chester has to choose between one of four roads which fan out to different parts of Wirral.

The original village of Gayton lay nearer the river. For 600 years there was a ferry crossing from here to Flintshire on the Welsh coast; Edward I is believed to have crossed from here in 1277 on his way to the invasion of Wales. The old Ferry House, now called Gayton Cottage, still stands at the foot of the lane, looking out across the lonely marshes of the Dee. The five-mile crossing must have been a fair enough trip in calm weather, but a hazardous journey when the Dee was rough.

The greater part of Gayton is now well-to-do suburbia. The seventeenth-century Hall, however, facing the broad estuary in its charming setting down a narrow cobbled lane, is one of the fine old halls of Wirral. It was originally the home of the Glegg family, one of the oldest Wirral families with connections dating back to the year 1380, and whose name is perpetuated in the popular Glegg Arms Inn at Gayton roundabout. Gayton Hall, like so many other Wirral halls, has been altered and added to many times over the years. It was a place of hospitality for travellers *en route* to Ireland in the days when Parkgate was an important sea port. King William III stayed here in 1689 while on his way to the Battle of the Boyne in Ireland; and he was apparently so pleased with his overnight reception that he knighted his host, William Glegg, who subsequently planted two fir trees in front of the Hall to commemorate the occasion. They became known as William and Mary, and stood as prominent reminders of the Royal visit for nearly 250 years. One was blown down during a gale in 1936, and the other had to be felled shortly after. The flat roof of the Hall is said to have been used by smugglers as a hide-out during the eighteenth century.

In the grounds of the Hall (which was originally protected by a deep moat) stands a fine octagonal dovecot. Built of brick in 1663, this is one of only two dovecots or columbaria in Wirral, the other being at Puddington Old Hall. The keeping of pigeons in the Middle Ages was a pastime with a practical end, as they formed a much-needed part of manorial diet during the winter months when other food was scarce. There were often 500 or more pigeons to one dovecot. They reared their young, all the year round, in rows of niches built into the walls, a bit like a primitive chicken battery. Dovecots fell into disuse about two hundred years ago when the introduction of turnip fields meant that sheep and cattle could be grazed all the year round, giving fresh meat even in the depths of winter. The peasantry hated the dovecots, as not only were they the sole property of the lord of the manor, but the pigeons tended to eat the villagers' crops and grain supplies. There were once some 25,000 dovecots in Britain – about two to each parish – so the two Wirral examples are indeed important.

Before leaving Gayton, mention must be made of Gayton Mill, a red sandstone building at the side of the main road to Heswall. Now a private dwelling, the mill is believed to be the oldest on the west coast outside Anglesey, and it is certainly the oldest tower mill in Wirral. It bears the date 1735 and was last worked about 1875. Present-day folk trying to bring up a family in today's small, modern houses may be interested to note that the wife of the last miller at Gayton successfully reared a family of sixteen children within the narrow walls of the nearby miller's cottage!

There is a fine footpath from Gayton along the bank of the

Dee to Parkgate. Not that you would know that the Dee is there – even at high tide the river is far away across the salt marsh. Only the exceptionally high tides of spring and autumn cover the marsh – and then only to a limited degree. Less than twenty-five years ago it was possible to walk along this sea wall with the water lapping the stones and the wind throwing spray up over the top on to the pathway.

To the casual observer the acres of salt marsh stretching away from the sea wall into the distance may seem bleak and dreary. The marsh is, however, an important habitat for bird life of every description. Redshank, oyster-catcher, and lapwing regularly breed here, and many other waders feed and roost on the marsh during the winter months and on passage in spring and autumn. Heron can often be seen gracefully winging along the gullies and channels, while many smaller land birds forage for food on the drier areas. The Royal Society for the Protection of Birds recognized the importance of the marsh to the extent that it last year purchased some 5,000 acres between here and Burton from the British Steel Corporation to be set aside as a reserve. This acquisition is seen by many as one of the most significant events for bird conservation in Britain for many years and it is hoped that, with the appointment of a full-time Reserve Warden, much more may be learned about patterns of bird life in this part of the estuary which until now has been rather neglected.

Bird-lovers from all over the north-west gather along here on the rare occasions of an exceptionally high tide. Expectation mounts as the tide creeps ever so slowly higher, until the water flushes the birds out of the marsh. Clouds of birds fly towards the land, startled by the sudden rude washing-out of their hiding-places! But the disturbance is brief; after half an hour the tide recedes and the birds can once again settle in peace.

In summer the marsh's edge is bright with plants and flowers unique to this special environment: sea aster, sea purslane and scurvy grass grow on the marsh, while the pretty seaside centaury bedecks the red sandstone blocks of the old sea wall.

A reminder of the days when these parts had trade links with

Ireland can be seen midway between Gayton and Parkgate. The slipway here was used by cattle pushed overboard from the boats to swim ashore. Near here, too, a footpath cuts across the golf course to the Wirral Way or beyond to Backwood Hall, a delightful mansion set up on the slopes above the Dee.

A mile or so further along the sea wall is Parkgate, with its neighbouring town of Neston. I have at my side fifteen or twenty books about Wirral. All of them devote more space to Parkgate than to almost any other part of Wirral except Wallasey and Birkenhead. This is not surprising, since these one-time ports have had the most colourful history of all Wirral's townships. Although now seemingly sharing little in common, the two places 250 years ago were linked together by a common interest: shipping. Looking out across the vast acres of marshland today, with scarcely a drop of water in sight, the visitor might be forgiven for being unable to imagine that, during the seventeenth and eighteenth centuries, Parkgate was one of the busiest ports in the land. And yet the evidence is still here in bricks and mortar; a mile or so of inns, shops and cottages within a stone's throw of the redundant sea wall, all looking out across the marshlands of Dee. "All on one side like Parkgate" is an old Cheshire saying with plenty of meaning still today.

The story starts, not here at Parkgate, but a mile and a half up-river where, in the middle of the sixteenth century, a quay was constructed to cater for the shipping which had originally used the port of Chester. As we have seen, by the fifteenth century siltation had begun to cause serious problems for boats entering Chester: a document dated 1422 states that "the abundance of sands which had choked the creek" was lamentably decaying the commerce of the City. Anchorages had been established on the Dee at Shotwick and Burton, but these too had been made useless by the relentless march of the grass and mud.

The building of the quay at Neston (originally called the "New Quay") brought a vast amount of shipping to this anchorage during the second half of the sixteenth century and the early years of the seventeenth century, and was largely responsible for the rise in importance of Neston during this time. The New Quay, unfortunately, was never a very satisfactory anchorage; it provided little shelter from the storms which regularly sweep up the Dee, and it was not long until silting caused problems here too.

By the end of the sixteenth century, the authorities had begun to look elsewhere for the site of a new anchorage. The river shore by Neston Deer Park (Leighton Park), a couple of miles down-river from the New Quay, at a place known as the "parke gate", had on occasions been used by boats to unload their goods if they were too large to reach Chester. The site was not too far distant from Neston, where a considerable business had evolved in catering for travellers and the handling of goods, and so it was announced that "the water bailys of this city [Chester] do immediately demand anchorage at Parkgate and insist upon the same as this City's right". And so Neston's New Quay was abandoned and the stones used to form a new anchorage at Parkgate. The original site at Neston is a fascinating place today; all that remain are the ruins of the Old Quay House (which in its time has been used as a "House of Correction", a farmhouse, and a private residence), and the sandstone walls which were constructed to protect the farmland from the river. A smugglers' tunnel is supposed to have run from here to the old Vicarage at Neston. The site is now, confusingly, called the Old Quay!

The construction of the new anchorage at the "Parke Gate" at the beginning of the seventeenth century transformed a sleepy hamlet into a bustling seaport of national importance. The main catalyst in this transformation was undoubtedly the introduction of the Dublin Packet Service, a combined freight and passenger service which operated on a "demand" basis from its inauguration in 1710 to 1775. For nearly a hundred years the service to Dublin brought travellers to Parkgate from all over the country. Many were famous (or at least titled) and most were wealthy – poor people could not afford to travel in those times. The passengers brought money, and a small town of inns, hotels, coffee houses, gaming parlours, assembly rooms and even a theatre sprang up to cater for the demand. But surely, you say, Parkgate was only a stopping-off place, a

Shore Cottages, alongside the Dee, Thurstaston shore

Across the Sands of Dee

Hill Bark, Royden Park

Barn End Cottage, Burton

Old Gayton

The Parade and Marshes, Parkgate

Bishop Wilson's Cottage, Burton

Shotwick Church

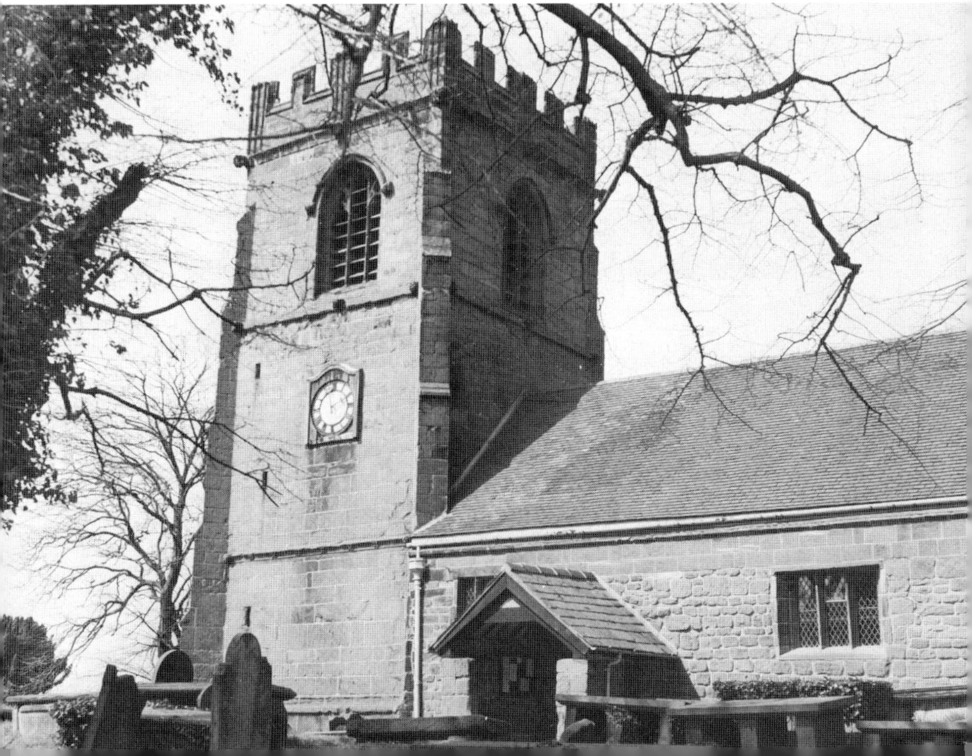

The East Float and Docks, Birkenhead

The Wirral Ferries

The Bridge and Lake, Birkenhead Park

The Windmill, Bidston Hill

port of call, a point of embarkation for the sea journey to Ireland? Yes, but the unpredictable weather of these parts (and the unpredictable vessels!) meant that the service was anything but regular. Passengers could wait days, even weeks, for the weather to change for the better. But if the passengers fretted at such delays, the local innkeepers rejoiced at the trade the inclement weather brought their way!

Mention must be made of the many famous people who passed through Parkgate during this period. Probably the most quoted was Handel, who came to Parkgate in November 1741 on his way to Ireland for the first performance of the *Messiah*. However, the weather knows no distinction between the famous and the unknown, and he too was prevented from sailing. Handel, though, made good use of the delay. Wanting to try out some last-minute alterations to the score of his oratorio, he went to Chester where he hired or borrowed some members of the Cathedral choir. He eventually sailed from Holyhead in North Wales, a longer overland journey, but with a sea journey much shorter than that from Parkgate. Handel did, however, return via Parkgate.

Jonathan (Dean) Swift, Dean of Dublin and celebrated satirist and author, often passed through Parkgate. John Wesley, the travelling evangelist, crossed to and from Ireland more than forty times during his lifetime of preaching the gospel to the folk of Britain. He, too, made good use of a delay caused by unfavourable winds; he preached at "the new chapel at Neston" in April 1762. Many more names are written in Parkgate's history – the Lord Deputies of Ireland; Oliver Cromwell; and Emma, Lady Hamilton, whom we shall meet again later.

The diaries and writings of these and other travellers of the time give highly descriptive accounts of the voyage across the Irish Sea. A young girl, Jane Reilly, wrote the following account of the arrival of her packed boat at Parkgate in 1791:

> After sailing close enough to the coast of Cheshire to see some fine houses we arrived about ten o'clock at Parkgate, but the tide not being in we could not get close to the shore,

but went some part of the way in a small boat and were carried by the men the rest of the way.

Accommodation on board varied according to the whim of the master of the vessel; John Wesley used to take his own chaise on board in preference to the discomfort of a cabin. Another traveller, though, commented upon the excellence of the accommodation being "subjects of praise among the first circles of the two kingdoms".

Mention has already been made of the delays in setting sail because of unfavourable weather. Even when the journey was under way, however, all was not always "plain sailing". Although the voyage could take as little as thirteen hours, it often took twice that time, and could even take as long as three days or more. On several occasions ships approaching Dublin were forced to return to Parkgate without reaching the safety of harbour:

> Being within a few leagues of Dublin Harbour, a strong wind sprang up, which obliged the "Murray" to put back and the next day return to Parkgate, where she now remains.

The passengers on that occasion were lucky to reach any port safely, for the violent storms which are common in the Irish Sea claimed many lives from the Packet ships. Poorly manned, overcrowded vessels with few navigational aids added to the risk of shipwreck:

> At Parkgate there also came women trembling and waiting for the packets aboard which were their loved ones, who had set out from Ireland. Day after day they waited for the overdue vessels; becoming at last uneasy, then anxious, and at length abandoning all hope, set out for home, knowing the sea would never give them back their dead.

One of the worst wrecks was that of the *King George* in 1806. This vessel, which local people had said had too sharp a hull for these waters, ran aground on a sandbank in the Dee estuary, her sharp hull causing her to lie over on one side. As the tide rose, a gale force wind got up which caught the boat. Water came pouring into the hold, which was full of passengers. In the ensuing *mêlée*, some 120 people drowned, the only survivors being four sailors and a boy.

The poet Milton lost one of his dearest friends, Edward King, in a shipwreck on his way from Ireland to Parkgate in 1637. King's death was such a blow to the poet that he composed what is now recognized as one of his best works:

> For Lycidas is dead, dead ere his prime,
> Young Lycidas, and hath not left his peer.
> Who would not sing for Lycidas? he knew
> Himself to sing, and build the lofty rhyme.
> He must not float upon his watery bier
> Unwept, and welter to the parching wind,
> Without the need of some melodious tear.

As well as the Packet service to Ireland, a ferry service plied across the Dee to the Welsh coast for some hundred years between 1750 and 1850. The ferry brought Liverpool-bound passengers from North Wales via the ports of Flint and Bagilt, saving them the long detour through Chester. The trip to Wales also proved popular with day trippers to Parkgate during the first half of the nineteenth century.

By the end of the eighteenth century, however, Parkgate's days as a first-class port were numbered. As well as the effects of the spread of the marsh, road travelling had improved to such a degree that most travellers preferred to travel through North Wales to Holyhead where a more reliable service to Ireland could be obtained, as well as a shorter crossing. Liverpool too was by this time a thriving port, and poor old Parkgate had to retire from the shipping scene; the last recorded reference to a boat landing passengers is 1811.

Parkgate's story does not end there; in fact, well before the last boat had left the quayside, fashionable society had discovered that here was the ideal venue for the newly found pastime of sea-bathing. We who take bathing so much for granted find it difficult to appreciate that, until the middle of the eighteenth century, "taking a dip" was almost unheard of. It was a Dr Russell who, in 1750, published a *Dissertation on the Use of Seawater on Diseases of the Glands* in which he advocated sea-bathing as a means of curing all such ills. And here, at Parkgate, was the ideal place to put the recommendations into practice. Firm yellow sands, bracing breezes, magnificent views across the estuary to the Welsh hills, pure sea-water, well-established communications (which were to improve with the coming of the railways), and excellent accommodation almost guaranteed Parkgate's success. And lest it be thought that the gentry of the time kept well away from such goings-on, note the following extract from a London newspaper dated 1802:

> Among the sea-dippers at Parkgate, near Liverpool, were the Hon. Colonel Crewe, Sir Boyle and Lady Roche, Sir Richard and Miss Hills, Colonel and Mrs Jepson, Lieutenant-Colonel Colston, Major Henchman, Captain Chandlers, Mr Trench, Mr Benson, the Hon. Mrs Foley, and the beautiful Miss Currie of Chester.

Parkgate had indeed become "much resorted to by the gay and fashionable world".

The kind of bathing indulged in at Parkgate in the late eighteenth and early nineteenth centuries was, however, different from the gay abandonment of today's sun-seekers. It was not done to be seen in the water with the body uncovered; and as such things as bathing-costumes had yet to be introduced, bathers had to use a contraption called a bathing machine. Tobias Smollett in his article "Bathing Machine", written in 1770, describes the machine admirably:

> The bather, ascending into this apartment by wooden steps, shuts himself in, and begins to undress; while the attendant yokes a horse at the end next to the sea, and draws the carriage forwards, till the surface of the water is level with the floor of the dressing-room; then he moves and fixes the horse to the other end. The person within, being stripped, opens the door to the seaward, where he finds the guide

ready, and plunges headlong for the sea. A certain number of machines are fitted with tilts, that project from the seaward end, so as to screen bathers from the view of all persons whatsoever.

Conditions inside the bathing machines apparently were pretty awful – dark, damp and musty, and crawling with insects. Small wonder, then, that not everybody used them. A visitor passing through Parkgate in 1813 was obviously shocked by the scene at high tide:

> We discovered a spectacle which a foreigner might have moralized upon with more seriousness than we of this free country can be permitted to do. Few of either sex thought it necessary to hide themselves under the awnings of bathing machines. . . . He would be a fool or worse who accused them of any intentional indelicacy, but I do think it would be as well were they not to despise bathing machines for the few plain reasons that induce so many to use them.

The crowds came to Parkgate until the 1830s, when the expanding road and railway networks made the more commercialized resorts of Blackpool and Southport (and even New Brighton) readily accessible. Local people still bathed at Parkgate until the 1940s, when the expanding saltmarsh finally reached the foot of the sea wall.

All through Parkgate's years first as a port and then as a resort, a small section of the community has earned its living from fishing on the Dee; few people, even today, have not heard of Parkgate Shrimps. Gone, however, are the days when fishermen's nets hung along the sea wall and trains of twenty or thirty trucks full of cockles and mussels would leave Parkgate Station bound for the towns and cities of the North and Midlands.

And what of Parkgate today? Well, Neston's suburbs have crept up to its very edge; there is no sea – you would be very lucky even to see it from here – but its "front" has survived as an interesting relic from the port's maritime days. Any fine day brings out visitors in their hundreds, to stroll along the prom, sample home-made Parkgate ice-cream, and take home a few ounces of Parkgate Shrimps. Most visitors remark on the attractive vista from Parkgate: westwards to the patchwork of the Welsh hills, or northwards to the cliffs about Thurstaston shore and the Hilbre Islands in the Dee estuary. Few of those who amble along this mile-long esplanade look at the many and varied buildings which make the town "all on one side". Fewer still know the historical background to them. There is not the space here to describe all the buildings in detail – besides, others have done this already – but any description of Parkgate would be incomplete without a mention of some of the more interesting buildings.

Most people start at the Neston end of the promenade and here, opposite the Old Quay Inn, is a row of eighteenth- and nineteenth-century cottages, one of which has the name Nelson picked out in stones on the ground in front of the house. This memorial is not, as many believe, to Admiral Nelson but to Nelson Burt, the son of a Chester artist Albin Burt who specialized in painting miniature portraits. Young Nelson was drowned in 1822 and his father set his name in the earth outside the front of the cottage. Nearer the parade, in a house on the corner, a young lady, Emma Lyon, stayed during the summer of 1784 to try to get rid of a skin complaint. The remedy (seaweed and salt water) evidently worked, for she wrote:

> My knees is well . . . there is hardly a mark, and my elbows is much better. If I stay a fortnight longer I shall not have a spot, for you can scarce discover anything on my knees and arms.

This young girl, unknown at the time, was to become the renowned Lady Hamilton, wife of Sir William Hamilton, and later the mistress of Lord Nelson. But more of Emma later. This part of the parade is somewhat dominated by the black and white timbering of Mostyn House School, a boys' preparatory school with a fascinating history. The oldest part of the school was originally a hotel, the George Inn, built about 1770 and at the time one of the most fashionable in Parkgate. It later became the Mostyn Arms Hotel until 1855, when a schoolmaster from Tarvin in Cheshire, Edward Price, bought the place and transferred his school here. From 1862 Mostyn House School came under the direction of the Grenfell family, first the Reverend A. S. Grenfell and later his elder son, Algernon. Wilfred, the other son, who was later to spend forty years of his life as a doctor in the frozen wastes of Labrador, passed his boyhood years exploring the wide open spaces of the Dee estuary. J. Lennox Kerr captures something of Wilfred's adventurous spirit in his biography:

> To the young Grenfell the wide, tide-shaped and rippled sands offered a new experience each day, a new challenge to what was a foolhardy daring. For those who sailed and those who went by foot the estuary could be a trap. The young Grenfell gave little thought to such dangers. The estuary or the patchwork green of the Welsh hills called him, and he went . . . searching for a new route each time and testing his hardy body in leaping water-filled guts or racing up newly discovered hillocks. The villagers considered both Wilfred and his brother Algernon foolishly reckless . . . and their escapades were a topic of wonder and worry to the whole village.

When Algernon became headmaster of Mostyn House in 1890, he greatly enlarged the school and turned it into a preparatory school, adding at the same time a fine chapel. The school possesses a carillon of thirty-seven bells, erected as a memorial to Old Boys of the school who fell in the First World War.

Just beyond the school, Drury Lane was a narrow "weint" forming the heart of Parkgate's social life during its day as a port. Here was a "home from home" for the travel-weary Londoner – a theatre, coffee-houses, gaming parlours – even the name of the passageway was guaranteed to make the homesick feel at home.

More houses and shops follow; the old Assembly Room (Balcony House), a nursing home, and the Red Lion, probably the oldest surviving Parkgate inn. Around and about Mostyn Square are the church, the old Schoolhouse, the coastguard cottages, and Mostyn Cottage, like many other Parkgate buildings reputedly the haunt of smugglers in the olden days. Beyond the square is another group of early eighteenth-century cottages, and then an odd-shaped building with an odd name – the Watch House. This was built about 1720 and was used as a look-out for the Customs officers who were able to keep watch on the shipping along the quayside. An attractive group of buildings towards the end of the parade consists of Pengwern, Sawyers Cottage (originally a public house and said to have a secret escape passage for smugglers) and Dee Cottages. These last-mentioned were fishermen's cottages and were subject to severe flooding at regular intervals. After one storm in 1802 the flooding was so bad that "an old woman was unfortunately drowned in her bed".

The last building along here, the Boathouse Inn, occupies the site of the Ferry House for the boat service across to Wales. In its latter days it became known as the Pengwern Arms. A short distance beyond the Boathouse, the picnic area for the Wirral Country Park occupies the site of an open-air swimming pool, said to be the largest in England at one time.

And so we are nearly back where we started – on the lonely stretch of river bank between Gayton and Parkgate. But tell me, what do you see now across the marshes? Ghosts of sailing ships leaving for Ireland? Bathing machines with their occupants coyly splashing about in the water? A young boy swimming across the swirling channels to the Welsh coast? Fishing boats returning, low in the water with their day's catch? A wreck, lying on its side in the sand? All of these, perhaps . . . and yet none.

Mention has already been made of Parkgate's neighbour, Neston. The name means "the town on the cliff or headland" – and if this seems a little strange today, we must remember that it is only in comparatively recently times that the sea has receded from this coast. Anna Seward, writing in 1794, confirms Neston's maritime situation before the marshes grew:

> The clean and lonely village on the extreme edge of the Peninsula . . . it is indeed a nest from the storm of the ocean, which it immediately overhangs. We find pleasure in contemplating its neat little church and churchyard on that solitary eminence lashed by the tempestuous waves.

Neston is old – there has probably been a settlement here since the ninth or tenth century – but its rise to become, at one time, the most populous place in Wirral, was due to the building of the New Quay in the middle of the sixteenth century. This development brought trade, commerce and custom to the town. Hotels and lodging-houses thrived and the place became an important market town and coaching station. Even the shifting of the sea traffic to the nearby port of Parkgate made little difference to Neston, for by this time the town was well established; and besides, Parkgate alone could not cater for the volume of business generated by the Irish Packet. At the beginning of the nineteenth century, Neston was the most populous town in the peninsula, with some 1,500 inhabitants compared with only a hundred or so for Birkenhead.

That a town of such historical importance has left us with so little of interest today is surprising; apart from a few eighteenth-century houses in Parkgate Road, the old red-brick tower mill, and a few old shops in the centre, there is only the parish church which is of any real architectural importance. Dedicated to St Mary and St Helen, the church has foundations going back at least to the twelfth century, and possibly earlier. The church's antiquity is evident in the carved Saxon stones which were found buried under the floor during the 1874 demolition and reconstruction. The oldest part of the present building is the short, square, fourteenth-century tower which has some Norman stonework incorporated into its lower part; the rest of the building was built 1874–5 using red sandstone. Inside the church the main attraction is four beautiful windows, designed by Sir Edward Burne-Jones and crafted by men working under the care of William Morris. The influence of both of these talented men is evident in these magnificent windows; especially, perhaps, in the figures of Justice and Humility.

In the graveyard several gravestones bear the words "accidentally killed at Neston Colliery" with dates spanning across two centuries. Colliery? Yes – it is but a short walk from the church to the banks of Dee. And here is a surprise: spoil-heaps from a coal mine! These ugly mounds are all that remain of the Wirral Colliery, an enterprise begun in 1750 by Sir John Stanley of Hooton, but later bought by a group of Lancashire merchants who called the business the Neston Colliery Company. For over 175 years men and boys laboured in vile conditions to bring poor-quality coal from seams two miles out under the waters of the Dee. Indeed, it seems that the very waters of the Dee, some sixty yards above the mineworkings, seeped into the workings in large amounts. The horizontal shafts were, in effect, miniature "canals" and tubs laden with the mined coal were propelled along by boatmen lying on their backs on the canals, their feet against the roof of the shaft. The mines closed in 1928, and photographs of the last shift to work there hang in the nearby Harp Inn.

It might be appropriate to recall here a remarkable Neston custom known as "Riding the Lord". On Easter Monday a man was mounted on a donkey and rode from the top of High Street to Chester Lane. The local crowds amused themselves by pelting the unfortunate rider with mud and rotten eggs all along the way. Needless to say, the rider was given a money prize for enduring this unpleasant performance!

Inland again, the village of Ness is now hardly recognizable as a village at all, more a suburb of Neston. According to Mortimer, this prosperous-looking place was "one of the most miserable in the hundred, consisting of a mere mass of hovels inhabited by the colliers; the greater part of the land is of very inferior quality and much of it absolutely worthless". Ness has two claims to fame. Mention has already been made in this chapter of Emma, Lady Hamilton. Emma Lyon (christened Amy, but soon called Emy and later Emma) was born on 26th April 1765 in a tall house (still standing) known as Swan Cottage. She was the daughter of a blacksmith who died while Amy was still a baby. Her mother returned to her home in

Hawarden shortly after, where she brought the child up.

Emma grew up to be one of the beauties of her age, a natural actress, a talented singer, the friend of politicians and other well-known personages, the wife of the British Ambassador to Naples, the theme of poets and painters (it is believed that Romney painted her portrait at least a couple of dozen times). She had an incredible personality – impulsive, vivacious, courageous, violent, yet tender and often docile. She became the devoted lover of Lord Nelson and appeared publicly at his side, her charm dispersing the inevitable insults. She bore his children, alone and in secret while he was far away at sea. After Nelson's death Emma battled with stubborn governments for financial recognition; and she fought against the cruel accusations of scandal-mongers and gossips. She fled to Calais to escape the debtors' prison and died there in 1815, in poverty. She was buried in a Calais cemetery which has since been built over.

There can be few Wirral people who have not at some time or another visited Ness Gardens. Now the Botanic Gardens of Liverpool University, these sixty acres of garden and woodland were originally the grounds surrounding the home of a Liverpool cotton merchant and philanthropist, Arthur Bulley. Here, on the banks of the Dee, Bulley built a large house and laid out the surrounding area as a nursery. The place became known as "Bulley's Gardens" and visitors were allowed a free access to enjoy the many rare and exotic plants cultivated here. In these grounds were the beginnings of the now famous seed firm of Bees of Chester.

Bulley delighted in the rare and unusual. He financed expeditions to Western China and the Himalayas, expeditions which regularly sent samples home to Ness. Many of these samples Bulley named after himself: *Primula bulleyana*, *Iris bulleyana*, and *Salvia bulleyana*, to name but three. The celebrated plant collector George Forrest and botanical explorer Frank Kingdon-Ward became associated with these expeditions; the plant *Pieris formosa forrestii* at Ness came from the first seeds sent to Britain.

Bulley died in 1942, and in 1949 his daughter gave the gardens to the University of Liverpool, on condition that they must remain open to the public at all times. The gardens have since been fully restored and expanded and are a delight at any time, but particularly from May to September, when a succession of blooming shrubs and flowers ensures a constant display of colour.

The association of the gardens with the university has resulted in a great deal of research into various aspects of botany. An example of the tremendous benefit of such work has been the recent development of grasses which are suitable for planting on derelict and polluted ground.

The people of Wirral have reason to be deeply grateful for the generosity of the Bulley family and others whose labour and dedication so deeply enrich our lives today.

8

VILLAGES BY THE MARSH

Burton – Puddington – Shotwick

"O Mary, go and call the cattle home,
  And call the cattle home,
  And call the cattle home,
  Across the sands of Dee;"
The western wind was wild and dank with foam,
  And all alone went she.

The creeping tide came up along the sand,
  And o'er and o'er the sand,
  And round and round the sand,
  As far as eye could see.
The rolling mist came down and hid the land:
  And never home came she.

"Oh! is it weed or fish or floating hair, –
  A tress, of golden hair,
  A drowned maiden's hair,
  Above the nets at sea?"
Was never salmon yet that shone so fair
  Among the stakes of Dee.

They rowed her in across the rolling foam,
  The cruel, crawling foam,
  The cruel, hungry foam,
  To her grave beside the sea;
But still the boatmen hear her call the cattle home,
  Across the sands of Dee.

CHARLES Kingsley, at one time a canon of Chester Cathedral, wrote the above lines in response to seeing a sketch by Copley Fielding of the Dee estuary, a sketch portraying

> a wild waste of tidal sands, with here and there a line of stake-nets fluttering in the wind – a grey shroud of rain sweeping up from the westward, through which low red cliffs glowed dimly in the rays of the setting sun – a train of horses and cattle splashing slowly through shallow desolate pools and creeks, their wet, red and black hides glittering in one line of level light.

The tale of the tragedy that went with the scene – of a farmer's girl caught by a sudden flow of the tide while bringing her father's cattle home across the sands and marshes – took possession of Kingsley, and "The Sands of Dee" was the result.

Pick a stormy late autumn day and walk the track along the edge of the marshes to Burton. The Welsh hills will likely be shrouded in mist, the forlorn cries of curlew and lapwing will be echoing across the sheep-specked marsh and, although the waters of Dee will remain distant, Kingsley's scene will come alive. Burton marshes are several thousand acres of land reclaimed from the river and sea by both man and nature; man through the construction of embankments and channels, and nature through siltation. Further up the estuary towards Chester, at Shotton, extensive use has been made of this reclaimed land by industry; but here, at Burton, the marsh is left relatively undisturbed as the haunt of sheep and wildfowl. The main game birds – teal, mallard and widgeon – frequent the marsh in large numbers, while the flock of pintail at 5,000 is among the largest in Europe. The list of birds to be seen here is endless – spotted redshank, greenshank, green sandpiper, golden plover, snipe, kestrel, short-eared owl, ruff, whimbrel, black tern, to name but a few. Geese of all kinds were once common on the marsh, but indiscriminate wildfowling reduced the numbers dramatically. Fortunately, conservation measures encouraged by such groups as the Dee Wildfowlers' Club, should ensure the survival of the marsh as a habitat for wildlife for the future.

The small headland shown as Burton Point on the Ordnance Survey map was at one time a rocky promontory jutting out into the Dee. The earthworks here are something of a mystery. It is possible that they were connected with the defence of the port and anchorage at Burton, under the shelter of the Point; or they may be earlier still, possibly even having given their name to the village of Burton, the Anglo-Saxon *Burh* meaning mound or earthwork. Beyond Burton Point, a stone embankment runs for some three miles across the marsh almost as far as Connah's Quay on the Welsh side of the river, forming a tidal defence which seems somewhat redundant today, but which during the eighteenth century was breached several times by the sea. Further inland, the original coastline of cliffs can still be seen stretching away towards Shotwick.

Nearby Burton must surely be one of the most attractive villages in Wirral. Despite the intrusion of twentieth-century developments, the main village street, with its old cottages and lanes hewn from the glorious red sandstone, still wears a timeless rural air. Gone though are the days when painters would congregate in the village street in large numbers, when it was "a common sight to see them sitting at their easels outside some picturesque cottage or in the extensive woods at the back of the church".

Burton's setting is glorious, and was probably the reason for its existence. Sheltered on the north and east from the worst of the weather by a tree-clad hill, with fine views across the Dee to Wales, it must have been a natural choice for a settlement. Originally a small fishing and farming community (Domesday population seventy-three), the place developed as a port and anchorage during the thirteenth century in response to the silting-up of the Dee towards Chester. The effect this had on the population was dramatic: between 1086 and 1296 the population of Burton grew some 300 per cent. The formerly sleepy community changed almost overnight into a place of great activity with the comings and goings of passengers and cargoes in and out of the Dee. In 1299 King Edward granted the village permission to hold a weekly market and an annual three-day fair in July for the feast of St James. Millstones for the Dee mills were shipped here from Anglesey in 1357, and by the turn of the century the main street was echoing to the sound of troops, mainly archers, leaving for Ireland to fight for King Richard II.

By the middle of the fifteenth century Burton had become an international port. Records give details of Spanish vessels bringing cargoes of wine, cloves, cork, sugar and raisins. At one time the village had ten inns (there are none now), to cater for the sailors, and the local people found themselves paying the highest taxes in Wirral. Burton's time of glory was not to last for much longer, however, for by the end of the sixteenth century the anchorage had become unsuitable for many of the larger vessels, and the New Quay at Neston had recently been built.

Burton's proximity to Chester was undoubtedly the cause of its being particularly hard hit by the plague in the middle of the seventeenth century, so that by 1801 the population was about the same as it had been 500 years earlier. Thereafter the village remained a fairly close-knit rural community until the 1920s brought about the dissolution of the Manor and its estate. This resulted in an influx of commuters which is still going on today, and will inevitably continue. The surprising thing about Burton is that it retains so much that is pleasing; the ancient cottages seem to have sprouted out of the sandstone like plants, so well do they harmonize with the surroundings. Many of these buildings are old farms and inns dating back to the fifteenth century, and are worthy of closer attention; alas I have space here to describe but a few.

The parish church of St Nicholas is a plain building of local red stone, set back from the main village street against a backcloth of trees. Built in 1721, this is the third church on the site; the original twelfth-century building was replaced in 1380 by a second church, little being known of either. All that remain of the Norman church are some carved capitals in the porchway; while the base of the wall in the Massey Chapel is the only remnant of the 1380 building.

There are several features of interest in and around the church. Above the porch doorway notice the names of the masons and carpenters who built the church; and the clock, one of only two in Wirral with one hand, the other being at Stoak. In the churchyard there is an eighteenth-century sundial, and several interesting gravestones. Inside the church, a finely carved thirteenth-century stone coffin lid and a Jacobean communion rail, thought to be the oldest in Wirral. The chair behind the rail dates back to the time of Charles II. The church possesses a small book *Prayers and Meditations* by Bishop Wilson, about whom more later, and a copy of John Foxe's *Book of Martyrs*, printed in 1562. Note the three money bags carved on the lectern; these are associated with the church's patron saint, Nicholas, who, the story goes, gave away three bags of gold to a poor family to pay for their daughters' weddings. For the same reason St Nicholas became the patron saint of pawnbrokers, hence the three golden balls often seen hanging outside their shops. In passing, I should add that St Nicholas is also the patron saint of mariners, a far more suitable association for a church situated in a one-time port.

On the plain tablet on the west wall of the church mention is made of "Thomas, Bishop of Man". Thomas Wilson was born in Burton in 1663, in the lovely thatched cottage, still standing, at the western end of the village. At the early age of thirty-four he became Bishop of Sodor and Man, a post which he held until his death at the age of ninety-three. The Manx bishopric was very poorly paid yet, despite this, he constantly refused offers of more rewarding sees in England and Ireland. He was a prolific writer; Young, in his account of the bishop, wrote,

> His works are now little read by the general public, but he has influenced the men who influence, and John Henry Norman praises his life and works highly, saying: "Burning indeed and shining, like the Baptist in an evil time, he seemeth as if a beacon lighted on his small island to show what his Lord and Saviour could do in spite of man." There was a time when no collector of books felt quite happy unless he possessed a large paper copy of Bishop Wilson's edition of the Bible.

It was also said of Wilson that he was the last survivor of the saints of the English church. In 1724 Bishop Wilson founded a school in the village, the building of which still stands today on a rocky outcrop by the Neston road.

Ellison, twenty-five years ago, asked of Bishop Wilson's

cottage, "Is there any reason why its appearance should not be a credit to the village today?" obviously a little disturbed by its uncared-for appearance. Last time I visited Burton, the cottage seemed well looked after and a credit to its owners. I think even Ellison would have approved! I believe the main beam supporting the living-room ceiling is a ship's mast, with the grooves worn by the ropes still visible.

Across the road from the cottage, but hidden from view, is Burton Manor. Once the home of the Congreves – a family with a colourful history too involved for these pages – and then the Gladstones, the manor is now put to good use as a conference and study centre.

Burton Woods, over twenty acres of pine wood rich in bird and plant life, were given to the National Trust by the Bulley family of Ness in 1928. A few years ago, red squirrels were plentiful in these and other Wirral woods; but now they are rare and our country walks are the poorer without these colourful little creatures. At the edge of the woods, at the side of a footpath behind the church, are two gravestones enclosed by iron railings. These are Burton's Quaker Graves, and they remind us of the days when the established Church looked upon Quakerism as "an active spirit of evil, and they saw contamination and disgrace in everything connected with it". In our times of religious tolerance, it seems to us incredible that these two people (possibly man and wife) were outcast to the extent of being buried in this unconsecrated spot in the centre of the pathway "where the men who had stood on their hearts whilst alive might daily trample over their heads when dead". The inscriptions on the graves have unfortunately worn away owing to the stones originally being in the middle of the pathway, but the date of burial, 1663, is known. It is also said that the two were buried in a standing-up position, but this is not known for certain.

Close to the summit of the hill behind Burton village are the overgrown remains of an old mill. There has been a mill here since the fourteenth century, for it is mentioned in the Magistrates' Accounts of 1360, and we know that "Burton milne was built new by Sir William Massey Knighte about the feaste of all Saints in anno 1629". This was presumably a rebuilding of the earlier mill, for it is recorded that in 1579 the miller, John Haggassman, was killed by a thunderbolt. Young tells us a bit more about the subject of milling:

> Milling in those days was a rich monopoly, and the lords of the manor provided a mill for the accommodation of their tenants, the charge for grinding being paid by the miller taking a certain percentage of the grain, and sometimes he would take twice from the same sack, just to be quite certain that he had not forgotten his share!

How many people, I wonder, know about Burton's well, which is situated just outside the village in Station Road? Hampston's Well – it is really a spring – served the Burton community from Iron Age days right up to the early years of this century. Such was its importance before the coming of piped water that strict by-laws were laid down to ensure the purity of the supply. The washing of clothes in it was prohibited, and the men of the village were obliged to help with the annual cleaning out of the well, subject to a fine amounting to as much as a couple of days' wages. Hampston's Well and its immediate surroundings have recently been tidied up after a long period of neglect and decay, and the site is now an attractive asset to the village.

A pretty country lane leads from Burton to Puddington, a mile away. Puddington was described by a local writer some sixty years ago as

> a tiny street of queer roofs, red steps, grey walls and green branches. There is no inn, no shoeing forge, no noise, and the only sign of life is now and again a faint flutter around the cottage post office. It is so quiet that it has never yet reached the fame of a picture postcard. A place in which it would be like a sacrilege to hear a gramophone.

Little has changed over the last sixty years to make those words any less true today. Only the prospect south-westwards of the smoke and chimneys of the Shotton steelworks reminds us of the age in which we live – an age far removed from the colourful times of the Masseys, who held the manor here for over five hundred years. The story of this almost legendary Wirral family is worth recounting, if only to remind ourselves that life in these apparently sleepy hamlets during the Middle Ages was not so peaceful as is often made out.

The Massey family, from Richard who settled here in the early thirteenth century, to William, who died in 1716, were zealous Catholics who were not afraid to go out and fight for their beliefs. Ever distinguished for love of war and courage, they went forth across the drawbridge of their ancestral home to battle at Poitiers, Crécy, and Agincourt, and no less fiercely on their native English soil. Sir John Massey, who took part in the French wars of the fourteenth century, and Sir William Massey, who remained loyal during the Civil War, both received knighthoods.

The last William, son of Edward, was true to form. A staunch Jacobite, he had joined the Pretender's forces at Preston in 1715 but, after the surrender to the Royalists, he fled for home, riding his favourite horse. Budden continues the story:

> He rode without slacking rein until he reached Speke Hall and knowing that the ferry at Runcorn was closely watched, he tried the desperate course of swimming the Mersey between Speke and Hooton, a distance of three miles. This meant, according to the contemporary plan of the river, that even if he chanced on a spring tide at dead low water, he would have had to swim his horse across two channels, each half a mile wide, and with a depth of water from one to two fathoms. From Hooton he pushed on without pause for Puddington, having ridden over 45 miles without a break, a wonderful performance for a man of nearly 60.

His faithful horse, however, dropped dead in the courtyard of the Hall, and was buried where he fell. Until recently, local people could point out the stone slabs indicating the place where the horse was buried. Massey himself realized that, although home, he was far from safe, for if the King's men learned of his escape he would be arrested and executed. He therefore is supposed to have created an alibi for himself, relying upon his speedy ride from Preston to make local folk think that he had been in Puddington at the time of the battle. To help his case, he thrashed a local farmer and, before the local court, used the affair as evidence that he could not have been at Preston on that date! All was in vain, though, for he was later arrested and imprisoned in Chester Castle where he was found, frozen to death in a dungeon, in February 1716. He was buried at nearby Burton.

Puddington Old Hall, "that gallant, lofty seat overlooking the sea", has been altered radically since its erection in 1490. Only the Tudor timber-framed courtyard with its traces of an open gallery remain as evidence of its antiquity. The drawbridge disappeared in the late part of the last century, and the remains of the moat are only just discernible. In the grounds are the remains of an eighteenth-century dovecot or columbarium, one of only two in Wirral; the other is at Gayton Hall. The tale is still told of a priest who, hounded by the Puritans in 1679, hid in a secret chamber in the chimney stack at the Hall, but was betrayed and captured. He too was kept at Chester Castle and was later executed.

It is a pleasant tramp across the pylon-straddled fields to Shotwick, the silent village of Wirral's southernmost border. Shotwick comes as a delightful surprise to folk who have never been here before. "We never even knew it existed until now" was the remark made by one family with whom I was chatting on my last visit to the place; and indeed this tiny cluster of houses, church and Hall form a peaceful backwater in stark contrast with the busy Welsh Road and Deeside industry just a short distance away. What is more, it is a cul-de-sac for vehicles, a real blessing for those who live and work here, or those who just enjoy its rare solitude.

Yet for centuries this was a busy place, the setting-off point for a ford across the Dee to Wales, and later it became a port. During Roman times, perhaps earlier, Cheshire salt was carried into Wales along this "Saltesway" which in 1339 was described as "the Kyng's Highway ner Chester to lede the host of our Sovregn Lord the Kyng in tyme of Warre unto

Shotwyck Ford". Traces of the ancient Saltway can be seen in the cobbled road and bridge below the church. Henry III and Edward I used the ford to lead their armies into Wales during the warring years of the thirteenth century. Peace-time travellers preferred the hazards of shifting sands, errant channels, and unpredictable tides to the risk of being waylaid by highwaymen on the more circuitous routes into Wales.

Shotwick's heyday as a port was during the thirteenth and fourteenth centuries. In the days when tidal waters lapped the wall below the churchyard (where you may still find an iron ring supposedly used for tying up the boats) armies of archers from Wirral and other parts of Cheshire assembled here to await embarkation for Ireland. "Fancy the great barons assembled there with their retinues, the street ringing to the tramp of armed men marching with warlike bustle, and in the mornings the famous Wirral Archers at practice with their longbows." Henry II left for Ireland from here, and the church registers record details of marriages performed on the eve of long voyages, voyages which often led to the loss of one of the newly married partners. But Shotwick, like the other anchorages along this coast, silted up too; and a giant steelworks straddles the marsh where the Dee once flowed.

What of the name Shotwick? Here is conjecture indeed! It could be from the Norse *wik* or creek which existed just south of the church; or from the Anglian "cattle station on the ridge"; or yet again it may have something to do with the manufacture of salt, as in the other Cheshire salt towns of Middlewich, Nantwich and so on.

The red sandstone church at Shotwick, dedicated to St Michael, is well worth inspection. It is mainly fourteenth century, but with bits of an earlier, Norman building incorporated into the fabric. Like so many of our old parish churches, St Michael's has been altered and added to a great deal over the years. Have a leisurely look around this old Cheshire church whose churchyard wall was once pounded by the waters of the Dee. There is space here to mention but a few of the church's many interesting features.

The church is entered through the finely decorated arched Norman doorway with its massive studded fifteenth-century door; note the grooves worn into the stones in the porch – made by the sixteenth-century archers sharpening their arrows. Of particular interest inside are fragments of fourteenth-century glass in the east windows; the seventeenth-century altar rails; the canopied Warden's Pew; the Georgian three-decker pulpit (the only one in Wirral) which housed the clerk on the lower deck, the minister taking the service on the middle deck, and the preacher speaking from the top deck. Note too the unique single-tier brass chandelier of the late eighteenth century; and the seventeenth-century octagonal font.

But what are mere words when describing such an ancient, holy building as this? Words alone cannot convey autumn sunlight filtering through coloured glass and tinting the rough-hewn stone walls; or the wooden box-pews dark with age; or the cold, grey stone floor trodden by centuries of worshippers' feet. Sitting alone in the church, one's mind seeks and searches for answers to questions. What kind of people worshipped here? What role did the church play in Shotwick's history? The parish registers throw some light on this latter question:

1722 – to 3 poor Sealors with a Pass.
1724 – to an outlandish Dub man taken by ye Spaniards and having a paper. Travel to get homewards.
1725 – to 2 poor passengers trying for a passage to Ireland 1s.
1725 – given to a distressed sailor.
1725 – to a decayed gentleman with a testimonial of his loss by ye South Sea, 1s.
1733 – to 2 poor persons come out of slavery.
1741 – paid to ye ringers for the good news of Admiral Vernon.
1741 – for going with a woman to Brumbrow (Bromborough) and into Wales, and our expenses.
1759 – the Ringers when Admiral Boskenon took the French fleet.

Lest it be thought that Shotwick church is just a decaying museum-piece in a forgotten backwater of Wirral, I must record the generous and loving response to the restoration appeal in the early 1970s. Many folk and organizations, some far removed from Shotwick yet with a deep affection for this ancient place of Christian witness and worship, gave generously to the appeal. And folk come from a wide area to worship within these hallowed walls on summer Sundays.

Just north of the church is the site of the ancient manor house of Shotwick; nothing remains of the building, but the dried-up moat is still discernible, surrounding a small clump of trees. A new hall was built in 1662 and this still stands, though a little off the beaten track up the little lane leading to the Puddington footpath. This well-preserved building in the late Elizabethan style was built by Joseph and Elizabeth Hockenhull, an ancient Cheshire family which held the manor from the reign of Edward I. The hall is of brick and stone in the form of a letter "E", with the small entrance porch set between the two wings. In the stone floor of the cellar a spring still rises between the flags; quite a convenient feature in the days when the nearest water supply was the village well!

The village buildings are mainly seventeenth century, one of the oldest being the Greyhound farmhouse, originally an inn of the same name. The old Greyhound Inn has connections with the Gibbet Mill not far from here on the Chester High Road. Back in 1750 two Irish labourers robbed and murdered a traveller after a heavy drinking bout at the inn; they were caught and hanged from an ash tree near the mill – hence the name. Smugglers are said to have used the sixteenth-century cellars of the vicarage as a hiding-place; all of these old buildings are now the subject of a conservation order.

Having reached this last outpost of Wirral, it would be senseless to miss seeing the site of one of the peninsula's few castles. The unlikely site lies in the fields between Shotwick and Great Saughall; a public footpath passes near the site, which may be missed if a careful look-out is not kept. For here are no battlements or decaying towers; no turrets or castellations; no rocky foundations high on a hill. All you will find are a few large mounds and trenches. Yet here was a fortress built on the bloody English-Welsh border, probably by the Normans, as one of a line of defences against Welsh invasions. Stand atop one of the knolls and picture the scene as it may have been eight hundred years ago, with the treacherous waters of the Dee swirling at the castle's base. Little is known about the castle's structure; it was probably rectangular in shape with several circular towers enclosing a square keep. It *is* known, though, that the castle was used by the kings of England during the twelfth- and thirteenth-century skirmishes against the Welsh. Henry II probably stayed here in 1156 when he led his army against the Welsh; and again in 1165 after returning from his defeat by the Welsh on the Berwyn Mountains. In 1245 Henry III led a great army against the Welsh and probably stayed here, as did Edward I in 1278. The castle was a base for such expeditions for over one hundred years until, in 1281, with the death of Llewelyn Prince of Wales, peace was made. From then on the castle became more or less redundant and gradually decayed; some of the stones were incorporated into local farm buildings.

9

"THE CITY OF THE FUTURE"

Birkenhead

WRITERS over the years have never been short of words – usually derogatory – to describe the town of Birkenhead:

> Birkenhead must always be considered as a dependency, or rather as a component part, of Liverpool.
>
> Birkenhead is almost entirely Liverpool's ugly little sister, and hardly at all a town in its own right.
>
> A desolate and disappointing town with most of what is bad in Liverpool and little of what is good.

And, indeed, their descriptions are not entirely without foundation. The visitor to Birkenhead, arriving from any direction, by road, rail or river, cannot fail to remark on its air of depression and failure. It is difficult to enthuse over vast expanses of derelict wasteland backed by rows of dingy houses, with a horizon of idle shipbuilders' cranes.

But, as any Wirral person knows, Birkenhead has another face. Beyond the scrapyards, docks and warehouses (which are certainly not unique to Birkenhead) are leafy streets of fine Victorian terraces and handsome stone-fronted villas, a public park designed by Sir Joseph Paxton himself, and a hinterland of the hills and heaths of Wirral's open spaces.

Over the years, Birkenhead has acquired many of the once outlying townships such as Bidston, Oxton and Prenton. However, these belong to Birkenhead for administrative purposes only, and few people who live in these areas would call themselves Birkonians. These communities, many with identities of their own, are therefore dealt with in other chapters.

The appearance of Birkenhead town today is the direct result of planning decisions made over a hundred years ago, in the middle years of the eighteenth century. But the town's true beginning goes back to the year 1150 when the Norman baron, Hamon de Mascy of Dunham in Cheshire, founded a Benedictine priory on the then remote headland on the north-eastern corner of the peninsula. This wooded headland was called Birchen Head, but there is dispute over whether this is the origin of the town's name, or whether it takes its name from its position near the head of the River Birket (or Birken).

The isolated position of the headland assured the monks' religious seclusion; at the same time, the existence of a landing stage and ferry nearby gave them opportunity to practise hospitality to travellers, one of the features of the Benedictine Order. The responsibility of the Priory for the ferry was confirmed by Edward III in the charter of 1330, which granted to the priory of Birkenhead and to their successors for ever "passage over the arm of the sea" and the right to make reasonable charges for that passage. Incidentally, the ferry tolls for the year 1357 were as follows:

Foot passengers, market day	¼d
Foot passengers, other days	½d
Foot passengers, with pack	1d
Man and laden horse	2d
Man and unladen horse	1d
Quarter of corn	1d

Right up to the Dissolution of the Monasteries in 1536, this corner of Wirral remained remote; the monks, and the few villagers who worked for them, were the only inhabitants of the headland, which changed little during the priory's 400-year existence. After the Dissolution the priory, with its estates and tenures (which included lands in Claughton, Tranmere, Higher Bebington, Bidston, Moreton and Saughall Massie), were bought by Ralph Worsley who became lord of the manor. Some of the priory buildings were converted into dwellings, but life for the few farmers and fishermen of Birchen Head continued much as before. A force of Cavaliers shattered the peace in 1643 when they "kept a guard about Berket Wood over against Liverpool, and did shoote over the river to Liverpool towne"; but after the Civil War life again became quiet and uneventful.

In 1716 the manor passed to the Price family; some houses and cottages were built and ferry traffic increased due to the rise of Liverpool; but the population remained stable. By the end of the eighteenth century, Liverpool was a flourishing port with a growing world trade, but Birkenhead, with a population of about one hundred, remained unaffected by the bustle across the water. Liverpool businessmen at this time must have gazed longingly across the Mersey to Birkenhead, which presented an attractive prospect of rocky foreshore backed by low sandstone cliffs and green wooded slopes. Few, however, were prepared to risk living on this shore while the crossing was dependent upon wind and tide, a journey which might take several hours in rough weather. Still, the introduction in the early 1820s of a regular steam ferry service brought an influx of residents, mainly Liverpool merchants and businessmen, who welcomed the prospect of living on the attractive Wirral side of the Mersey. The population doubled almost overnight.

Then, in 1824, a Scotsman named William Laird, seeing the possibilities of development on the Cheshire banks of the river, began to buy land in and around Birkenhead. He established a boilermaking factory on the shore of Wallasey Pool, but this soon expanded to become the basis of the shipbuilding industry. Laird's works moved to the present site in 1856, and shipbuilding and shiprepairing have continued here to the present day. Laird was also responsible for laying out Hamilton Square and the formal, gridiron pattern of long, straight roads radiating from the square. Not content with shipbuilding and town planning, he turned his thoughts and energy to the possibility of building a dock system to rival Liverpool's. Telford, who was called in to assess the possibility, exclaimed as he gazed over Wallasey Pool from Bidston Hill, "Liverpool was built on the wrong side of the Mersey!" However, opposition by Liverpool Corporation, who foresaw competition with their own trade, blocked the scheme.

Building of the "City of the Future" continued apace. The population had risen to over 4,000 by 1833, and the same decade saw the building of the first town hall and market. The railways came in 1840, and by 1844 the town had been given the go-ahead to build its own dock system. The population by this time had reached a staggering 40,000 (remember that there had been only one hundred people living here thirty years previously), and the area was rapidly losing its rural aspect as the roads and houses made inroads into the surrounding country. A magazine article of 1845 makes interesting reading:

> One of the facts which have most deeply impressed us lately, is the sudden rise of a new city in England. We allude to Birkenhead on the Mersey, near Liverpool . . . it is one of the greatest wonders of the age . . . the banks of the Mersey will present the grandest monument which the nineteenth century has erected to the genius of Commerce and Peace.

Two years later Disraeli wrote: "As yet, the disciples of progress have not been able exactly to match this instance of Damascus, but it is said that they have great faith in the future of Birkenhead." This, at the end of a passage in which he had mentioned such cities as London, Paris, Babylon and Rome!

This optimism was short-lived; the ambitious schemes ran short of money, political feuds developed, and by 1851 the population had fallen to around 24,000. A contemporary writer made this observation:

> The serious drawback in the township during the last year has been severely felt by all classes; buildings have been nearly suspended, property of every description has been much depreciated in value, and as a natural consequence the tide of immigration has been stopped; the town is at present, beyond all doubt, in a state of great depression.

With the eventual return to prosperity, Laird's original concept of a town built to a plan was largely forgotten, and the streets were built up in a mean and disorderly manner. During this period, though, the town had several notable "firsts", in addition to having been the first to develop a public park, in 1843–7. The first tramway service in Europe was inaugurated here, the first Member of Parliament was elected, and the first purpose-built library, workhouse and cemetery were erected in Birkenhead. The town became a borough in 1877, incorporating the townships of Claughton, Oxton, Tranmere and part of Higher Bebington. Thereafter the town's population continued to increase as cross-river travel made the journey to and from Liverpool easier, and as a variety of industries became established. At the turn of the century the population had reached 100,000, and this grew to a peak of about 147,000 in the late 1920s. About this time the borough's boundaries were extended again to include Landican, Thingwall, Prenton, Bidston, Noctorum, Upton, Woodchurch and Arrowe.

Birkenhead, along with its neighbour Wallasey, suffered heavy wartime damage, and the post-war period saw much rebuilding on the outskirts of the borough. A policy of inner urban demolition (I hesitate to say renewal) has continued and, as I write, acres of land lie derelict in the town centre, fulfilling a useful function as overflow car parks for shoppers. Much of old Birkenhead is in an advanced state of decay, and the town's list of jobless grows ever longer as shipbuilding and docking decline. On the bright side, a new shopping centre attracts shoppers from all over Wirral; but shopping precincts are all the same, whether in Birkenhead or Brighton, so let us see what else Birkenhead can offer that might be of interest.

This is a riverside town, yet the river is for the most part unseen and unnoticed. Unlike Wallasey, with its miles of riverside promenade, Birkenhead has no access to the coast, the banks being lined from end to end with docks and shipbuilders' yards. It is difficult to picture the days before the docks, when

> The Woodside beach, north of the slip, was composed of hard, dry sand, well suited for bathing. The water was always clear; and the bathing machines were well patro-

> nised. Donkeys were on hire and the merriment ran high. The beach south of the slip was rocky and covered with beautiful seaweed; periwinkles and crabs abounded; and much we enjoyed gathering and eating them.

However, the docks and shipbuilding industries came, and the beaches and cliffs disappeared under thousands of tons of masonry. From the world-famous yards of Cammell Laird have come ships that have made history. In the face of many obstacles and almost unconquerable prejudice they pioneered the use of iron instead of wood for shipbuilding and, shortly after, the use of the screw propellor. During the latter years of the last century the yard was turning out some of the biggest ships afloat, and was responsible in the 1920s for building the first-ever all-welded ship. Wartime production at the yard was high, and the names of the great fighting ships of the war – *Ark Royal*, *Prince of Wales*, *Achilles* – live on. Post-war days brought orders for liners, tankers, cross-channel steamers and, in more recent years, nuclear submarines. With courage and foresight, Laird's undertook a massive reconstruction and refurbishing programme in the early 1970s. Alas, the downturn in the world shipbuilding industry has hit Birkenhead badly, and near-empty order books have been reflected in redundancies and lay-offs. The docks, too, have seen trade decline, although the modern oil terminal at Tranmere is one of the few in Europe which can accommodate the supertankers of today.

Birkenhead Priory stands aloof and unconcerned, cheek by jowl with the cranes and derricks of the riverside industries, unnoticed by the thousands of tunnel-bound motorists who pass by every day. How many Wirral people have ever visited this, one of Wirral's oldest and most interesting sites? Recent demolition has cleared the approach to the priory, and the ruins once again enjoy an open outlook landwards. Much restoration work has been carried out since the ruins were acquired by the Corporation in 1896, and the priory has been regularly used as a place of worship since the closure of the adjoining St Mary's Church a few years ago.

The centre piece of the ruins is the twelfth-century chapter house which, even before restoration, has been remarkably well preserved. Remains of the great hall, kitchen, and crypt are also well worth seeing. Stories are told of underground passages leading from the priory to various places; at the time of the Dissolution one of the monks fled down one of these passages with some treasure. A large stone fell and killed him, and his bones – together with the treasure – are supposed to be still hidden underground in the vicinity of the priory ruins.

Only a stone's throw from the priory, that epic of twentieth-century engineering, the Mersey Tunnel, consumes and spews out thousands of vehicles each day. To dig a hole nearly three miles long under a river might not pose many problems or cause much excitement today, but in the 1920s this was considered a major feat of planners' ingenuity and engineering skill. There had long been a need for vehicular communication between Birkenhead and Liverpool. A train tunnel had established a rail link with Liverpool as early as 1886, but increasing trade between the two centres had put great strain on both ferries and trains. Plans had been put forward for a bridge across the Mersey, but the tunnel was chosen. Work started on the tunnel in 1925, and it was opened to traffic nine years later. (I often wonder at how two teams, each digging towards the other from opposite banks of the river, managed to meet up at a precise point under the river!) The tunnel's ventilating shafts, over 200 feet high, are significant, if not attractive, features of the skylines on both banks of the river.

Excellent though the tunnel scheme was, only thirty years passed before congestion at peak periods was such that another river crossing was necessary, and the Birkenhead Tunnel (named Queensway) acquired a neighbour (Kingsway) in 1971, the Wirral approach this time being in Wallasey.

As well as being a pioneer in sub-river roadway construction, Birkenhead had, as early as 1860, become the first town in Europe to establish street tramways. Aspinall wrote:

> Tramways are a remarkable development of vehicular traffic. To George Francis Train, a clever, persevering American, belongs all the glory of the initiator. Snubbed on all sides, he finally came to the poor little "City of the

Future"; where in spite of the abuse freely bestowed upon the benighted place, the man of ideas was listened to; facilities were afforded; and the first tram-cars in Europe began to ply between Woodside Ferry and Birkenhead Park. Other cities quickly followed the lead of despised Birkenhead.

It is entirely appropriate that Europe's first tramway should have had its terminus at the first purpose-built public park in the land. Birkenhead Park was conceived as part of the total plan for the development of the town, but was designed to present a complete contrast to the formal grid layout of the inner areas of Birkenhead. At the time of its conception, in 1842, the site was a low, foul-smelling swamp. Sir Joseph Paxton, the celebrated landscape gardener, on visiting the site for the first time, remarked that he considered it would be almost an impossibility to do what was proposed. However, Paxton drew up a plan for turning the 225-acre site into a park which would contain "extensive drives, beautiful walks, and elegant gardens, adorned with groves, fountains, ornamental waters, and numerous sources of pleasure". The park was opened in 1847 by Sir William Jackson, who had been the driving force behind the project, amidst scenes of great rejoicing and celebration; the day was declared a public holiday, and the whole town was *en fête*. During excavations for the foundation of the park a bronze axe-head was found; this can be seen at the Williamson Art Gallery.

Paxton's design for the park was used as a basis for other public parks in this country, and Olmsted borrowed some of Paxton's ideas for the creation of Central Park, New York.

The park consists of two parts – an upper park and a lower park – separated by a public road. Sandstone lodges (recently cleaned and undergoing much-needed renovation) at the various entrances were built to reflect different styles of architecture. So there is the Gothic Lodge, the Norman Lodge, and the Italian Lodge; while the monumental main entrance was modelled on the Temple of Illysus in Athens. The park has two lakes, one in each part, the lower lake having a boathouse and an ornate "Swiss Bridge". The lakes were formed by excavating and draining the surrounding marshes, the waste from the excavations being used to create the many mounds and hillocks. It is sad that so many of the original trees were elms; their loss has destroyed much of the intended landscape of the park.

Paxton's intention was for the perimeter of the park to be built up with tastefully designed houses which would complement the layout of lakes, driveways and open spaces; alas, few of these were built, and for the most part the present buildings surrounding the park are a hotch-potch of styles.

It is, perhaps, inevitable that a fine open space in the centre of a large urban area should suffer from overuse and misuse. This has certainly been the case with Birkenhead Park. What is surprising is that the park still retains much that is worthy, and is an asset which the town should strive hard to maintain and improve.

Birkenhead has few buildings of merit, but it does possess a grand square, described at its erection as "scarcely excelled by any in the kingdom". Built in 1847 as part of the rectangular scheme for the town, Hamilton Square is reminiscent of some of the Edinburgh work of its architect, Gillespie Graham. Hamilton Square is large (perhaps too large?) and the buildings are of Storeton stone, of similar (but not identical) design all the way round. Most of the premises are now used as offices, some of which have had the stonework façades cleaned to reveal the underlying pale sandstone, giving the square an unharmonious, "toothless" appearance. Public gardens, bereft of any decent trees, occupy the centre of the square. Aspinall, in his recollections of early Birkenhead, recounts the following tale relating to Hamilton Square in the days when the buildings were occupied as private houses:

> A romantic incident occurred at one of the first houses erected in Hamilton Square. The gentleman residing there had three charming daughters, whose pretty faces and lovely figures excited the admiration and imaginations of the few young men resident in the neighbourhood. It was the girls' custom to enjoy, each Saturday night, a primitive sort of bath in tubs at the top of the house. The room was

> lighted from the roof by means of a hinged skylight; which, unless specially secured, could be easily opened from without. One Saturday night, the girls were presiding as usual over their respective tubs, when suddenly a shadow fell across the skylight; the window was quietly opened; a man's hand appeared; and three beautiful roses, bearing the legend "to the three Graces", were silently dropped at the feet of the astounded and, let us hope, indignant nymphs.

The Town Hall, set in the middle of the south side of the square, is in the classical style, and is obviously modelled on that of Bolton. Built in 1883, the building was extensively damaged by fire in 1901, the repairs entailing some alterations to the original design of the clock tower and dome.

Birkenhead's other public buildings – Central Library and Williamson Art Gallery – are interesting, but not outstanding. The museum contains some good local collections of pottery, hand-woven tapestry and maritime items.

The presence of a large cultural centre like Liverpool so close to Birkenhead has resulted in a marked absence of theatres and other places of entertainment in the town. This has not always been so. Birkenhead's Argyle Theatre was for nearly seventy years the country's leading music hall. Built in 1868, the Argyle was the venue for the first performance of moving pictures outside London. Here Harry Lauder and George Formby rose to fame. Here Flanagan and Allen first sang "Underneath the Arches" to a roof-raising reception. The list is endless – Hetty King, Stan Laurel, W. C. Fields, Charlie Chaplin, Webster Booth, Donald Peers, Pat Kirkwood and many more. The Argyle was the first music hall in the country to go on the air, and the first to broadcast direct to the U.S.A. It was the London Palladium of the day. But seventy years of entertainment came to a sudden end in September 1940 when the theatre was hit by an enemy bomb. Despite gallant post-war attempts to resurrect it, the Argyle remained closed, and the building was pulled down in 1974. The Clarke family, however, associated with the theatre since its inception, are still in the entertainment business in Wirral.

As has been said, Birkenhead has expanded to absorb many

former villages and hamlets. Most of these (Bidston, Oxton and others) are dealt with elsewhere, but two townships close to the centre of Birkenhead are so much part of the town that it would be fitting to mention them here.

South-west of the town centre, Tranmere ("the town on the hill") occupies high ground overlooking the Mersey. It was, from earliest times, considered an ideal site for occupation; in the early 1800s it was the most populous township in Wirral, apart from Neston. In 1843 work commenced on the creation of a "villa estate", subsequently named Clifton Park, along the same lines as that at New Brighton. Unfortunately the scheme was never completed, as the establishment of gas works and other industries made the area less than desirable. Many of the original buildings remain but in general the area, like much of inner Birkenhead, wears a sad air of neglect.

One of the principal routes out of the town centre, Borough Road, winds its way to inland Wirral through lower Tranmere. This busy thoroughfare was built on the site of a pretty brook, hence the road's wayward nature. Aspinall gives us a glimpse into the beauty of the area before the roads and houses came:

> At the west end of the wood was a beautiful valley (known as the pleasant or happy valley) which abounded with wild flowers. The district is now covered with houses and shops; and the Borough Road runs through the midst of it.

Claughton (formerly Claughton-cum-Grange, the Grange being the farm of Birkenhead Priory), west of the park, was also planned as a "leafy suburb" for the wealthier citizens of Birkenhead. Large houses set in spacious grounds still occupy much of the upper part, but monotonous rows of terraced houses fill the lower reaches.

Birkenhead's oldest inhabited house, Toad Hole Farm Cottage, is at the junction of Tollemache Road and Bidston Avenue. Its date of erection is uncertain, but it is thought to have been built around 1550 as a tied cottage of Toad Hole Farm which stood a short distance away.

On the outskirts of Claughton, almost on Bidston Common, is Birkenhead School. Founded in 1860, it moved to its present site in 1871. This has long been regarded as one of the finest schools in Wirral. F. E. Smith, later Lord Birkenhead, said this of the school: "No Public School in England could show such an extraordinary record of success."

No account of Birkenhead would be complete without reference to the Birkenhead Plan of 1947. This bulky 200-page document was one of several prepared in the immediate post-war years "to repair the scars left by the enemy, and to plan the town in its entirety for the future". Sir Charles Reilly, an outstanding town planner, was its author. Similar words had been uttered by Laird 120 years previously, with as much optimism for the future. Both plans were laid with noble intentions for the town. And the results? Well, we have seen what happened to Laird's plans for Birkenhead. What about Reilly's?

He started off the report by saying,

> In the rebuilding of the large part of the town the work will be . . . more worthy of Birkenhead, both as regards design and materials, than that carried out during the past half century. The final hope for the town's appearance must lie mainly in two directions; in a return to the clearer physical atmosphere of the past and, under the guidance of trained architectural taste, in straightforward contemporary modern architecture. The aim of the Plan is to harmonize and improve where possible the relations between the individual elements of the town for the happiness and prosperity of all.

There followed suggestions for the location of industrial zones, improved communications by road, river, rail, and even air (by means of a new airport at Saughall Massie). Then came Utopian ideas for "Neighbourhood Units" – area units of accommodation and facilities for up to 10,000 people per unit. The town would be divided into twenty such units. Here is a description of a typical Neighbourhood Unit:

> Dwellings around oval greens would be in a more friendly relation to one another than dwellings on roads, and if the greens radiated like the petals of a flower from the community centre, the inhabitants would all naturally gravitate towards it. At the other end of the greens could well be the nursery and nursery school. Flats would be best placed near a public open space.

There followed plans and models for typical units; civil and commercial centres; amusement centres; theatre centres, academic centres; nothing was left out. All this to be accomplished in forty years, by 1986.

Reilly's plans, like Laird's, were ambitious – too ambitious for realization. With just five years to go before the deadline set by Reilly, few (if any) of his suggestions have been put into practice. True, the air is purer thanks to smoke-control measures; but the architecture and redevelopment? The vast areas of derelict land in central Birkenhead, the physical and social problems of the peripheral housing estates, the run-down industrial areas, tell the story far better than words. The "City of the Future" is still very much in the future.

10

LOST IN A TIDE OF HOUSING

Bidston – Ford – Noctorum – Oxton – Prenton

THE western limit of Birkenhead town proper is clearly defined physically by the hill ridge which extends roughly north-south from Bidston to Storeton. Birkenhead's housing, however, knows no such physical barriers, and the town's suburbs have inexorably spread across the ridge and down into the Fender Valley beyond, submerging once-rural villages in a tide of bricks and mortar.

A hundred years ago Birkenhead's more prosperous residents, viewing with alarm the spread of industry's noises and smells to their own doorsteps, took to the hills and erected palatial residences set amongst pine woods and heathland. These high-class suburbs of secluded mansions, within easy reach of Liverpool and Birkenhead, but far enough away for their owners to forget about their place of work after hours, are now sandwiched between Birkenhead town on the one side and high-density council housing estates on the other, and as such are an attractive buffer between the two. Although many of the older residences have been demolished and "luxury flats" built in their place, much of the area retains a strong country atmosphere, enhanced by large areas of public open space such as Bidston Hill, which is as good a place as any to start a description of the area.

Mention of Bidston Hill conjures up, for me, fond memories of long childhood hours spent playing in its woods, picnicking on its springy turf, and hiding in its secret places. And, always, the feeling that this was no ordinary place. And indeed, few other parts of Wirral can offer so much of interest in such a small area. Where else in a few hundred acres can you find open, gorse-covered heathland with fine land and sea views, pine woods and rhododendrons, a lighthouse, an observatory, a windmill, rock carvings, and a fascinating seventeenth-century village?

Bidston Hill's unique history begins in 1407, when the top part of the ridge was enclosed for use as a deer park by the lord of the manor. Parts of the enclosing wall, known as the "Penny-a-day dyke" because of the rate of pay of the men who built it, still survive today, albeit in a rather neglected state. During the seventeenth and eighteenth centuries a number of farms sprang up on the hillside below the wall, followed in the late nineteenth century by large houses built for Liverpool merchants and shipowners. The top of the hill, however, still owned by the manor of Bidston, remained untouched, used only by walkers. In 1893 local residents, fearing the eventual development of the whole area, urged the corporation to purchase the remaining land, and as a result 141 acres were acquired for public use over a period of twenty years.

Most visitors to Bidston Hill are attracted in the first instance by the windmill, which is a prominent landmark for miles around. This mill replaces earlier, wooden peg mills which occupied the site as early as the mid-sixteenth century. Evidence of such a mill can be seen about twenty yards north of the present mill, in the remains of the base trenches and a circle of small holes where the tail-piece was wedged. Similar tread-holes can also be made out close to the wedge holes.

The present mill, a tower mill, was built after the previous wooden mill had been destroyed by fire in 1791, caused by friction from the sails revolving at high speed during a gale. Harry Neilson, in his *Auld Lang Syne*, recounts milling life a hundred years ago:

> I distinctly remember a walk over Bidston Hill when a child with an elder sister, about the year 1868. A fresh breeze was blowing and the sails of the mill were turning round in full swing, grinding corn. A cart, laden with sacks of flour, stood just ready to leave by the stony cart-track to the road below while the miller stood by chatting to the carter. As we stood watching, the loaded cart moved off and the miller

> asked us if we would care to look inside the mill. His invitation was gladly accepted and in we went. My first and lasting impression was of the loud buzzing noise of the machinery, very like the sound of a swarm of angry bees but much louder, and my next, the whiteness of everything inside the mill, caused by the coating of fine white flour dust which nothing could escape, not even the miller himself.

Neilson goes on to recount how one of the miller's predecessors had been killed by one of the great sails striking him on the head as he stepped out of the mill one dark night, and also how a mischievous youth had daringly grasped one of the sails as they were revolving and had been lifted high up into the air before the sails could be stopped!

This mill, too, has suffered damage by fire several times, as well as structural damage caused by the severe gales which frequently blow on this exposed ridge. Milling ceased about 1875, but the mill has been restored and reconditioned several times since, and is in a fairly good state of repair. Stand beneath the massive sails on a blowy day, and picture the scene as it may have been 150 years ago, the great sails racing round, the machinery humming, and cartloads of flour trundling down the track to be made into bread at the local farms.

It is a short walk along this rocky ridge to the Observatory; much has been said about the view from here which, although extensive, is certainly not "unrivalled in Cheshire". It is, if anything, depressing. Urban sprawl in every direction reminds us of the changes which have taken place in this part of Wirral over the years; only far away in the south-west do bricks and mortar, motorway and flyovers, give way to green fields.

Nearer at hand, a number of circular holes, set at regular intervals into the rock along the ridge, are a reminder of a unique signalling system employed here over 200 years ago. In those pre-radio days, Liverpool shipowners were able to receive advance notice of their ship's homecoming by the sight of a flag hoisted on the appropriate flagpole. Of the 58 poles on the hill at that time, 49 belonged to Liverpool shipowners, the other 9 being used for sending advance warning of the approach of warships.

Unfortunately, such notice was often too short to be of much use, and in 1827 the system was extended to Anglesey so that news of a ship's approach as far away as Holyhead could be sent. This was achieved through a series of nine signal stations along the North Wales coast, each station having a semaphore system by means of which almost any message could be conveyed. The first message sent on the system, announcing the sighting off Holyhead of the American ship *Napoleon* on 26th October 1827, took fifteen minutes to travel the seventy-two miles to Liverpool. Eventually, shorter messages took much less time to transmit, the fastest recorded time being only twenty-three seconds; the average message took eight minutes. Some idea of the importance of Liverpool as a trading port in the mid-nineteenth century is gained by the fact that some 1,300 vessels were "on tap" to the system of the time. The semaphore system turned out to be short-lived, for by 1860 a cable had been laid between Holyhead and Liverpool, eliminating the obvious problems of using the semaphore in foggy weather.

Bidston Hill has been closely associated with Liverpool's shipping in other ways too. The Observatory (now the Institute of Oceanographic Sciences) at the extreme northern end of the hill was built in 1866 to assist in the accurate setting of ships' chronometers before a lengthy sea voyage. This was done using accurate observations of the sun, moon and stars, a job which was originally carried out in a building at Waterloo Dock in Liverpool. Observing conditions there, however, deteriorated due to the atmospheric pollution from the city's chimneys, and the equipment was moved to Bidston where the air was comparatively cleaner. Weather predictions for local shipping were also a feature of the Observatory's early days.

Over the years, the Observatory's work has gradually changed and developed. In between the more "routine" tasks of weather forecasting, tide predicting, and measuring land movements, the Observatory has undertaken the measurement of the width of the Atlantic Ocean and the firing of the

"One o'clock gun". The latter was a loud time-signal fired each day from a cannon at Birkenhead Docks, the electrical impulse being transmitted from Bidston. The gun could be heard over a wide area, and was used by many Birkenhead and Liverpool workers as the signal for a return to work after their lunch break. The gun was fired for the last time in 1969.

Perhaps the Observatory's most celebrated achievement was the inventing and perfecting of the tide-predicting equipment. This brilliant mechanical calculator, a forerunner of today's computers, was able to predict, with amazing accuracy, the height and time of high tide anywhere in the world for any particular date – past, present or future. Although now superseded by sophisticated computerized equipment, the original machine, together with the original telescopes from the observation domes, are carefully preserved and on view in the Liverpool Museum.

Cheek by jowl with the Observatory, and seemingly miles from the sea which it served, Bidston lighthouse remains as a reminder of the days when, together with its partner at Leasowe, ships entering the Mersey had to line up the two lights to ensure a safe entry through the narrow channel. The first light here was built in 1771, to replace the original "lower light" at Leasowe which had been washed away; Bidston thus became the "upper light" of the pair. The original building at Bidston was "a substantial stone building with an octagonal tower, which from a distance had the appearance of a church"; it was pulled down when the Observatory was built in 1866. The present lighthouse was built 1872–3 but the light has not shone since 1908.

A keen eye on Bidston Hill will soon search out other, less obvious, features of interest. The rock carvings, for example. On a flat sandstone outcrop near the Observatory are several carvings of figures – a "Sun Goddess" with outstretched arms whose head points exactly to where the sun sets on Midsummer's Day; and a cat-headed "Moon Goddess" with a moon at her feet. Another outcrop bears the figure of a horse. Who carved these, and why? No one is sure, but a date of about the second century has been tentatively suggested.

A circular hollow cut into the sandstone on the top of the hill behind Bidston Hall is said to be the remains of a cockpit, used by villagers taking part in the cruel but popular sport of cock-fighting.

Most of the cottages which at one time were scattered about the slopes of the hill have gone. A few, however, remain; and one in particular has an interesting history, and a romantic link with the Scotland of two hundred years ago. Tom o'Shanter's Cottage was built in 1837 as a small farm, holding about six acres of the surrounding land. Its tenant in 1841 was Richard Leay, a master stonemason and probably a Scotsman. It is likely that Richard Leay carved the stone set in the gable end of the cottage, the stone which gave the cottage its name. The stone depicts a scene from the poem "Tam o'Shanter" by Robert Burns. In the poem, Tam was riding home after a day at market, a little the worse for drink. The night was dark and stormy, and on the way he disturbed a party of witches in the old haunted Kirk of Alloway. The drunken Tam roared out "Weel done, Cutty Sark" at the leader, and was immediately chased by the witches. Tam managed to get across a bridge and the witches, who would not dare cross running water, caught the horse's tail. Tam escaped, but "Poor Maggie" lost her tail:

> Now, do thy speedy utmost, Meg,
> And win the key-stane of the brig;
> There, at them, thou thy tail may toss,
> A running stream they dare na cross.
> But ere the key-stane she could make,
> The fient a tail she had to shake!
> For Nannie, far before the rest,
> Had upon noble Maggie prest,
> And flew at Tam wi' furious ettle;
> But little wist she Maggie's mettle –
> Ae spring brought aff her master hale,
> But left behind her ain grey tail:
> The carlin caught her by the rump,
> And left poor Maggie scarce a stump!

The cottage continued as a small farm for over a hundred years but, after being burnt down several times in the 1950s, was on the point of being demolished completely when the Birkenhead Historical Society, backed by the Council, stepped in with a scheme to restore it. With the help of local schools, organizations and individuals, Tam o'Shanter's Cottage has been completely restored and is now a fully equipped field study centre. The annual rent on the cottage – one pine cone – is paid over to the Mayor of Wirral by the trustees each spring as part of a tradition which goes back to the days when squatters moved into the area. Another custom – that of egg rolling – has recently been revived here too. Crowds gather on Easter Monday to roll gaily coloured hard-boiled eggs down the field in front of the cottage, the object being to get an egg into a hole cut in the turf at the foot of the slope. Egg rolling was popular in several parts of Wirral – the "bonks" of Birkenhead Park and Irby Hill were popular venues – and had its origin in the early days of Christianity, the egg being regarded as a symbol of hope and resurrection.

The township of Bidston at one time covered an extensive area, incorporating the parishes of Bidston, Claughton, Moreton and Saughall Massie. The village itself is an architectural and historical gem which, to the casual passer-by, appears to have been preserved (not too well) for looking at, but not for living in. Hemmed in by a council estate, a by-pass and a steel mill, all erected within the last ten years, Bidston village has changed surprisingly little over the years. It was described in 1847 as "a little, quiet, grey village" – words which still hold true today. Bidston's peace has not, however, been easily obtained. Up to the middle of the 1970s, all through traffic between Birkenhead and Moreton had to pass through the village's main street. An endless stream of traffic, much of it commercial, pounded the narrow, twisting road, shaking the seventeenth-century foundations of the grey stone cottages along the way and stretching the nerves of their twentieth-century inhabitants. After much pro-ing and con-ing, the Council at last recommended that the village be by-passed. With its opening, the village has become virtually a backwater, for the only way out is into the housing estate at Ford.

Much has been said and written about the disastrous planning (if indeed it can be called planning) which has resulted in the virtual destruction of Bidston's immediate environment; suffice it to say that the damage has been done. It is to be hoped, though, that lessons have been learnt by many; not only by the local authority, but those ordinary folk of Wirral who should have done something, who should have stood up and shouted long and loud, to save Bidston from the ravishes of insensitive planning. Some did fight; as a result of a "Save Bidston" campaign in the late 1960s the Council declared the village the first Conservation Area in 1971. Yet even as I write, plans are afoot to convert one of the old cottages into a restaurant, and the Hall into a country club.

But what's all the fuss about, you ask. To find out, let us take a closer look at the buildings in and about Bidston village.

Bidston Hall is set back from the main street along a rough, sandy lane. It is a grey sandstone building, probably built about 1535, and rebuilt in 1620 by William, sixth Earl of Derby, as a country seat of the colourful Stanley family. James, who succeeded William in 1642, was a staunch Royalist and during the Civil War fled to the Isle of Man where he apparently succeeded in holding out against Cromwell. In 1649 Cromwell offered James a free pardon and the return of part of his surrendered estates if he would surrender the Isle of Man. James's reply was characteristic:

> Sir, I received your letter with indignation and scorn. I scorn your proffers, disdain your favour, and abhor your treason, and am so far from delivering up this Island to your advantage, that I will keep it to the utmost of my power to your destruction. Take this for your final answer and forbear any further solicitations, for if you trouble me with any more messages I will burn the paper and hang the bearer.

Shortly after, learning that Charles II was advancing from Scotland, James rushed to England to join his monarch. He was captured at the Battle of Worcester, and was beheaded at Bolton a few days later.

The last of the House of Stanley to live at Bidston Hall was Charles, the eighth Earl, and he lived there until 1653. Thirty years later the property passed to Sir Robert Vyner, the one-time Lord Mayor of London and maker of the Coronation regalia, in whose family it remained for nearly 300 years.

Today the Hall is a private dwelling, having been lovingly and painstakingly restored fifteen years ago from what was a virtual ruin. It is a romantic place, each niche telling a story; some say secret passages beneath the Hall connect with Mother Redcap's old tavern, away across the once-treacherous Moss in Wallasey. Hall Farm, just below the Hall, is, like the other farms in Bidston, a farm in name only, and the outbuildings are now used as stables.

Bidston's parish church, St Oswald's, stands dominating the village on a steep grassy bank. Evidence indicates that there has been a church of some sort here since the twelfth century, but the oldest part of the present building is the tower, early sixteenth century; the remainder was rebuilt in 1856 in a style similar to the previous church. Prominent amongst the heraldic shields above the west doorway is that of the Derby family, the three legs of Man. The church received its main support for a long time from Sir Edward and Lady Cust of Leasowe Castle. The arrival of the family for Sunday services must have been quite a sight, for it is recorded that they brought with them a retinue of castle servants, butler, footmen and maids! Before the rebuilding of the church in 1856, the roof was most likely thatched; the parish records frequently mention the "mowing and buying of rushes". The reredos is a coloured glass mosaic by Salviati of Leonardo da Vinci's *Last Supper* and is considered to be "one of the finest examples of Italian mosaic work in this country".

The fine grey stone buildings dotted about the village are worthy of close inspection. Immediately east of the church is The Lilacs (formerly the Old Vicarage), built in the late seventeenth century, with its massive stone chimney-stacks. Nowadays our central heating with its attendant cleanliness is often taken for granted; the primitive method of cleaning these massive old chimneys makes entertaining reading:

> The method of sweeping chimneys adopted by the Bidston people in old days was to procure a good gorse bush, a long

> rope, and a brick or stone. A lad then climbed on to the roof and dropped the stone with the rope attached down the chimney, then the bush was pulled down two or three times until the chimney was clean. Unfortunately no provision was made for the catching of the soot, which descended in clouds and smothered everything with its sticky blackness.

Attached to the house is the old Tithe Barn, a sturdy building with its thick walls and supporting buttresses.

Across the road from The Lilacs is Yew Tree Farm, half-timbered and dated 1697; and Church Farm, again seventeenth century. Church Farm is believed to have been an abbey or monastery and once housed a party of monks. It has traces of underground passageways or hides; and inside there are no less than thirteen different floor levels.

At the top of School Lane, at the junction with the main street, is Stone Farm, originally the Ring o' Bells Inn immortalized by Albert Smith in his book *Christopher Tadpole*. The inn was known far and wide as the "Ham and Eggs House":

> At certain stated times, such as Easter, people came in crowds to consume ham and eggs. On such occasions the inn yard would be crowded with gigs, spring-carts and traps of every description. On one such day as an Easter Monday, during the 1860s, between thirty and forty hams, and a proportionate number of eggs, were polished off.

Simon Croft, the inn's landlord, was apparently quite a character; he erected a sign above the entrance:

> Walk in my friends and taste my beer and liquor;
> If your pockets be well stored you'll find it comes the quicker;
> But for want of that has caused both grief and sorrow,
> Therefore you must pay today; I will trust tomorrow.

Liquor smuggled across the boggy Moss from the wrecks along the Wirral shore undoubtedly found its way into

Simon's cellars. Simon, alas, was one of the inn's best customers; he failed in his duty of keeping order over his customers to such an extent that it was common to see drunken men lying beneath the church wall on a Sunday morning. This apparently upset the churchgoers so much that they petitioned the squire to have the inn closed. This was carried out in 1868, and the village has been without an inn since.

The footpath from Bidston village along the lower western side of Bidston Hill to Noctorum was, before the houses were built, a pleasant walk indeed, looking over the green valley of the Fender. The path still exists, but is now thoroughly suburban. It comes out at Ford Hill, at a tortuous hairpin bend on the Upton Road. For the walker, a steep, rugged path cuts across this bend; this ancient track, part of the old pack-horse route to Upton, is known locally as the "Pass of Thermopylae"; why, no one knows. Thermopylae Pass skirts the ground of Bidston Court, the original site of the house called Hill Bark which was removed and re-erected in Royden Park, Frankby; the old site here has been transformed into a pleasant public garden. A grand view of western Wirral is to be had from here; the houses of the Fender Valley give way to the trees and fields of Arrowe, while in the distance the hills and mountains of North Wales form a purple backcloth.

Here we are on the outskirts of Noctorum, "a spacious, leafy district of late Victorian houses, many very large and very red". Much argument has raged over the origin of this unusual name; it is called Chenotrie in the Doomsday survey, and it has been said that this developed into its present form as follows: Chenoctre, Kenoctre, Knocktory, Knocktorum, and Noctorum. Chenotrie means "oak town", this area being particularly noted as abounding in oak in earlier times. Another authority gives the place Celtic/Gaelic origins: *knock*, being a hill, and *torran* a grave or tomb – the Doomsday Chenotrie being an error of the scribe. To add to the confusion, thirteenth-century documents show the place as "Knocttyrum".

There is no village. The higher parts of the suburb are extremely attractive; large houses with suitably large gardens off country-type lanes appeal as much today as they did a hundred years ago. The lower parts are, in contrast, unattractive; modern, high-density housing right up to the motorway.

Oxton ("the town of the oxen") takes up where Noctorum leaves off. Like Noctorum, much of it is leafy, even though many of the grand houses have been demolished and replaced by modern flats. It has obviously been (and to a degree, still is) prosperous. Its prosperity began in the 1840s when, as in so many other parts of Wirral, wealthy Liverpool merchants began building high-class residences. What attracted them to Oxton is difficult to say, for Ormerod writing only twenty years earlier, said this of the place:

> The village of Oxton is mean and small, composed of wretched, straggling huts . . . no degree of civilization or improvement has reached this part of the opposite shore, which is a scene of solitude broken in upon only with the voice of the cowherd or the cry of the plover. Bleak and barren moors stretch round it in every direction, and exhibit an unmixed scene of poverty and desolation.

Oxton's inhabitants at that time had acquired an "unenviable celebrity in their own neighbourhood". The population then was about 150; by 1847 it had grown to 1,400. Perhaps the attraction of Oxton was its commanding situation, with an extensive prospect in all directions: westwards across the fields and woods of Wirral, and eastwards across the busy Mersey to the developing port of Liverpool and beyond.

Oxton today is perhaps a bit of a surprise to those who think of Birkenhead only in terms of docks and slums. Many of the narrow lanes which constitute the older "village" area still retain their red stone walls and are overhung in summer with the dense foliage of many fine trees. Quaint cottages (some seventeenth century) rub shoulders with large Victorian dwellings. The parish church, St Saviour's, a fine sandstone building of 1890, has much of interest inside – see the inlaid ornament in the chancel screen, choir stalls and altar. The stained glass in the vestry came from a nearby house called Point of Ayr. Recently Wirral Council, in an endeavour to limit the piecemeal demolition and redevelopment of many of the buildings which give Oxton its charming character, have made Oxton village a Conservation Area. Too late, some would say.

Before leaving Oxton, mention should be made of the Arno, a miniature park set on a hill on the outskirts of Oxton. Besides being a delightful oasis, this was the site of an important find, in 1834, of a hoard of Roman coins. In view of its prominent position, was this at one time a Roman settlement?

> At Prenton are some of the best examples on Merseyside of early twentieth-century domestic architecture, and the summit of Prenton Hill forms an attractive Edwardian suburb, created amongst existing pinewoods, with views westwards across Wirral to North Wales.

So wrote Pevsner just over ten years ago. Prenton, like so much of outer Birkenhead, is almost entirely suburban. The area referred to above is, unfortunately, not really typical of the area. Post-war semi-detached houses have engulfed the former hamlet, which was noted in the Doomsday Book as Prestune, the priest's town or farmstead. Neither is there any trace now of the extensive wood also mentioned in Doomsday. One of the few surviving remnants of the past is the "Roman Road" or "Monks' Stepping Stones", a paved path across the fields to Storeton. Local people have for centuries ignored the opinions of historians who have tried to set down the truth about this pathway, probably unique in Wirral. Irvine, in his *Notes on the Old Halls of Wirral*, had this to say:

> Our way from Prenton to Storeton lies along an ancient lane popularly called the Monks' Stepping Stones, also sometimes called the Roman Road. Both names are quite misleading. That an occasional monk may have stepped along these stones is quite probable, and there can be little doubt that sometimes a stray Roman may have used this very lane nearly two thousand years ago, but it has no more right to either name than any other lane in the neighbourhood. These stones were probably placed in their present position

some time in the Middle Ages, just as stones were put in any miry spot, when the locality could afford it, in other parts of the country. They were mainly used by the heavily laden pack horses that carried merchandise from village to village in the days before wheeled traffic became possible.

But whatever the truth, it is a pleasant enough tramp across these green acres; even more so knowing that the houses are far behind, and ahead lie only the hedges and fields, paths and woods of mid-Wirral.

11

WHERE THE HOUSES MEET THE FIELDS

Upton – Woodchurch – Landican – Arrowe

UPTON – "the farmstead on the hillock" – stands at the meeting-place of two busy roads: the one from Birkenhead to West Kirby, and the other from Wallasey and Moreton to Chester. Unlike many other Wirral villages, Upton's busyness is not peculiar to the present day, for the place was formerly considered "the metropolis of the lower mediety of Wirral". Its central position in northern Wirral made it an important meeting-place for people from the surrounding villages, although Upton itself had few inhabitants (less than 150 by 1800). The bi-annual fairs, held in the spring and autumn, and weekly market, attracted folk from Bidston, Greasby, Woodchurch, Moreton and other villages in the area. Dancing, racing and other sports were held in the fields around the village, and were apparently well patronized by the farm workers and servants who constituted the greater part of the population at the time.

Even by the middle of the last century, Upton was still a self-contained rural community, unaffected by the rapidly emerging town of Birkenhead, unseen and unthought of beyond Bidston ridge. That there were few buildings is borne out by Mortimer's description of Upton in 1847: "The surrounding country is very bare of foliage, but the scenery is enlivened by the distant prospect of the sea and the numerous vessels trading to and from the port of Liverpool." Today, trees and buildings completely obscure the view, even from the highest point in the village.

Inevitably, like so many other communities situated near important business and trading centres, things had to change. Upton's catalyst of change was William Inman, a shipping magnate. Inman's influence on the community was such that it is worth while taking a closer look at this exceptional man.

Described by Aspinall, who knew him well, as "a strong Conservative and a man of no ordinary ability", Inman was responsible for the introduction of screw-steamship passenger emigration to America. The Inman Line was, at the time, the leading line in passenger transport to America, Inman himself being responsible for the design of the vessels in the fleet. T. H. Ismay, one of Inman's contemporaries, once remarked that he considered Inman's *City of Rome* one of the handsomest ships afloat.

Inman came to live in Upton Hall in 1855. Two years later he built his own residence, Upton Manor, on the outskirts of Upton near Overchurch. The manor still exists as part of the Upton Convent School, bounded by Moreton Road and the motorway spur. Like several other local buildings, the manor was designed by John Cunningham, architect of the first Philharmonic Hall in Liverpool. It is of Storeton stone.

William Inman changed the character of the area by planting his estate with small woods and coppices, many of which remain and greatly enhance the area. He improved the roads, laid sewers, and replaced some of the older houses with new ones. He established a Free Reading Room and Library in the village, and provided for a new church (the present building) and a new school. His concern for the well-being of his fellow-men is expressed in the words on his memorial plaque in the church, "both in his public life and social relations an upright, generous and just man".

Inman's was not the only estate in Upton in the middle of the nineteenth century. Aspinall gives us a glimpse of life at Upton Hall, home of Squire Webster:

> Squire Webster, of Upton Hall, was a thorough sportsman and a preserver of foxes. He had near his residence many fine covers and plantations with good lying for foxes. Upton Hall was a recognized meet; and breakfast was ready for anyone who chose to call. At Upton Hall, the best spermaceti candles were used, and no candle was ever lighted a second time. Every Saturday Broster, the butter

> farmer of Upton, brought the candles to the Abbey [Birkenhead Priory].

Upton Hall stands in a dominating position overlooking the crossroads, and is now part of the Convent School.

The creation of these, and other estates around the village (at Overchurch, the Salacres, and the Elms) brought employment to the area and this led to an increase in population. Improved transport systems encouraged people to move away from Liverpool and Birkenhead, and by 1911 the population of Upton had reached 1,000. Even so, the influx was not great; photographs of the village taken at the turn of the century show Upton as still a rural community. Dr Pullan, in his history of the parish and church, describes the growth of Upton during this century:

> Through the period between the two world wars the character of Upton changed only slowly. It was becoming a dormitory suburb of an expanding conurbation, and large detached and semi-detached houses were being built. Still surrounded by extensive countryside on all sides, it was a most attractive place to reside in. Expansion continued after the war in 1945 and through the 1950s with the building of small estates and housing developments with smaller detached houses. As the population quickly reached 10,000 new shops, petrol filling stations, schools, and other services became part of the scene. The "village" now existed only in the minds of the people.

It is, perhaps, interesting to note that the main road through the centre of Upton is still "The Village", in name if not reality.

I have in front of me the Outline Plan for Birkenhead, prepared just after the Second World War (Upton was incorporated into the borough in 1933). In those optimistic days it was proposed to develop "Neighbourhood Units" of 8,000 to 10,000 people per unit. The Upton Unit was to be bounded on three sides by permanent open space and on the fourth by the by-pass. A village green was to be the focal point of

Upton, together with the church and the Victory Hall, "to enhance the appearance of the centre and retain the rural atmosphere which now prevails". As I write, bulldozers have just moved into the last of the "permanent open spaces", and the by-pass plans have been shelved yet again! The area for the proposed "village green" is on the main road through the village, forever busy with traffic.

And yet, for all the expansion in building, the loss of fields and hedgerows, Upton retains (or, more correctly, has built up) a sense of community which is uncommon in this faceless age. Perhaps it is the compactness of the village itself – shops, pubs and churches packed closely together; or the social mix of the inhabitants; or Inman's influence which still lingers.

Upton's present church, in a commanding position on the main road, is the third church to have been built for the parish of Overchurch. Each has been built on a different site. The first was a Norman building, which stood at Overchurch Hill, three quarters of a mile from Upton in the direction of Moreton, on the site of an even earlier Saxon building. Overchurch means "the church on the shore" and, hundreds of years ago, would have been an apt description of this part of Upton. It is the highest ground from the present shore-line, and it is not too difficult to picture the waters of the Irish Sea lapping up to here. Not too difficult either to imagine this as an ideal point for early settlers to found a church.

The Norman church was in such a dilapidated condition by the middle of the eighteenth century that it had to be pulled down in 1813. The site of this building at Overchurch remains as one of the wildest, most romantic places in Wirral. Only yards from the busy Moreton Road and motorway junction, and surrounded by housing, these few acres from a bygone age have a fascination of their own. Here you will find moss-covered gravestones lying at all angles, their inscriptions almost illegible. It is an eerie place to be in, alone, at any time of the day, but particularly as dusk is falling and the owls are calling. Make the most of this little patch of history, for the proposed motorway extension is likely to destroy much of the site.

As the Norman church was pulled down, a new one was

erected almost in the centre of Upton, at Greenbank on the Greasby Road, using stones from the Norman building. This second church, built on a site described at the time as "the best and most commanding situation in the township" was referred to as a temporary church, and had seating for only 150. Its graveyard remained until 1973, when a funeral parlour was built over the site. It was during the demolition of the Greenbank church in 1887 that one of the most remarkable finds in Wirral's history was made. Amongst the stones from the original church was an inscribed block of sandstone. The inscription on the stone has been translated as "The people erected this memorial . . . pray for Aethelmund". Who was Aethelmund? A leader, a chieftain, a priest? We do not know. He was obviously a hero of some sort, much respected by his people. The stone dates back to about the ninth century, and is one of the oldest inscribed stones in the north of England, and certainly the oldest in Wirral. The original is housed in the Grosvenor Museum, Chester, but a plaster-cast replica can be seen in the present church.

The parish church of St Mary, Upton, was erected in 1868 to a design of John Cunningham. It too was constructed of Storeton stone, a much paler stone than that from the western side of the peninsula. Young, in 1909, described the church as "modern and uninteresting", but the passage of seventy years has left Upton with a building which is anything but modern, and certainly not uninteresting.

The original entrance under the tower is now rarely used, the main entrance being around the side in Church Road. This new entrance is part of an extension made in 1977 to the original building, which had become too small to cope with a growing congregation, an uncommon situation in these times. Perhaps the main attraction of the interior is the bay-shaped chancel; the finely detailed marble pulpit is worth close inspection, and the church possesses a "Breeches Bible" of 1663.

A short distance along Ford Road from the church, a pair of sandstone gateposts inscribed "The Priory" are all that remain of a large house of the same name formerly used as a vicarage to the church. There is little else of interest in Upton today.

Tucked away in odd corners of the village are small cottages and terraces; but suburban housing predominates.

The main road out of Upton towards Arrowe Park is modern; the original highway was narrow Rake Lane. Where Rake Lane meets the main road a wide belt of waste land cuts between the houses and tower blocks of the Woodchurch Estate. This is the route of the Upton by-pass, first proposed in the 1940s and designed to ease the congestion of through traffic in the village. Looking eastwards, it is difficult to imagine how this part of Wirral looked in 1909, when Young described it as "a pretty country . . . this excellent land, full of good seventy or eighty acre farms all the way between Woodchurch and Upton". For this is now the outer part of a post-war overspill housing estate, a "garden town" which, at its inception, aimed to provide smoke-weary town dwellers with fresh air and elbow room. More than 3,000 houses stretch down the slopes of the Fender Valley from the ancient hamlet of Woodchurch to the motorway along the valley floor.

The original plan of 1944, by Sir Charles Reilly, was for a "village green" layout with the estate divided up into small "communities" each centred around its own green. This scheme was rejected, and in 1946 work began on an alternative layout, the results of which can be seen in the older parts of the estate (along Woodchurch Road and Home Farm Road for example). This "open" arrangement with attractive, varied, cottage-style homes was unfortunately discontinued in 1952, when faceless, repetitive, high-density housing was implemented. Tower blocks came in the 1960s and, coupled with other social problems, heralded the estate's decline. The estate today is an area of contrasts. The older, original parts have matured and are pleasing to look at, the broad lawns lending an air of spaciousness. The later parts are drab, soulless and seem uncared for. Many who left their grimy two-up, two-down terraced homes in inner Birkenhead, with promises of a new start in the wide, open spaces of Wirral, yearn for their cosy, friendly back-to-backs which were, at least, home.

Most of the original village of Woodchurch and its surrounding fields and copses were destroyed during the building of the estate; all that remain are the church, rectory and school.

Even the fine tall elms around the church and its narrow approach lanes have gone, victims not of man but of nature. This site undoubtedly had a commanding view over north Wirral and the Fender Valley before the houses were built. It was also one of the largest parishes in Wirral up to the nineteenth century, containing the townships of Arrowe, Barnston, Noctorum, Landican, Oxton, Pensby, Prenton and Thingwall – a total of 4,820 acres.

I recently spent an evening browsing through the parish registers of Woodchurch. The earliest entry is 1571, and as I turned the pages of yellow parchment I tried to picture life as it was here over four hundred years ago. Hamlets set amidst rolling acres connected only by muddy tracks and field paths; people from the outlying districts of Irby, Prenton, Noctorum, Oxton and Arrowe converging on the church on a warm June evening. People whose livelihoods seem a far cry from the office and factory workers of today: yeomen, millers, shoemakers, wheelwrights, weavers, coopers, husbandmen. But also the paupers and servants – and "a poor man from Chester" who was buried here in 1729. Men married girls from their own or a neighbouring village; not until the later years of the eighteenth century does the name Liverpool appear in the marriage registers – and then only occasionally. Woodchurch slept on in its peaceful backwater until the 1940s and its rude awakening by the building of the estate at its doorstep.

The church of the Holy Cross is well worth a visit. It is old (the earliest part dates back to the twelfth century, although there has probably been a church on this site since Saxon times) and is said to be built on a Druid burial ground. It is therefore possibly the earliest Christian church in Wirral. Whether the parish's name means "wooden church" or "the church in the wood" is uncertain; there is strong supportive evidence for both.

The church is approached through a lych-gate and along a sunken path flanked by yew and holly trees. It seems likely that the wood of the yew was used for making bows and that the deep grooves in the stonework of the outer arch of the porch result from the repeated sharpening of arrows by the archers; a similar example can be seen at Shotwick. The building is of red stone, probably from the quarry at Irby Mill Hill, and is a hotch-potch of architectural styles spanning more than 700 years. It has a twelfth-century nave; a tower, south aisle, and chancel of the fourteenth century; a sixteenth-century porch; and a twentieth-century north aisle. Date stones set in the walls around the church record the different building work over the years. The exterior is distinguished by the tower with its massive buttresses, the one nearest the porch bearing a mass-clock (a kind of church sundial) of the Middle Ages.

The heavily studded oak door set into the porch is at least 400 years old, and has a spy-hole cut into the wood. Inside the church, at the back of the aisle, hang a pair of seventeenth-century bread racks, on which loaves were placed every Sunday for distribution to the poor. The church was evidently aware of its social obligations to the needy of the parish, as the charity board of 1741 indicates. This gives details of the cow, bread, and other charities established for the benefit of the poor by various benefactors – a medieval Social Security?

Do not dismiss the faulty alignment of the chancel as bad workmanship; this could be an example of a "weeping chancel", said to symbolize the head of Christ inclined on the Cross. The rood screen is quite modern (1935), in contrast to the bench-ends of the clergy stalls which are said to be the best examples of medieval woodwork in Wirral, and date from the fifteenth century. The sense of history and antiquity in this fine building is surely heightened by its twentieth-century environment; one wonders if it will weather the next five hundred years as well as the last.

Close to the church are the Rectory (built 1861 but with a cellar surviving from an earlier house and bearing a date stone of 1631), a couple of modern church buildings, and the church school. The first school was founded in 1665; the present buildings date back to 1873, with extensions added since. Recently, the children of the school performed a play based on stories and accounts from school records and the memories of people who lived in Woodchurch at the time of the First World

War. Parts of the play provide a fascinating insight into parish life at that time.

> The ploughing matches at Landican, Prenton, Home Farm, and Arrowe were really exciting events. Remember how the ploughmen used to groom their horses; they brushed their horses' coats till they shone and gleamed in the light, they plaited the horses' manes and tails and hung them with ribbons. And the horse brasses – they shone like gold.
>
> A scheme had been drawn up to use schoolchildren to pick the blackberries for the jam factories in Liverpool. Every Tuesday and Thursday afternoon the school would be closed and we'd set out to pick blackberries. We went all over the place – Thingwall, Barnston, Thurstaston, Prenton, Landican. I think the most we collected in one afternoon was 24 lbs.
>
> The war was hard and we were often reminded of it. There was the day the aeroplane landed in the fields at Landican. Lots of people went to see it. I mean, we'd not seen an aeroplane before, had we?

If Woodchurch is the hamlet which mushroomed into a sizeable community, then its neighbour, Landican, is just the opposite. The only indication that such a place exists at all is a small sign pointing down a country lane off the main Woodchurch Road. At Landican you will find no shops, no church, no inn; only a couple of farms and cottages skirting the lane as it twists and turns towards Thingwall. Yet here is a corner of Wirral steeped in history. The origin of its name is uncertain, although it seems likely that "Lan" is a corruption of *Llan*, the Welsh word for "church". Mortimer is of the opinion that the "dechene" of the "Landechene" mentioned in the Doomsday survey, is the French or Norman word for "of oak". There is no evidence of a church ever having been here, but a priest is mentioned as residing here in the Doomsday survey. Several authorities refer to Landican's importance in pre-Norman days; Mortimer adds: "It is stated to have been, in the reign of the Confessor, more populous and of greater value than any township in the Hundred except Eastham, which far exceeded all the others." Whatever its age and origins, there must be few places in Wirral which have changed as little in recent times as Landican. A local man visiting the place in the early years of this century wrote:

> Landican's most outstanding distinction seems to be its completeness. No brazen-looking new villas start up here thrusting inartistic proportions between the time-toned roofs. Here at least is picturesque isolation. It is very small and very old – far older than the coming of the Norsemen. Seemingly a place without history, and yet not unknown to fear and bloodshed. Tradition has it that a headsman of the sixteenth century claimed at least one trembling victim from Landican.

Perhaps the only significant change this century has been the development of a vast cemetery in the fields between the hamlet and the main road at Arrowe Park.

Several fine field-paths radiate from Landican – another indication of the place's past importance. One meanders down the slopes of the valley to Storeton; another cuts across to Thingwall; and a third, although overgrown in places, emerges at Arrowe Park roundabout. This latter is shown on early maps as a fairly respectable track, and was probably the original route between Landican and Woodchurch.

Originally a township of the parish of Woodchurch, Arrowe ("Well-farmed land") with its park, fields, and woods, is a greatly treasured "lung" for the people of this part of Wirral. There is no village as such, although there is a cluster of houses and shops on the main road at Arrowe Hill. But to most people, the great feature of Arrowe is the park. It was originally the private estate of John Shaw, a wealthy Liverpool warehouse owner, but was bought by Birkenhead Corporation for public use in 1928. John Shaw subsequently left the estate to his nephew, John Ralph Shaw (commonly called "Nicholson" Shaw), High Sheriff for the county of Chester. Aspinall gives us an insight into the character of "Nicholson" Shaw:

> He was devoted to shooting, but I never remember seeing him on horseback. He closely preserved the estate (about 1,000 acres); and planted near the Hall a large and warm pheasantry, with plenty of shelter and good lying. Unfortunately, he made a mistake common to many country gentlemen who favour the strict preservation of game. Believing he could not have foxes as well as pheasants, Squire Shaw did not hesitate to say he would trap or shoot any foxes on his estate. This made him very unpopular. My father wrote young Shaw (as he called him) a strong, friendly letter, advising him to discontinue the destruction of foxes. Squire Shaw replied in an equally friendly spirit and said he would destroy no more foxes.

Subsequently, Mr Shaw held a "meet" at the park, where he gave the hunt breakfast of jugged hare, laid on a billiard table in the hall!

Today we can enjoy the careful planning and hard work of the Shaw family. For on their estate they planted trees by the thousand and erected a magnificent mansion, Arrowe Hall, as their residence. Built in 1835 of local stone, it has been extended several times over the years, and as I write is undergoing further alterations for conversion to a school. Some fine carved oak furniture of 1684, brought from York for Arrowe Hall, is now on display in the Williamson Museum, Birkenhead. With its backcloth of fine trees and a vista of rolling parkland, the Hall is a splendid piece of neo-Elizabethan architecture worthy of protection for future generations.

The main entrance to the park is for pedestrians only, and has a fine set of ornamental gates. They have an intricate design incorporating the arrow motif, the whole being set in sturdy sandstone pillars and painted a tasteful green and cream. From the gates a well-wooded path leads to the Hall through a fine avenue of beech trees. This side of the park has been turned over to golf, bowls and other recreations, but a cinder track leads across the fields to the best part of the estate, alongside the Arrowe Brook. This has its source not far from here, in the fields beyond the park's boundary, and it babbles (like all good brooks) through a pretty wooded valley rich in flowers and bird life. Ferns, bluebells, violets, primroses and campion provide a colourful setting for the brook as it twists and turns through the trees. Kingfisher and wagtail zip along the banks; woodpecker cling to the tree trunks; and grey squirrels scamper teasingly amongst the trees. The brook flows into an ornamental lake, its waters reflecting the pinks and purples of the rhododendrons in spring, and the glorious tints of beeches and horse chestnut in autumn. Here also is one of the only waterfalls in Wirral; seldom spectacular, except after heavy rain, but come on a frosty morning and see the sides of the cascade draped with icicles. Footpaths from this side of the park go across the fields of Arrowe to Irby and Thurstaston, a rambler's paradise.

I have in front of me a book commemorating the Boy Scouts' World Jamboree – *The Quest of the Golden Arrow* – held at Arrowe Park in the summer of 1929. A fascinating, illustrated account of two weeks during which over 50,000 scouts from all over the world came to Arrowe. Why here? Well, the Jamboree was to celebrate the 21st birthday of the Boy Scout Movement's inauguration, only four miles away in Birkenhead, in 1908. And so, for two weeks the park became converted into a colossal camp for the scouts of the world. But after a few days the Jamboree became known as the "Mudboree" for it rained, and rained, and rained. Special raised walkways had to be laid. One Scottish scout was heard to remark cheerfully, "It's a good thing we're no' centipedes!" However, in spite of the mud (or because of it?) spirits remained high. The book states: "It is difficult to feel that the Jamboree would have been anything of a success without that mud!"

The peace and goodwill generated by the Jamboree was amazing; Lord Baden-Powell, the Chief Scout, in his final speech to the 100,000 scouts and visitors gathered together, said,

> From all corners of the earth you have journeyed to this great gathering of World Fellowship and Brotherhood. To-day I send you out from Arrowe to all the world, bearing my symbol of peace and fellowship, each one of you my

The Bridge over the Dell, Port Sunlight

Tam o'Shanter's Cottage, Bidston Hill

The Stonehouse, Upton Village

Arrowe Park gates

Capenhurst Church

St Andrew's Church, Bebington

The Gatehouse, Thornton Manor, Thornton Hough

Thornton Manor

The Old Mill, Willaston

A Summer scene, Wirral Country Park

Hadlow Road Station, Wirral Country Park, Willaston

Eastham Ferry and the Mersey, Eastham Country Park

The Old Flaybrick Forge, Eastham Country Park

> ambassador bearing my message of love and fellowship on the wings of sacrifice and service, to the ends of the earth. From now on, the Scout symbol of peace is the Golden Arrowe. Carry it fast and far so that all men may know the Brotherhood of Man.

To the four corners of the compass the Chief Scout sent four golden arrows of peace and friendship. Swiftly they radiated from hand to hand until they had travelled throughout the nations of the world. A great silence fell. The shaft of the Scout Promise and the Scout Law lived out at Arrowe had transfixed the hearts of the Scouts of all nations.

The park has changed little in the fifty years which have passed since those words were spoken. Its rolling acres, its wood and paths remain. However, by the time these words appear in print, the massive 800-bed Arrowe Park Hospital should be open. Occupying a prominent and commanding site on the highest point around here, the hospital will provide a long-overdue and much-needed replacement for the grim, urban buildings which Wirral patients have long endured. Here, set amidst majestic trees and looking out across the rolling Wirral countryside to the far Welsh hills and the open sea, the hearts of the sick will surely be uplifted and recovery hastened. Let us hope that the effects of such a huge building on the rest of the park are minimal, so that here, where the houses meet the open spaces of Wirral, people may still find the beauty of nature almost on their doorstep.

12

ALONG THE MERSEY BANK

Rock Ferry – Port Sunlight – Bromborough – Eastham – Ellesmere Port

THE Wirral frontage to the River Mersey is in stark contrast to its Deeside counterpart. Southwards from Woodside Ferry stretches a twelve-mile ribbon of industry, commerce and housing, with only a short break at Eastham before the petrochemical industries of Ellesmere Port. The Mersey is for the most part out of sight, for access to the coast is extremely restricted. Yet barely 150 years ago, Liverpool merchants and businessmen looked across the clean waters of the Mersey to the green fields and woods of this Cheshire bank. Liverpool, at the beginning of the nineteenth century, was probably the most congested area in the whole of Britain, its 100,000 inhabitants packed into a square mile of mean streets and alleys. How they must have cast envious eyes on the few lucky enough to be able to retreat to their homes on the Wirral side. Few, though, were willing to undertake the hazardous and unreliable journey across the Mersey. At Woodside, for example, there was a causeway formed of large boulders and logs, but when the tide was out travellers had to wade ashore, or be carried on the backs of the boatmen. Daniel Defoe, in his *Tour Through England and Wales* in 1724, recounts his own experience of the landing:

> This narrow slip of land . . . is called Wirall. Here is a ferry over the Mersee, which, at full sea, is more than two miles over. We land on the flat shore on the other side, and are contented to ride through the water for some length, not on horseback but on the shoulders of some honest Lancashire clown, who comes knee deep to the boat side, to truss you

> up, and then runs away with you, as nimbly as you desire to ride, unless his trot were easier; for I was shaken by him that I had the luck to be carry'd by more than I car'd for, and much worse than a hard trotting horse would have shaken me.

Boats were frail, boatmen reckless and dishonest, crossings infrequent, and in rough weather dangerous. "All Wirral indeed was in those days a kind of Africa, inviting and daring the young Bruces and Mungo Parks of Liverpool to explore it."

It was the steamboat which was to break Wirral's isolation. The *Elizabeth* was the first to be seen on the river, used in 1815 on the service to Runcorn, then a bathing resort. A year later steamships were plying to Ellesmere Port and Eastham, and in 1817 the *Etna* made the first journey to north Wirral, crossing between Queen's Dock and Tranmere. The advertisements were full of promise: "In crossing the river in a calm or in any state of wind or tide, the passage will always be very short, and the inconvenience to passengers and the risk to horses, carriages, etc, which is inseparable from the use of sail boats will be almost entirely removed." In the early years, however, the promise was unfulfilled. The passengers were often tossed about, and frequently had to choose between being half-drowned on deck or half-suffocated near the boilers below. But things gradually improved; in particular, floating landing-stages meant that passengers could embark and disembark without risk at any state of the tide.

As we have seen, Laird's development of Birkenhead provided the impetus for the growth of the Wirral side of the Mersey, and by the middle of the nineteenth century there were no less than ten ferry services connecting Wirral with Liverpool. These were (from north to south): New Brighton, Egremont, Seacombe, Woodside, Monks', Birkenhead, Tranmere, Rock, New and Eastham. Birkenhead Ferry, inaugurated in 1819, was designed to service the fashionable Birkenhead Hotel, near the priory, which became not only a stage-coach terminus but also the headquarters of the Wirral Meet, to which Liverpool merchants came across the river in hunting kit! Monks' Ferry was inaugurated, illegally, in 1838;

it became used specifically by passengers using the terminus for trains on the railway to Chester. Woodside and Tranmere, Rock and New Ferries were almost exclusively used by local daily commuters.

It was inevitable that, in the face of such competition, some of these services would have to close. The first was the Birkenhead Ferry in 1870, followed soon after by Monks' (1878) and Tranmere (1895). The opening of the Mersey Tunnel, and improved sub-river railway services, precipitated the closure of the New Ferry (1922), Eastham (1935), Rock (1939), and Egremont (1940). Today, even the remaining Woodside and Seacombe Ferries are under threat of closure.

As may be expected, the earliest development was alongside the river, but growth was rapid to the south and west until today suburban housing has reached Storeton Hill in Higher Bebington; further south, the railway has formed an effective barrier to the spread of suburbia. Inevitably the older areas have tended to decay as industry has made inroads, and the stretch of New Chester Road through Rock Ferry to Port Sunlight is probably one of the most depressing areas in Wirral.

At Rock Ferry, though, there is access to the river side. Make the most of this half-mile, for it offers a rare prospect of south Liverpool seen, as it were, across a lake. Immediately across the water the terraced houses of Dingle give way to the leafier suburbs of Aigburth, Mossley Hill and Woolton. Downriver, beyond the jetties of the Tranmere oil terminal, the prominent features of the city's principal buildings acquire an unusual perspective seen from here. Upriver the Mersey broadens out towards the flat expanses of Speke Airport.

"The river would be a pleasanter object, if it were blue and transparent, instead of such a mud-puddly hue." Modern-day sentiments perhaps? No – these words were written in 1853 by the American Consul in Liverpool, Nathaniel Hawthorne, who spent his four years as consul living here in Rock Park, just above the promenade. Rock Park a hundred years ago was a fitting place of residence for persons of Hawthorne's rank and station. He himself describes it:

> Rock Park is covered with residences for professional people, merchants, and others of the upper middling classes . . . it is the quietest place imaginable . . . never were there more noiseless streets than those that give access to these pretty residences. On either side there is a thick shrubbery, with glimpses through it of the ornamented portals, or into the trim gardens with smooth shaven lawns, of no great extent, but still affording reasonable breathing-space.

During his four years here, Hawthorne, the prolific writer who studied alongside the poet Longfellow, added to his list of novels and stories. He was obviously very charmed by this part of the world. He recorded thumb-nail sketches of strolls into Bebington, Eastham and other Wirral villages, and paints a vivid picture of a winter's day in Rock Ferry:

> This is the most beautiful day of English winter – clear and bright, with the ground a little frozen and the green grass brightly growing along the waysides at Rock Ferry, and sprouting up through the frozen pools. England is for ever green. On Christmas Day the children found wall-flowers, pansies, pinks, and a beautiful rose in the garden.

Rock Park remained an oasis along this part of the Mersey bank until the early 1970s, when a by-pass was slashed right through the middle of the estate, an unforgivable act of vandalism in the minds of many.

Just beyond New Ferry the traveller is surprised to see a sudden change from run-down shops and grim industrial premises to smart red-brick and half-timbered cottages, of varying styles of architecture and obviously well cared for. This is Port Sunlight, a colourful gem set in this grey industrial hinterland; a garden village born out of one man's vision for a product and the people who make that product.

William Hesketh Lever, later to become the first Viscount Leverhulme, was born at Bolton, Lancashire, in 1851, the son of a wholesale grocer. By the mid-1880s he had begun to specialize in the manufacture of soap, owning a factory at Warrington in partnership with his brother. Right from the start, Lever's product was just that bit better than everyone else's. It was made from vegetable oils rather than tallow; it had a fine lemony scent (to hide the smell of the oils); it was sold neatly wrapped in individual bars; and it had an attractive name, Sunlight. Coupled with a well-organized advertising campaign, the soap sold; so well, in fact, that Lever had to look around for new premises in which to manufacture Sunlight Soap. Hearing of a site near Bromborough Pool for sale at the reasonable price of £200 per acre, he paid the place a visit. He must have been dismayed when he saw the site for the first time, for it was liable to flooding at high tides both by the Mersey and the Pool itself; a wasteland of mud and slime. Yet close by were the great ports of Liverpool and Birkenhead, good rail and road links with the rest of the country; and potential wharving facilities in Bromborough Pool. The merits apparently outweighed the disadvantages, and Port Sunlight was born.

But this was going to be no ordinary manufactory. Lever had had first-hand experience of unplanned industrialization in his native Lancashire. He had seen (and probably experienced) at close range life in the serried rows of two-up two-down terraced houses thrown up around the mills and factories. He had observed the effects of people living in overcrowded conditions, seeing little in the way of daylight, with little or no space to call their own. He now conceived the idea of a "garden village" for the workers – "cottages" pleasing to look at, and comfortable to live in, set in wide, curving roads planted with lawns, trees and shrubs. This indeed would be a Port Sunlight in every sense of the words.

Lever took up residence at Thornton Manor in 1888 (we visit this lovely place later on), the same year as work was begun on constructing the factory. His words on that occasion sum up his hopes and aspirations for the project:

> It is my hope, and my brother's hope, some day to build houses in which our workpeople will be able to live and be comfortable – semi-detached houses, with gardens back and front, in which they will be able to know more about the science of life than they can in a back slum, and in which

> they will learn that there is more in life than the mere going to and returning from work, and looking forward to Saturday night to draw their wages.

High hopes; high ideals. Did Lever's vision work out? Let us take a stroll around this masterpiece of planning and see for ourselves.

The original layout for the village was drawn up by Lever himself; he planned the estate around a series of old channels – tidal inlets from the Pool – with curving roads skirting their edges. Most of these channels were eventually filled in, but one, the Dell, remains, forming an attractive sunken garden.

Most of the cottages are in small groups of between two and ten and the variety of architecture is such that no two groups are the same. Much of the red brick and timberwork reflects Tudor and Elizabethan influences, but the hipped roofs and large corner stones of the Queen Anne style are also evident. Note the variety in the use of materials – rustic brick, half timber, weatherboarding, stone, roughcast rendering, pebbledashing – and the endless variety of doors, windows and chimney stacks. Most of the cottages are complemented by well-tended lawns and gardens, although the stately avenues of elms are sadly depleted. Note the brass plaque on the wall of No. 20 Bolton Road, directly opposite Hulme Hall. This commemorates the visit in 1914 by King George V and Queen Mary who, having been thoroughly impressed by the external appearance of the cottages on the estate, cast doubts on whether their interiors could be as attractive. Without further ado, the Royal pair were shown inside the nearest house – No. 20 – to see for themselves.

Of the public buildings (all of which contribute to the overall beauty of the estate) the Bridge Inn, Gladstone Hall, the Lyceum, the Lever Library, and Hulme Hall are all worthy of inspection. The gem, though, which should be visited by all who come here, is the Lady Lever Art Gallery.

It is unusual to find such an outstanding collection of art treasures as this outside London or the main provincial centres; yet here, housed in a building itself worthy of acclamation, is a magnificent collection of paintings, sculpture, ceramics, furniture, textiles and other fine pieces. The gallery was built by Lord Leverhulme in the years 1914–22 as a memorial to his wife, Elizabeth Ellen, who died in 1913. It is built of Portland stone in the form of a broad-stemmed cross with slightly projecting arms; Ionic columns give the building a sturdy, permanent appearance. Its ground area is said to be greater than that of Westminster Abbey.

Wander around these elegant rooms and marvel at the discerning taste of the donor – Lord Leverhulme himself. The great painters are worthily represented – Constable, Gainsborough, Romney, Reynolds. Marvel at Holman Hunt's *The Scapegoat*; shed a tear over Rivière's *Fidelity*. Study the loving workmanship in the fine furniture in the Tudor and Stuart Room, the Adam Room, and the Early Eighteenth-century Room. The Napoleon Room contains many pieces from the palace of the French Emperor Napoleon I including, it is believed, Napoleon's own bed! The Wedgwood Room houses a beautiful collection of pottery by the great master, together with a fascinating description of the process of manufacture. The colourful collection of Chinese pottery and porcelain offers an interesting contrast to the Wedgwood. A word of advice: do not hurry over the gallery. And come often, for each time you will discover a new pleasure, some detail previously unnoticed, such is the richness of this collection.

Lord Leverhulme died in 1925 and is buried alongside his wife in the village church. The business which he founded, however, continued to grow; in 1929 Lever Brothers amalgamated with a group of Dutch-founded margarine-companies to form the Unilever organization, a worldwide group of companies with interests as diverse as computers, margarine, packaging and frozen foods. Lever started a business which was to become the sixth largest concern in the world. An exceptional memorial to an exceptional man.

Just beyond Port Sunlight, but on the other side of the New Chester Road, the River Dibbin flows into Bromborough Pool. Like Wallasey Pool, the Pool at Bromborough has long been used for industrial purposes. Mortimer described it in 1847:

> A winding branch of the Mersey is also navigable for nearly two miles, at the head of which piers have been built, for the accommodation of small vessels that trade on the Mersey with coals and other materials.

Nestling amongst the industrial complex in the flat expanse beyond the Pool are the remains of the moat which once surrounded Bromborough's original manor house, held by the monks of St Werbergh's Abbey at Chester. Until recently, a seventeenth-century Court House stood in the group of trees beyond the moat, held for many years by the Hardwares, a celebrated Chester family. The site is now criss-crossed by gigantic pipelines carrying chemicals across the Pool; the only evidence of there ever having been a residence here are a few clumps of daffodils and overgrown rhododendron bushes.

At the far end of Pool Lane, sandwiched between the storage tanks and factories, is a small community unknown to most travellers who tear along the busy A41 a short distance away. This is Bromborough Pool Village, or Price's Village, created in 1853 by the owners of "Prices Patent Candle Company" (later to become Price's Chemicals), specifically for their employees. This, one of the earliest planned workers' estates, older even than Lever's, was simple in concept; just a chapel, school, two hospitals and, of course, the houses. The village is much smaller than Lever's – just a few rows of houses – and the architecture quite plain. But the houses were, at the time, considered to be quite outstanding examples of "houses for the workers". They had, for example, an inside toilet – generally unheard of at the time – and a garden; many also had three bedrooms. The whole estate was set in generous open space. There is, I think, something vaguely surrealistic about this nineteenth-century community surrounded on all sides by the sights, sounds and smells of the twentieth-century chemical industry; an impression reinforced by the sight of an Italian-looking ornate clock tower peeping through the pipes and towers of the adjoining works.

Bromborough itself is a growing residential area, surprisingly isolated from the industrial banks of the Mersey by the A41, which also by-passes the town centre. The Birkenhead-

Chester railway line and the Dibbin valley have in the past effectively prevented suburban development from spreading into the rural hinterland, although there are indications that this is being overcome as new houses spring up on the hills overlooking Dibbinsdale.

Bromborough is old, although there is little left as evidence of its antiquity. We know that in 912 King Alfred's daughter, Ethelfreda – "The Lady of the Mercians" – founded a small monastery here. During the Middle Ages, Bromborough must have been one of the most important places in this part of Wirral, for in 1278 a charter was granted allowing a weekly market and an annual fair. These are known facts, which is more than can be said for other stories frequently told about Bromborough. It is said, for example, that this was the site of the great Battle of Brunanburh in 937, when

> Five Kings lay
> On that battle field:
> In bloom of youth
> Pierced through with swords:
> So also seven
> Of Anlaf's Earls.

During this legendary battle, the Saxons under Athelstan defeated the combined forces of the Danes, Irish and Scots, destroying Norse hopes of supremacy in England. Did 30,000 men land on these banks to do battle in the meadows of Bromborough, meadows still called "the Wargraves" today? Or was it at one of the thirty-odd other places which also claim to be the site of that battle? We may never know. Just as we may never know whether St Patrick landed here in 432 to baptize the heathen English at the well in Brotherton Park still bearing his name. It *is* likely, though, that this well gave Bromborough its name – from the Norse Brunbrae meaning "the town of the well or spring".

Bromborough in 1801 had 52 houses and 277 inhabitants – still very much a rural community. It was inevitable that, with the growth of commerce along the Mersey's banks, and improved communications, people should want to settle here.

By the middle years of the nineteenth century, Mortimer was to describe the village as containing "several good houses and possessing an appearance of comfort and respectability beyond many in this part of the hundred". At the turn of the century, its population had risen to over 2,000 and in 1937 the town was incorporated with other villages in the area into the borough of Bebington, a move which has since been regretted by many.

Why have some 15,000 people made Bromborough their home? What is there here that makes it, in the words of one resident, "a pleasant place in which to live"?

As we have seen, the town centre has been by-passed. Traffic is also barred from the main shopping area, a move which, although unpopular at the time, has made shopping a more leisurely and less hazardous affair. A fine new library and community centre adorn one end of the main street, while at the other end, marking the centre of the original village, stands the Bromborough Cross. The time-worn steps are thirteenth century, but the head is modern, a gift from the Bromborough Society to replace the 1874 cross which was stolen in the late 1960s.

Across the road from the Cross, the parish church of St Barnabas occupies a prominent site overlooking the town. Built 1862–4 by Sir George Gilbert Scott on the site of a small Norman church which was demolished in 1828, it is of red sandstone with a square tower supporting an octagonal steeple. The interior is good but not outstanding; outside are the remains of two Anglo-Saxon crosses. On the pavement outside the church, unnoticed by the majority of passers-by, is a large granite boulder brought down from the Lake District by a glacier during the Ice Age.

There are still a few old buildings dotted about the place, although many have been demolished in recent years. The oldest is Tellett's Farm, 1685, now an insignificant-looking building forming part of a row of shops; it has been gutted to house a betting shop. Stanhope House, in Marks Rake, is an attractive three-storey stone building of 1693, narrowly saved from demolition in the 1960s by the action of the Bromborough Society, and restored through the generosity of Mr

Raymond Richards of Gawsworth, Cheshire. And there is Pear Tree Cottage, a quaint two-storey house dated 1699.

The people of Bromborough are fortunate in having, close at hand, an area of great natural beauty. The River Dibbin rises in the mid-Wirral countryside and flows in a meandering course through the woods and dales below Poulton and Spital, to come out at Bromborough Pool. This is Dibbinsdale, an area crossed by paths and tracks where the public can roam at will. Its Bromborough entrance is through Brotherton Park, a gift to the borough of Bebington by Lord Brotherton. Here, below Spital Road, you will find St Patrick's Well, a fresh-water spring with legendary healing properties. Here, too, on the opposite side of Spital Road, was the site of a water mill which worked almost continuously for over 500 years; it was demolished in 1959, but the massive cog-wheels remain, rusting away on the river bank.

Nature-lovers will find something of interest here at any time of the year; I recall a sunny April morning with a north-westerly breeze sending masses of fleecy clouds scudding across a blue sky. In the valley the brook sparkled on its way to the Pool; moorhen stalked amongst the reed-beds, foraging for food; the electric blue of a kingfisher flashed above the water and was gone. In the woods the yellow and green pussy-willows stood out against the still-bare oak trees. The hawthorns were clothed with their fresh emerald-green raiment. A squirrel on the path ahead paused, listened, and scampered up the far side of the nearest tree. The valley slopes were a mass of wood-anemones, their delicate pink and cream heads nodding in the breeze; fresh green shoots of dog's-mercury peeped through the carpet of decayed leaves; the bright yellow flowers of lesser celandine shone like miniature suns in the green banks; and clumps of hart's-tongue fern sprouted out of the sides of a wet ravine.

The track through Dibbinsdale eventually comes out into the fields of Poulton Lancelyn or, as shown on the Ordnance Survey maps, Poulton-cum-Spital. The township of Spital, as its name suggests, contained a leper hospital founded in 1183 and dedicated to Thomas à Becket; Spital Old Hall is built on the site. During the nineteenth century Spital, like

Bromborough, developed as an area of large Victorian houses, the only survivors of which are a few entrance lodges. Mortimer wrote this of Spital in 1846:

> The Spittal estates will probably be soon covered with detached villas, as they are advertised for that purpose, and from their easy distance from the ferries, and the accommodation afforded by the Chester and Birkenhead Railway, combined with their secluded situation and the undulation of the surface, they are peculiarly adapted for the residences of the affluent traders of Liverpool.

The area is now being increasingly built over by residential estates.

Poulton Hall has been the home of the Lancelyn family since the eleventh century at least. They built themselves some kind of castle or fortified mansion at the highest point in the area, near the present Poulton Hall; the earthworks of the original building can still be made out. Poulton Hall was built about 1653 and has been greatly altered and enlarged over the years. It is L-shaped in plan, with pebble-dashed rendering. Amongst the outbuildings is a seventeenth-century brewhouse of brick and stone.

From here, attractive byways lead to Raby Mere and Thornton Hough, places which we shall be visiting in another chapter. Our goal now, though, is Eastham, worlds away from these rural lanes overlooking the Dibbin.

How can you describe Eastham? Unlike Bromborough, and many another Wirral village, Eastham still has a nucleus of old buildings worthy of the name "village"; it was by-passed by the busy A41 many years ago. Yet here is a village surrounded not by fields, farms and hedgerows, but by, on the one side, modern suburbs and, on the other, chemical and oil-storage tanks!

Eastham itself is a mile or so inland from the Mersey shore; in Doomsday it was described as being the largest and most valuable place in Wirral. It has always been a busy place, with nineteenth-century Liverpool-bound passengers passing through on their way to the boats at the nearby ferry, and later when the woods and fields adjoining the ferry became the "Richmond of the Mersey". Yet even during the nineteenth century it remained essentially a rural community. The American Consul in Liverpool, Nathaniel Hawthorne, who visited the place in 1854 on one of his frequent excursions from his home in Rock Ferry, described it as "the finest old English village I have seen, with many antique houses, and with altogether a rural and picturesque aspect. It was not merely one long wide street, as in most New England villages, but there were several crooked ways, gathering the whole settlement into a pretty small compass".

The description still applies, to a degree, but take any of the roads out of the village and you are reminded, with great force, of the twentieth century. Fast roads, houses, and row upon row of metallic storage tanks shatter any illusion of its "rural and picturesque aspect". Even its "village life" is non-existent, as most of the houses of Eastham are on the other side of the murderous A41, where a virtually self-contained community complete with shops, pub and other facilities for present-day living has developed.

The greatest blight on the Eastham scene, the ugly storage tanks – which have almost reached the residents' gardens – are closely linked with the development of the Manchester Ship Canal. This great monument to human skill and ingenuity – both physical and verbal, for it was built only after long-drawn-out wrangles – was opened in 1894 to provide ocean-going ships with easy access to the port of Manchester. It has its massive entrance-gates at Eastham, but this is not the problem. The storage tanks have arisen with the development of the nearby Queen Elizabeth Dock into an off-loading dock for chemicals of all kinds. It is not only the tanks which have made local people see red. In the early 1970s the road tankers used for the transportation of these chemicals – some of them highly dangerous – had to pass through the narrow, twisting roads of Eastham village. Several hundred a day thundered past these old cottages, shaking foundations loose and tearing away chunks of wall. The village made headlines. Now all is quiet again. The tankers have their own road; but the storage tanks remain.

We shall be looking at the history of the old Eastham ferry, and its woods (now a Country Park), in a later chapter; but the village of Eastham is well worth a visit in its own right. Dominating the village group in a setting of fine trees is the church of St Mary, a red stone building with an odd-looking broached spire – a tower surmounted by a spire. The original church was probably built about 1150, when the parish was given to the monks of St Werburgh's, Chester. As it is, the tower and spire are possibly fourteenth century, but the main fabric is the result of a nineteenth-century restoration and alteration. The church is approached through a handsome lych-gate, and in the churchyard is Eastham's famous yew tree. Conservative estimates make this tree at least 1,000 years old; some say it is nearer 1,500. Whatever its age, it is showing signs of decay, and one wonders whether it will survive for many more years. Nearby is a well-preserved sundial dated 1798.

Inside the church are several interesting things to see: a massive sixteenth-century oak chest, a circular tenth-century barrel font; and the shields of three notable Wirral families – the Pooles, the Buertons and the Capenhursts – carved in wood on the panels of the organ screen.

The buildings dotted about the village are interesting, but not outstanding. Some, like the church, are of local stone: the Dower House, 1711, complete with "battle scars" from passing tankers; the old school building, 1851; and Holly Cottage. Many, though, are of rendered or painted brick, and in consequence show the dust thrown up by passing traffic. The village's inns – the Hooton Arms, the Glyder Hotel and the Stanley Arms – remind us that at one time twenty to thirty coaches passed through here *en route* for the ferry.

What does the future hold for places like Eastham, of which there seem to be many in Wirral? Will Eastham, like the other ferry towns along the Mersey's banks – Rock Ferry, New Ferry – be overtaken and completely submerged by a tidal wave of commerce and industry. Or will someone at last say enough is enough?

South of Eastham the village of Childer Thornton survives intact, a quiet backwater of houses tucked away behind the ever-busy A41. Set in fields outside the village, the church, St Paul's, is like an over-decorated wedding cake. This spectacular building was designed in 1858 by James Collins who only a couple of years before had built the fine Albany building in Liverpool city centre. You name it, this church has it – domes, arches, tracery, pyramid roofs, columns, towers – and all in a colourful combination of red and white stone. Alongside the church the entrance to long-demolished Hooton Hall still survives, a semicircle of Ionic columns flanked by a pair of box-like lodges. Beyond is a golf course and Thornton Woods, where squirrel, fox and woodpecker survive, heedless of the encroachment of twentieth-century man all around. For Childer Thornton is at the gateway to Ellesmere Port, a "new town" on the industrial bank of the Mersey.

Ellesmere Port? What, you ask, is there to say about Ellesmere Port? After all, Ellison wrote but ten lines about the place, and those were hardly complimentary. Other visitors too have tended to denigrate the place; for example, "There is probably no town in the kingdom which presents so dull, so gloomy an appearance." Is this attitude justified today? Let's find out.

Ellesmere Port grew from nothing to become the largest industrial town in Cheshire in less than 200 years. Before Ellesmere Port there was nothing. A census of 1801 shows that only 25 families lived in the area, an area represented not by Ellesmere Port as we know it today, but an area of small rural townships or settlements. Ellesmere Port was a product of the canal-building age; an age of speculation and optimism born of the Industrial Revolution. An Act of Parliament was granted in 1793 to build a canal "from the River Severn at Shrewsbury in the County of Salop to the River Mersey at or near Netherpool in the County of Cheshire". The idea was to create a network of waterways linking the Severn, the Mersey and the Dee; such a scheme would, it was said, enable the wares of Shropshire to reach the sea, and at the same time provide better transport for the coal and iron of the Wrexham area and the minerals and agriculture of the Welsh border.

Work was begun on the canal almost immediately and the

first section, which followed the Vale of Broxton to Chester, was opened in 1795 with the name Ellesmere Canal. At the canal's junction with the Mersey, Ellesmere Port was born. Naturally enough, the town's early development was based entirely on the canal. Warehousing and docking facilities, and canal workers' houses formed the nucleus of the town which, despite ups and downs in trade, grew steadily. A popular passenger steamboat service soon became established between Liverpool and Chester, a rival to the Eastham service a few miles down-river.

By the late 1820s, with the prospect of increased trade through the planned Birmingham and Liverpool Junction Canal, the great engineer Telford was invited to design improved terminal facilities at the Port. These were opened in 1843 and included docks, quaysides and warehouses. Much of Telford's fine work is, alas, no more; but many remember the magnificent "Great Warehouse" with its graceful arches. During this period the canal company built many houses for its staff, some of which still stand today. Note particularly four finely proportioned houses near the flour mills in Lower Mersey Street, built in 1835 for the company's senior employees.

The coming of the railway in 1863 was viewed with some anxiety by those with vested interests in the canal, but in fact it had little effect on the volume of trade handled by the port. What *did* affect the port – but in an entirely different way – was the cutting of the Manchester Ship Canal in 1891. This turned Ellesmere Port into a "transport centre" and heralded a new phase in the town's growth. For trade and industry saw in Ellesmere Port an ideal site for the setting up of manufacturing works, with good communications and transport to all parts of the country (and the world) via land and sea, and a large pool of labour over the Mersey in Liverpool. In line with this new era, the town linked up with the nearby townships of Whitby, Overpool, Netherpool, Great Stanney and Stanlow to become an Urban District Council in 1902.

The canal, meanwhile, was still doing well. The canal company, which right from the beginning had played a large part in the development of the town, undertook civil commitments such as the provision of a gas works. Sadly, the First World War resulted in a down-turn in trade (but even as late as 1929 the canal still carried almost half a million tons a year); and in 1958 the Ellesmere Port dock estate was closed down for good. That was not the end of the canal story, as we shall see shortly. But the decline in the canal's trade coincided with the coming of oil refining, and this has developed eastwards along the banks of the Mersey almost to Helsby. Vauxhall Motors came in 1958 and is today one of the area's biggest employers.

So Ellesmere Port today is a thriving town of some 60,000, in Cheshire but of Merseyside, an industrial centre which has spread its tentacles miles outwards from its original nucleus around the canal port to submerge once-rural hamlets, fields, farms and hedgerows, beneath a tide of housing.

The town's modern centre is the former hamlet of Whitby, where there is a very twentieth-century civic centre, shopping precinct and other municipal buildings. There is really little here to dwell on; but by the Mersey, the original port site has been turned into a fascinating boat museum, a place well worth a visit. Here you can see work in progress on boats in the dry dock, trace the history of inland navigation with exhibits of traditional canal boats, painted ware, equipment, tools and documents. The Pump House, once the source of hydraulic power, has been reopened and one of the horizontal hydraulic steam pumps has been restored to working order. The Museum is said to contain the largest collection of historic canal craft afloat in Europe. From here too is a fine view of the Manchester Ship Canal and the Mersey as it sweeps around to Runcorn, the huge arched road bridge being clearly visible, with the higher land behind Helsby and Frodsham beyond.

In the near distance, though, industry predominates, particularly at Stanlow, the heart of the area's petro-chemical refinery. Stanlow itself is an island in the Mersey, cut off from the mainland by the Ship Canal. Before the oil came, this was a bleak place – "a scene of comfortless desolation", surrounded by barren marsh. Small wonder then that the Cistercian monks, an austere order which tended to choose lonely situations for the abbeys, founded an abbey here. Its founder was

John de Lacy, Constable of Chester, who built the abbey in 1178 shortly before setting off for a crusade in the Holy Lands from which he never returned.

How the monks must have regretted de Lacy's choice! The Gowy empties into the Mersey here, and the surrounding marsh was regularly flooded when the river was high and the Mersey rough. The abbey was almost destroyed by gales and floods in 1279, and further catastrophes caused them to move, in 1296, to Whalley Abbey in Lancashire, although a small cell remained here at Stanlow. The only remains of the abbey today are a few stones and foundations, and this lovely poem written by an unknown monk from Stanlaw, as it was known then:

> Stanlaw! where I hope to lie
> When my hour shall come to die,
> Hard thy lot and brief thy fame
> Still thou teachest by thy name –
> STAN and LAW together blending
> Name all neighbour names transcending.
> LAW is hill – I lift my eyes
> To the hills beyond the skies.
> STAN is stone – O! Corner Stone!
> What art thou but Christ alone?
> Altar stone, on thee there lies
> That blest Bread of Sacrifice.
> Stanlaw! 'tis the Lord above
> Gave thy name to tell his love.

The first oil dock was built here in 1916–22, but the big expansion started in 1949. Now the island's docks handle over five million tons of oil products each year. Miles of pipelines connect the giant oil tankers which berth at the island to the main refinery complex on the mainland. Living amidst this space-age landscape are several families; they have their own ferry service, their own fire brigade and police force. There are no cars, and smoking is prohibited on most of the island. It is a weird place yet, amazingly, it is a sanctuary for wildlife! Stanlow looks out across the broad Mersey mudflats, and is a favourite resting place for a great variety of birds.

As I have said, Ellesmere Port has spread its tentacles, and once-rural villages are now just part of the outlying suburbs. Westwards the Suttons, Little and Great, straddle the A41, their contrast with former times quite amazing. Just over fifty years ago a traveller described Little Sutton:

> Little Sutton is not a noisy place. Beyond the rattle of an intermittent train little disturbs the peace of the village except the clank of milk-cans in some paved dairy yard, the querulous murmur or drowsy poultry, the snip of the shears in some cottage hedgerow, or the high-pitched conversation of the cottagers as they stake and tie young fruit trees in preparation for the loud tempests and the wrath to come.

In an earlier stage still, before the establishment of the Chester and Birkenhead Railway, these streets resounded to the sound of the stagecoach *en route* from Chester to the ferry at Eastham or Birkenhead. What, I wonder, would those travellers of a bygone age think of these places if they could pass through today?

13

THE RURAL HEART OF WIRRAL

Bebington – Storeton – Brimstage – Thornton Hough – Raby – Willaston – Capenhurst – Ledsham

THE "borough" of Bebington occupies a large chunk of the eastern side of the Wirral Peninsula, extending from Birkenhead's southern suburbs right down to Eastham. It is an area of sharp contrasts: an industrial waterfront, which we have already described, mixed suburbs, and picture-postcard villages. It includes some of Wirral's richest agricultural land, and some of its best-known beauty spots. Its urban areas are remarkably well defined so that, once clear of the streets and houses and into the green belt, the countryside can be enjoyed with the knowledge that there is no ugly factory lurking around the next bend.

Bebington itself occupies only a small part of the borough, and is an almost wholly residential area. The map shows two Bebingtons – Lower and Higher – but to all intents and purposes they are now one. Older maps show Bebington as an area of small hamlets with quaint names – Primrose, Woodhey and Trafalgar – but these too have disappeared, their only memorials being in street names. A writer has recently described the town as "lacking in character" yet at the same time "open, green, and wholesome". Pick a sunny day in May, when the cherry blossoms are in flower and the suburban gardens are at their best and I think you will agree.

Yet the suburbs have not obliterated *all* traces of Bebington's past. Dotted about the place are unexpected links with another age. The Puzzle Stones, for example. These stones, now incorporated into the wall inside the Mayer Park, were originally part of the Two Crowns Inn by the old Chester road in Lower Bebington. Each has the inscription in the form of a riddle, the first being:

My name and sign is thirty shillings just
And he that will tell my name shall
have a quart on trust
For why is not five the fourth
Part of twenty the same in all cases?

The solution:

Name:	Mark	i.e.	13s 4d
	Noble		6s 8d
Sign:	Two crowns		10s
			30s 0d

or Mark Noble, of the sign of the Two Crowns.

The second riddle stone has the following inscription:

Subtract 45 from 45
That 45 may remain.

The solution:

  987654321 (=45)
− 123456789 (=45)
  864197532 (=45)

Another stone was apparently used a lot by loafers, and the inscription was for them:

AR
UBB
I
NGS
TONEF
ORAS
SE
S

The last stone:

From six take nine,
From nine take ten,
From forty take fifty,
Then six will remain.

And the answer?

S I X = S
I X = I
X L = X

The stones were cut by an eccentric villager, Thomas Francis, who lived in Bebington about 150 years ago. Francis was one of those rare but much-loved characters who add a little spice to local life. As well as the puzzle stones, he erected a crazy brick turret with battlements and miniature cannon. And he gave dinner parties to the gentry, only to serve up a few cockles or a roast sparrow as the *plat du jour*! When I last visited the puzzle stones, I noticed that the inscriptions were weathering very badly, and it can only be a matter of years before they are almost completely illegible. Shouldn't these invaluable relics of Bebington's past be safely installed under cover in a local building or museum before it is too late?

Another local personality, but of a completely different kind, was Joseph Mayer, a Staffordshire man who retired in Bebington after having made his fortune as a Liverpool merchant. He came to love the place so much that he erected a free library and museum, stocked from his own collection of books, prints, paintings and sculptures. He also gave Bebington a small park behind these buildings, still called the Mayer Park to this date.

St Andrew's Church, Bebington, is a lovely old church. It is built of local Storeton stone, and it is this which probably caused it to be called the White-church in its early days. It has Saxon foundations but, like so many other Wirral churches, has been altered and enlarged many times over the centuries. There is much to see in and around this fine building; a list means little, so go and see for yourself. Several legends surround this church. It was originally intended to build the church at Tranmere, but it seems that each night the stones were moved in some mysterious way to the present site, and as it was thought unwise to argue with such supernatural agencies, the church was erected here.

The other legend concerns a prophecy by Robert Nixon, a celebrated Cheshire poet and prophet:

When that spire's vane shall clasp
Ivy with its fatal grasp,
Then the last stern trumpet's call,
Live and dead shall summon all.
Then shall hap the crash of doom,
Then the dead shall burst the tomb,
Together crushed the world shall roll,
Like the parched flame-shrivelled scroll.

Much has been said and written about this prophecy. Perhaps the best are the verses, complete with Moral, written by Mr Egerton Leigh:

Many years since then have passed,
Still the world and spire last;
Nor yet the ivy's fatal grasp
Dares the fatal point to clasp.
Once it almost reached the height,
Filling Cheshire with affright;
When the lightning's scorched blast
Through the threatening ivy passed.
Twice since then in utmost need,
Chance hath baulked the ivy's greed;
Still the tendrils seek the sky,
Struggling towards the spire on high.

Moral:
May our hearts to heaven rise,
Then we ne'er shall fear surprise;
E'en should the ivy top the spire,
And the doomed world wrap in fire.

It would seem that local people are not willing to leave the outcome to chance, for the ivy has now been well and truly cut away!

Village Road in Higher Bebington has some attractive-looking cottages evidently dating back to the days when the nearby quarries were in full production. The tramway serving the quarries wound its way down to Bromborough Pool about here; the only evidence today is in the name Quarry Avenue, which was built along the line of the old tramway.

Let me quote you a description of one part of Bebington some seventy years ago. The area concerned is Peter Price's Lane, a roadway still in existence but unrecognizable from this description:

> This has the appearance of an occupation road for some yards, but it soon takes you between a towering thicket, whose beauty of branch and leaf is so luxuriant that it deserves a better title than merely "Peter Price's Lane". Spreading sycamores, graceful ash trees, and stunted oaks throng in on either side, while rising to meet them is every conceivable manner of briar and bramble known to Cheshire wildness. . . . Under the gnarled boughs are glimpses of half-hidden pools as you follow the narrow pathway, and the odour of gorse and bracken goes with you all the way.

Many first-time visitors to Wirral express surprise – and delight – that so much of the peninsula is rural. Although much of the northern and eastern parts are heavily built over, a wide wedge-shaped slice of agricultural land stretches from Landican southwards to the outskirts of Chester. Within this area mixed farming is carried out on land which, although classified as being only of "medium quality", provides many a farmer with a living. Scattered about this rural, gently indulating mid-Wirral landscape are small communities whose inhabitants still largely live off the land, and where the invasion by "commuter housing" – thanks largely to the Green Belt policy – has been minimal. A network of twisting lanes, bridleways and field-paths links these villages with each other and with the urban areas to the east and west, offering the walker and cyclist unlimited opportunities for exploration and relaxation.

Storeton, the most northerly village in the group, is situated on a slight eminence at the confluence of no less than five roads, four footpaths and a "causeway". The last-mentioned is one of a network of long, straight, tree-lined avenues (most of which are prohibited to traffic) radiating from Thornton Manor. They were the work of Lord Leverhulme during the early years of this century, and total about six miles in all. Storeton village is a hotch-potch of old and new, the old being brick and sandstone cottages of local character, the new being two-a-penny twentieth-century houses. Most of the older buildings are constructed of stone from the long-disused quarries on nearby Storeton Hill. Note the difference in colour between this grey stone and the rich red stone from the western side of Wirral.

The remains of fourteenth-century Storeton Hall are now incorporated into a large farm complex, Storeton Hall Farm, which stands at the highest part of the village. All that remain of this once-great Hall, built about 1360, are the grey ivy-covered walls and gable end of the great hall. Yet this was the first Cheshire home of a family, the Stanleys, whose descendants were destined to play so large a part, not only in the history of Wirral, but in the history of England.

There used to be a racecourse at Storeton. This was a steeplechase course of about 2½ miles which ran towards Barnston and back. Lodge Farm was built as a hunting lodge with an outside verandah from which guests of the Brocklebank family, who owned the course, could view the races. The marks where the verandah used to be can still be seen on the building.

This seems a fitting place to mention that trademark of Wirral, the Wirral Horn. The story of this almost legendary horn goes back to about 1120 when Ranulf II, fourth Norman Earl of Chester, granted one Alan Sylvester "Stortun and Pudican, in fee and heredity to him and his heirs, for his service, to wit for half a Knight's fee and I will and decree that he have and hold the said townships with all appurtenances, in wood and in the open and everywhere, freely and honourably and quickly". This, in effect, was an official appointment of Alan Sylvester as master-forester of Wirral, an appointment confirmed by the presentation of a forester's horn as his badge and title of office. The Horn has been carefully handed down from generation to generation, and is today in the possession of the third Earl of Cromer. Would it be too much to ask that this fine token of Wirral's history be put on permanent public display, for the people of Wirral to see? The only Wirral Horns to be seen today are the sandstone replicas on many of Wirral's older station buildings – New Brighton and Birkenhead North, for example.

A narrow lane, hewn out of the sandstone, cuts across the fertile plain beyond Storeton to Storeton Hill. This is a wild area of pine trees and brambles criss-crossed by numerous footpaths where the public can freely roam. Its proximity to a large urban area is, however, evidenced by the vast amount of rubbish indiscriminately dumped in the undergrowth. One can only wonder at the mentality of people who deliberately desecrate these areas of potentially great beauty in this way. The extensive quarries which used to scar a large part of the hill have now been filled in, but in their day they provided characteristic pale grey stone for many of the buildings on this side of Wirral, and further afield too. London, Colchester and Ireland are but a few of the places boasting buildings constructed of Storeton stone. A hundred yards or so down Rest Hill Road on the way to Storeton you can see evidence of the Storeton Quarry Railway which carried the stone down to Bromborough Pool for export. The two worn railway lines sticking out of the tarmac at the side of the lane, and the old stone sleepers set into the wall near the Traveller's Rest inn, are all that remain of this once-busy branch line, possibly the first in Wirral, built in 1837 of lines from the original Liverpool-Manchester railway.

It is likely that Storeton stone has been used since Roman times, for among the Roman remains in Chester Museum are several sculptured stones fashioned from Storeton stone. Amongst the relics is a monument of a Roman centurion, set up by his freedman and heir, Aristio, thought to date from about A.D. 44.

Many fossils were discovered during excavations in the quarries. Ellison describes them:

> The discovery in 1838 of the footprints of the Cheirotherium, a long extinct animal, in the Higher Bebington quarries brought them international fame. Whenever the "footprint bed" was reached, the slabs containing the prints were carefully cut out and eagerly acquired by museums all over the world.

Cheirotherium was a dinosaur-like creature who left his giant footprints on this once muddy shore; the prints were dried by the sun and filled by blown sand. The sand eventually became sandstone, and the footprints remained as "plaster casts", hidden for millions of years until nineteenth-century man brought them to light. Some fine specimens can be seen in the Williamson Art Gallery and Museum in Birkenhead, and locally at Christ Church and in the Victoria Hall, Bebington.

A pleasant by-way from Storeton Hill wends it way down to Brimstage, passing beneath the M53 motorway. Brimstage, or Brunstath as it is referred to in ancient records, was the original settlement of the Domvilles, "a house of high consideration among the gentry of Cheshire". The holding passed to the Hulse family with the marriage of Margery Domville, heiress, to Sir Hugh Hulse, Sergeant of the Bridge Gate at Chester. Although the setting of the village is quite pleasant, with its "green" and babbling brook, the only building worthy of mention is Brimstage Hall. Study the Ordnance Survey map and you will see here the word "Tower" picked out as an antiquity, one of the few in Wirral. And this particular tower, part of Brimstage Hall, is indeed ancient. When it was built is not known, but we do know that in 1398 Sir Hugh Hulse and Margery obtained a licence to build an oratory – a small chapel or place for private worship – at their residence in Brimstage. Evidence seems to suggest that this was in the base of the tower, which must therefore make it earlier still. Several writers have suggested that the tower is all that is left of a larger, fortified stronghold of some kind, but Pevsner and Hubbard are not so sure:

> Neither is there reason to assume that the structure forms a fragment of a much larger building. It does appear to have extended further, at least at the E. end, where the present external wall has obviously been much altered, but the building has every appearance of having been a tower house, i.e. a compactly planned fortified dwelling of the pele-tower type.

That it was a defence system of some sort is obvious: it is set on a slight eminence and, without the trees which surround it today, would have commanded far-reaching views. It has slit windows for archers, and provision for molten lead to be poured down upon attackers; and there seems to have been some kind of moat around the site.

The building adjoining the tower is more recent; its exact date is not known. It might be worth mentioning, in passing, that in part of the garden near the tower, several bodies have been found, laid out in a regular pattern which suggests that the ground was at one time used as a cemetery.

The Hulse family retained possession of Brimstage until 1440, when Margaret, the only heiress, married Sir John Troutbeck, Chamberlain of Chester. Sir John fought against the Earl of Salisbury in the Wars of the Roses and was killed, with two thousand others, in the Battle of Blore Heath in 1459.

Young, in his *A Perambulation of the Hundred of Wirral*, an account of Wirral life seen through the eyes of a travelling writer during the early years of this century, recounts the following tale:

> Brimstage is known in Tranmere as "the three mile limit" for, crossing the fields from Tranmere and passing through Higher Bebington, and over the fields to Brimstage, entitles you to be called by the high-sounding name of "A Traveller", and you can demand reasonable refreshment at closed hours. A country man who gave me this information said, "I'm fond of a glass of beer myself, but I'd be damned if I'd walk three miles for it."

How things have changed! In these days of high-speed travel, you would have to have travelled from Timbuctoo before a local would look twice at you! And besides, there is no inn in Brimstage now; the Red Cat was demolished in the 1930s.

Wherever you may be in Wirral, you will never be far away from public footpaths; and this part of the peninsula is particularly rich in them. Several lead southwards from Brimstage to the next of our mid-Wirral villages, Thornton Hough. Alternatively, there is a pleasant tree-lined by-way, and it is this which we shall take today, for by so doing we shall get as near to Thornton Manor as we are able.

When William Hesketh Lever, the first Viscount Leverhulme, came to Wirral in 1887 to set up his new soap factory at Port Sunlight, he undoubtedly wanted a residence for himself well away from the sight and smell of his product. A large early Victorian house just outside the hamlet of Thornton Hough caught his eye; set in acres of rolling countryside, yet just a short journey from his business, here was the ideal retreat for an up-and-coming tycoon. Lever moved into Thornton Manor in 1888, renting it at first, and bought it outright in 1891; from then on he altered it, added to it, and generally transformed it into a grand neo-Elizabethan stately home. Inside, he furnished it with his much-loved art treasures; outside he laid out gardens, woodland walks, and lakes. The result survives today, still the home of a Leverhulme – the third Viscount, Lever's grandson. Go, if you can, on one of the manor's open days. In May, when the blossoms are in full flower and bright fresh greenery is reflected in the rippling waters of the lake. Or later in the year when the trees are turning to gold and the falling leaves carpet the woodland floor. At any time, admire the picturesque half-timbered entrance lodge, with its finely detailed carving, framing the statue in the middle of the gravelled courtyard.

I have just heard that part of the Lever collection is to be shown in London; amongst the items on view, and of particular interest, is the Augustus John portrait of the first Viscount Leverhulme. A brief account of this controversial painting might not be amiss here:

> Some time after Leverhulme died, his grandson discovered the head of the Augustus John portrait folded in the back of the safe at Thornton Manor. He had never seen it before, indeed, any mention of the portrait within the family circle was forbidden by his grandfather. The portrait head was framed and put on display at the Manor and in due course brought to the attention of Sir Gerald Kelly of the Royal Academy. At Kelly's suggestion, the Viscount with some

misgivings about the effect of a letter signed "Leverhulme", wrote to John to ask him if by chance he had the rest of the picture. The response was a charming letter from John saying that far from being bitter enemies, he and Leverhulme had parted friends. John promised to look for the "body" but nothing more was heard. It was only in 1950 when the "head" was hanging in the Royal Academy Exhibition that the "body" was rediscovered by John and his wife, after they had visited the Exhibition. The picture was restored and John paid for the restoration bill to make up for past grievances. It now hangs in Thornton Manor.

Beyond the manor on the road to Thornton Hough, other fine buildings catch the eye: Copley, a sandstone house in the Gothic style, and Hesketh Grange, built in 1894 for Lord Leverhulme's father. These, though, are but a prelude to the village itself, several times winner of the Best Kept Village competition. Can this be the same place as that described by Mortimer less than 150 years ago?

> Most of the land is of very indifferent quality, which indeed may be said of the whole parish. The entire township abounds with rock . . . presenting a very unpleasant appearance, and though it possesses a few tolerably good houses, the greater portion are of a very inferior description.

Before Lever came and transformed the place, Thornton Hough was just another Wirral hamlet, with a handful of decaying and insanitary dwellings. It was mentioned in Doomsday Book as Torintone, and was held by one Roger de Thornton in Edward II's time. De Thornton's daughter married Richard del Hoghe, whose name was later added to that of Thornton.

Joseph Hirst, a Yorkshire textile manufacturer, was the first to do anything with Thornton Hough. He built the parish church, the adjoining vicarage and former school, and built for himself a fine residence, Thornton House. But it was Lever who was to transform Thornton Hough into the place we see today. Using some of the architects from Port Sunlight, he turned the hamlet into a model estate village of character and charm. Farm workers were given half-timbered cottages beside a broad village green. He built a smithy (complete with spreading chestnut tree), a school, a village club, and a shop. Last of all, in 1906, as a crowning glory, he erected a church, now generally considered to be one of the finest "modern" churches in Wirral. This he built in the purest Norman style, sparing no expense. Existing Norman work in many parts of the land was carefully studied to ensure accuracy. Such was Lever's desire for authenticity that special plain glass was commissioned for the windows, at great cost. Admire this fine building, the brain-child of a grocer's son from Bolton. Examine the intricate carving inside; stand beneath the covered entranceway outside. Pevsner and Hubbard summed it up: "Very thorough and costly"; true words, indeed.

Hirst's church, in comparison, is rather ordinary. It was built in 1867 of the red stone which occurs throughout the village. Apart from the attractive stone reredos, the only other interesting feature is the additional clock set in the east side of the steeple. Hirst apparently could not see the original, lower clock face from his bedroom window, so he had another placed above it! Hirst himself lived in Thornton House, the white house opposite the primary school. Lever got hold of this, too, and reconstructed it in 1895 for his brother.

The amazing thing about Thornton Hough is that it has hardly changed since it was built; it has, if anything, improved as the buildings have mellowed over the years. It really is a gem set in the rural heart of Wirral.

It is but a short distance from here to one of the most popular beauty spots in Wirral – Raby Mere. Some of my earliest childhood memories are of summer days spent picnicking by the waters of this, one of the few lakes of any size in the peninsula. In those days, the woods round about here were carpeted with bluebells; few have survived years of constant uprooting by thoughtless townsfolk. Take a tip: if you want to see Raby Mere at its best, come mid-week or at evening time. Then you can linger in the leafy glades, the background of bird-song uninterrupted by the roar of car and motor-cycle.

The builder is making rapid inroads into the open spaces on

the Bromborough side of Raby Mere, and the mid-Wirral motorway passes close by the other; yet the village after which the mere is named sleeps peacefully on, relatively undisturbed by twentieth-century life. The village of Raby is, surprisingly, some two miles from Raby Mere. It is not so much a village as a group of farms, for it has neither church nor shop. It *does* have, however, one of the most picturesque inns in Wirral – the Wheatsheaf. This is an old inn, dated 1611, and thatched, with some half-timbering. But do not expect to find local farmers and yokels propping up the bar, passing the time of day over a well-earned pint; for this is the haunt of the evening motorist from the suburbs. Young reminds us of the real function of these country inns in times past:

> Probably you will refresh, and pay, and travel on, thanking your lucky stars that you have not to sleep there; but there was a time when to sleep under that roof would have been counted a great luxury, and many a tired traveller in those far-off days has drawn his breath more easily on beholding its lights, knowing that inside he would find supper and a hearty welcome.

Across the way from the Wheatsheaf, by a tiny white thatched cottage, is the start of a pretty path which passes between high hedges rich with foxgloves and honeysuckle. This path eventually passes through Cherry Wood and comes out on the lane to Willaston.

Willaston was one of the first places in Wirral to be colonized by the invading Anglo-Saxons during the seventh century. Such was its importance that it gave its name, as Wilaveston, to the whole of the peninsula or Hundred; but it was not until the thirteenth century that the name Willaston appeared. Whether the so-called Wirral Stone a mile or so from the village at the junction of the Willaston and Chester High Road has anything to do with the place name or not is uncertain. Some say that the stone was part of the Roman system of topographical measurement, a kind of milestone; others, that it marks the old meeting-place of the Hundred. I go for the less romantic theory that it was some kind of mounting-stone, which fits in with its step-like appearance and its position by the main Chester highway. That there was at some early date a stone of some kind at or near Willaston seems fairly certain; in fact some folk say that the "Wirheal-stone" itself lies buried under the road near the Old Red Lion Inn in the heart of Willaston.

It seems fairly certain that, because of its central location in the peninsula, Willaston has been an important centre since Saxon times, and probably earlier. The village's green (it was considerably larger than it is now) may have begun life as a Saxon meeting-place, functioning later as the meeting-place for the Hundred. The earthworks in a field north of the village may be the remains of a Saxon burial ground. And did the Romans pass through here *en route* from Chester to the north Wirral coast? Certainly their way must have passed somewhere near here, and a metalled surface has been identified by excavation at Street Hey, to the east of the village.

After the disafforestation of Wirral, Willaston became the centre of a thriving agricultural area; in 1831, 38 of the 48 families living here were living off the land, and a large sheep and cattle market was held regularly. A hundred years later Willaston's population had grown to 1,300, and it has almost doubled again since then. Yet, despite its growth and the influx of commuters, Willaston retains much of its rurality. True, the old farm buildings dotted about the village now serve as shops, banks and private houses – but a short walk in any direction will bring you to "real" farms and fields.

Willaston's focal point is the village green with its ancient buildings, the oldest dating back at least to the sixteenth century. I have not the space here to describe all the buildings in and around the village in detail; a few points of particular interest must suffice. A recently created waymarked Village Trail takes the visitor to most of the buildings and points of interest round and about Willaston; an imaginative idea, and one which could well be copied by other Wirral villages.

Ash Tree Farm, now a private house, was originally a sixteenth-century (or earlier) timber-framed wattle-and-daub building; during restoration work carried out a few years ago part of a cannon ball was found embedded in one of the old timber frames, suggesting that they possibly came from a wreck off the Wirral coast. Corner House Farm, at the south-west corner of the green, boasts a recently discovered ingle-nook fireplace and a cellar with its own well. The black and white timbered building next to Corner House Farm is the old Red Lion Inn, mentioned so often in nineteenth-century guide books as a place offering warm hospitality. This sixteenth-century building began life as a private dwelling, but was converted into an inn at the beginning of the nineteenth century. It remained a popular focal point in the village for a hundred years; it served as a kind of news-room before the days of T.V. and newspapers, a place where villagers came to take their ale and learn the latest news. The building was left in a state of disrepair for over thirty years until it was restored as a private house. It may seem strange that such a land-locked village as this should have maritime connections, yet fishing-boats for the Parkgate fishing industry were built at the Red Lion in the days before it was an inn.

Like all good Wirral villages, Willaston has its old hall. This is a red-brick three-storey building, thought to be seventeenth century, with three bay windows projecting from the front to form a symmetrical E.

One of the landmarks of this part of Wirral is the old windmill, down a lane north of the village. This is a fine example of a tower mill, and was built in 1800 as the successor to several mills on the same site. This tower mill was one of the largest of the Wirral mills, and was in constant use right up to 1930 when a storm destroyed the sails. The story is still told of the Willaston miller who had a reputation of being one of the most efficient in the country; he had the corn cut and threshed in the early hours of the morning, immediately ground it and made it into bread, and had it delivered to London the same night! The mill is in excellent condition (minus sails) as a private house.

As I look around Willaston today and see the smart new houses, well-fed and well-clothed families, I cannot help but recall Young's description of life in this village nearly a hundred years ago:

> The standard wage paid to a good farm-hand is 18s per week, and the best hands receive 20s. But their rents have advanced considerably of late years; cottages which formerly rented at 2s 6d per week now command 4s and 4s 6d – a large slice out of the 18s, on which, however, large families are brought up in some hardship, but in most cases in great respectability.

To most people Capenhurst is synonymous with atomic energy, and indeed this vast establishment with its innumerable cooling towers is overpowering. The village itself, though, is a neat little place, still predominantly agricultural, and with several features of interest well worth seeing.

The church was built 1856–9 and is of sandstone; its pagoda-like wooden tower, with lych-gate to match, is certainly unusual in this part of the country.

A short distance from the church, on the same side of the road, is the old pound or pinfold. This is a square sandstone enclosure whose origin goes back almost a thousand years to Norman times. In this enclosure, under the care of a pound-keeper, domestic animals were kept, usually for debt, until they were redeemed. It was the practice for the creditor to seize the cattle of anyone who owed him money, and drive them into the pound, where they were kept at the owner's expense. The pound was also used for retaining stray animals; they were kept here until any damage caused was paid for by the owner. Sounds like an idea worthy of revival today!

Ledsham is a village in name only, for all there is here is a cluster of farms and cottages. Yet this is an old place; it is mentioned in Doomsday and, like Capenhurst and Willaston, may be on the course of the old Roman highway from Chester.

Hooton is best known as the start (or finish) of the Wirral Country Park, and that is the subject of the next chapter.

14

THE COUNTRY PARKS

Wirral Country Park – Eastham Country Park

WIRRAL is fortunate in having within its relatively small area two Country Parks, each with its own unique atmosphere and flavour. I fell in love with the Wirral Country Park years before its official designation and, like many others, return time after time to discover something new to interest and excite me.

Do not be misled by the term "Park". In these parks you will find no bowling-greens or tennis courts, no trimmed edges or flower beds, no "Keep off the grass" or "Gates shut at sunset". What you *will* find are hedgerows and honeysuckle, estuarine sunsets and rolling landscapes, glow-worms and ghosts of trains long since gone.

Many times in the past the people of Wirral have benefited from the foresight of a few; but for their determination and action the hills of Bidston, Thurstaston and Caldy, the open spaces of Dibbinsdale and Arrowe Park, would now be covered by houses. The designation of the two Country Parks has assured their safekeeping for future generations – generations which will need the parks' facilities and treasures far more than we can imagine.

The Wirral Country Park

The Wirral Country Park has the distinction of being one of the first in the country to be recognized as such following the Countryside Act of 1968. The Wirral Green Belt Council (a body active on all matters of local countryside conservation) was among the first to recognize the potential of the course of the former West Kirby to Hooton railway, and in 1969 Cheshire County Council (backed by the Countryside Commission) started work on converting the track. The park was officially opened on 2nd October 1973 by Lord Leverhulme, Lord Lieutenant of Cheshire. I well remember walking the route one dreary March day in 1969 and, up to my ankles in mud barely a mile out from West Kirby, having passed through rubbish tips and overgrown bramble bushes, wondered if it was possible to do *anything* with this "outsize ditch", let alone make it into a country park.

But let us go right back to the beginning of the route's history, over a century ago, when in 1847 an Act of Parliament was passed giving authorization for the construction of a railway line between Parkgate on the west Wirral coast, and Hooton four miles inland. Parkgate's popularity as a resort in the first half of the nineteenth century accounted for the railway's terminating here, but the coal workings at Neston Colliery would also have benefited from its construction. The terminus at Hooton was on the Birkenhead-Chester line. This first section of line was opened in 1866, but was extended along the Wirral coast to West Kirby in 1886. For over twenty years the line prospered, linking the small agricultural communities of west Wirral with Chester, Birkenhead and Liverpool, and bringing townsfolk to the seaside resorts on "cheap day excursions".

Here is a glimpse of those times:

> The busiest train from Heswall was the 8am which easily caught the 8.40 boat at Woodside Ferry and so most businessmen used this train. The railway company considered the train to be important enough for a "club" carriage to be attached to it. This was a LNW coach fitted with armchair seats and bridge tables. All the dignitaries used this, schoolboys like myself were packed into the third class carriages. The corresponding busy train returned from Woodside at 5.50 and was usually crowded. It was a great sight to see a busy train arrive at Heswall. On the bridge, and in Riverbank Road, there would be at least six horse-drawn cabs and as soon as the train branched out of the cutting the drivers would stand up on their boxes and wave their whips to attract custom!

Thereafter the line's story is one of decline. The seaside resorts silted up, the colliery closed, but above all, the motor car became established as a popular means of transport. The opening of the Mersey Tunnel in 1934 provided commuters and trippers with an alternative to the railways, and the heavy losses suffered by the Hooton-West Kirby line could result in only one thing – closure. The last passenger train ran on 17th September 1956, although goods trains used the track until 1962. The hardware was removed in 1965, leaving only the grass and brambles to creep across the chippings and reclaim what was originally theirs.

To the walker today, the railway's past is continually present. The chippings underfoot form a constant reminder of the route's original purpose. Hidden in the undergrowth at the side of the path the diligent searcher will find gradient posts; old platforms and sidings now serve as picnic areas and car parks; whilst almost every section has its smoke-blackened bridge under which the rain-drenched walker can shelter. And it is rumoured that in the dead of night the whistles of long-forgotten trains echo through the cuttings and red tail-lamps disappear into the darkness. . . .

The park today reflects the enormous amount of work put in by Cheshire County Council and the team of Rangers. Rubbish has been removed, drains installed, trees planted, fencing, signposts and picnic tables erected, and car parks unobtrusively laid out. A first-class visitor centre at Thurstaston caters for the user's every need. And all is totally in sympathy with the landscape. The ongoing work of repairing fences, trimming bushes, conserving wildlife is, rightly, virtually unnoticed by the majority of people who use the park.

The Wirral Way (as the pedestrian route is called) can be walked as a complete twelve-mile stretch, but shorter, circular walks have been made possible by the use of associated footpaths and tracks which connect with the Wirral Way. Many sections of the park have a route for horse riders parallel with the pedestrian way, helping to ease the problem of horses churning up public footpaths.

The main route can be walked in either direction, but my preference is to start at Hooton rather than West Kirby. Walking in this direction offers the attraction of the ever-widening Dee opening out into its glorious estuary. Start out early afternoon, to arrive at Caldy and West Kirby just as the sun is setting over the estuary, and take away memories not readily forgotten. The walk in the opposite direction is good, but the dreary prospect of the industrial zone beyond Burton marshes is less than uplifting.

The wooden steps leading down from the roadway at the start of the walk, at Hooton, are the original steps to the old station platform. A section of this platform still exists as the first part of the walk, and its peaceful setting amidst a canopy of greenery is in marked contrast to the modern station and railway only a few yards away. The sounds of Hooton's factories are soon left behind as the way curves around a seemingly never-ending bend to Heath Lane bridge. This is the first of many such bridges carrying roads, lanes and paths across the former railway. A straight section follows, looking across open countryside, but the path soon enters a cutting which leads to the parking and picnic areas of Hadlow Road station on the outskirts of Willaston. Glow-worms have been found in the long grass along this section, their bodies shining in the fading light of summer evenings.

Hadlow Road is the only station in the park to have retained its original platform buildings. These have been lovingly restored to their original appearance in the early 1950s, complete with the Brooke Bond Tea and Bovril signs common at the time. Milk churns await collection on the platform, in front of which railway lines add a touch of realism. Step inside the Waiting Room, and you are transported back to a bygone age. Everything is just as it was on a typical working day in 1952. The Ticket Office is so realistic that the visitor almost finds himself asking at the counter for a return ticket to West Kirby! Ticket racks, date stamps, oil lamps, and the associated paraphernalia which only railway offices can accumulate, all are here; not neatly laid out for display but cosily untidy. Even a fire burns in the gate. All that is missing is the sound of the train approaching the platform . . . but perhaps the plaque on the wall outside can help to make even that a reality:

> Stop a moment, and imagine. It is 1952. The train will soon be in . . . you hear its whistle, faint on the wind. Behind you, business men and shoppers on their way to the city move aside for a porter pulling a trolley load of mail and country produce. From inside comes the sound of jingling coins and the thud of the date stamp as the clerk issues tickets. A late-comer rushes on to the platform as the train steams in.

It would have taken but thirty minutes to reach West Kirby from here by train; the walker still has another four to five hours' walk ahead, so it is best not to linger here too long.

Shortly after leaving Hadlow Road Station, the hum of traffic along the A540 Chester-Hoylake road gradually increases, but the way goes under this busy road. This section passes through the grounds of Leahurst, the University of Liverpool's Veterinary Research Establishment, and was originally closed to the public. However, a right of way was successfully negotiated, and we must thank the Leahurst authorities for allowing this. I well remember the detour that had to be made, ending with a hair-raising dash across the A540!

The short stretch between here and Cuckoo Lane is, to my mind, one of the prettiest in the park. Raised on an embankment, the path passes through a stretch of woodland, alive with bird-song and fresh greenery in spring, and the home of many woodland birds – long-tailed and marsh tits, woodpecker and jay. Wild strawberry plants line the sides of the path, their ripe fruits a source of pleasure in summer. The wooden bridge across Cuckoo Lane was constructed in 1969 across the original sandstone abutments by the 106 (West Riding) Field Squadron Royal Engineers.

The Lees Lane picnic area with its 'mod. cons." is reached soon after leaving the woodlands. The ponds here (formerly disused marl pits) are a rich source of water life. This area was a rubbish tip when taken over for the park, and much of the underlying ground is infilled rubbish.

The approach to Neston is probably the most spectacular section of the park. For three-quarters of a mile the way is along the floor of a deep rock cutting, its dripping sandstone walls green with ferns and mosses. In summer the cutting is a grotto, overhung with a canopy of leaves and branches; in autumn the October sun filters through the golden leaves, setting the red sandstone glowing as if on fire. Now a nature trail, it was proposed to fill the cutting with Neston's rubbish, hence the raised concrete manholes. Go very early on a bright morning in spring, and be thankful that this unique piece of Wirral was saved at the last moment as a sanctuary for nature.

From the end of the cutting the walker emerges into Neston's suburbs, for houses have been built over the site of Neston Station, one of only two breaks in the continuity of the park. A short walk along Station Road, across Burton Road (where the stone abutments of the original railway bridge across the road can be seen), and the peace of Wirral Way is soon regained. This contrast between the way and its surroundings in the urban areas is a striking feature of the park. Beyond the hedges and shrubs which line the path, all is twentieth-century noise and bustle; within, all is quiet, the green way stretching invitingly ahead.

The section between Neston and Parkgate gives the walker his first glimpse of the Dee and the hills of Wales, which will keep him company off and on for the rest of the walk. The path curves gently round towards the coast, and just before the sandstone bridge at Moorside Lane, the observant walker should be able to see the spot where the colliery branch line left the main route.

The Parkgate picnic area is situated on the site of the original terminus station, part of the old platform still being visible in one of the picnic bays. The sidings here were used by the goods trains taking coal from the Neston Colliery and fish caught off Parkgate; the red-brick house in Station Road was the station master's house. The walker has to cross the Parkgate road here (resisting the temptation to take the alternative walk along the old quay wall), regaining the Wirral Way by means of a cobbled path. This is the site of the second station at Parkgate, built when the line was extended in 1886, and of which only the concrete roof of the subway and some foundations remain.

The way continues northwards, skirting Parkgate's back gardens, crossing another wooden bridge erected by the army and similar to the one at Cuckoo Lane crossed a few miles previously. The route soon enters a deep cutting at Boathouse Lane bridge, where large anthills skirt the path at the foot of the cutting's slopes. Birds love this section, and many kinds can be seen pecking at the anthills. As the cutting opens out on to Heswall Golf Course, neat boundary signs mark the transition from the County of Cheshire to Merseyside. This open stretch to Gayton gives fine views of the marshes bordering the Dee, which can be gained by an access path which crosses the Wirral Way. In the other direction the golf course stretches luxuriantly up the hillside to its clubhouse, set amidst woodland. A short cutting ends in a picnic area on the outskirts of Heswall, and modern houses form an abrupt barrier across the way.

The terraced cottages a short distance from the picnic area were once homes for the railway staff who manned Heswall Station, which was situated here near the junction of Davenport Road and Station Road. Half a mile of suburban road walking breaks the continuity of the path, for houses were built across the track before the route's designation as a park. The path is regained at a cutting beyond the houses, and the brief contact with Heswall is soon forgotten. The slopes of this cutting are luxuriant with vegetation which hides the buildings above, only access gates indicating their presence. The cutting opens out on to an embankment and, if the way's proximity to the coast has been forgotten during the last mile, it cannot be forgotten for the next two and a half. Sky, sea, hills and fields combine to give the walker an ever-changing landscape. Nearer at hand, bridges and other railside remains are a reminder that engines once steamed along this route, towards West Kirby and the setting sun. Away up on the hillside on the right, the ravine of the Dungeon, clad with greenery of beech, oak and sycamore, forms a distinctive scar (the Dungeon can be reached by taking the footpath leading off the Wirral Way on the right of the track).

The sandstone tower of Thurstaston church nestling in the trees a little further on heralds the "hub" of the entire park.

The Thurstaston Visitor Centre is approached from this direction between sewage tanks on one side and a camp site on the other. This alone should be enough to encourage the serious walker to pass quickly through without stopping. But this is no "entertainment centre". Attractive buildings, well-planned nature trails, exhibitions, guided walks, film shows, attract hundreds from Merseyside's towns on fine Sunday afternoons. Overflow car parks often cannot cope. Grassy picnic areas give direct access to the cliffs and shore. The Centre is indeed the "honeypot" it was intended to be, relieving other popular spots of the pressure they have suffered over recent years.

The Visitor Centre is laid out around the site of Thurstaston Station, the platform of which still remains, preserved in remarkably good condition. Cars now park where sidings once echoed with the rattling of goods wagons. The site is a mile from the village it served; the owner of Dawpool Hall in Thurstaston village objected to the proposed railway's proximity to the hall, and so the line was laid nearer to the coast. Modern-day visitors should be thankful for Ismay's protestations, for the Centre's location atop the cliffs is surely its main attraction. The grassy area between the main buildings and the shore was an army gunsite during the Second World War, protecting Liverpool from foreign raiders. I suspect few of the children (or grown-ups) who play up and down the "bonks" here realize that gun emplacements lie buried beneath their feet!

But do not linger here today; return on an afternoon in early January, when the gales are whipping the waters of the estuary up the cliffs and you can barely stand upright. You will find no one else here; only the sky, the sea, the wind; and the prospect of returning home to a warm room, a cosy fire and a mug of soup.

Before you leave to continue along the way, take a look at the memorial plaques set in stone outside the Visitor Centre. Read, and be thankful for the vision of Captain Beswick, who was dedicated to "the conservation of the countryside in Wirral and Cheshire and his association with the concept of the Wirray Way".

It is but two and a half miles to West Kirby, and the section to Caldy is for the most part in a shallow cutting, giving occasional glimpses of the Welsh hills across the golf course which sweeps down to the estuary. The picnic site at Caldy marks the beginning of the end of the way. Cubbin's Green, just beyond the picnic area, is the last open space before suburban West Kirby is reached. Stand on top of the cliffs hereabouts, and watch the sun sink behind the Hilbre Islands. The hills on the far side of the Dee are already studded with lights twinkling in the gathering dusk. The broad waters of the estuary are grey and unfriendly. Turn inland, back on to the path which now cuts behind West Kirby's houses right into the town's heart. West Kirby's sidings are no more; a massive leisure complex occupies the site, and gives the walker a rude re-entry into twentieth-century Wirral.

The Wirral Country Park is an achievement of which the people of Wirral can be proud. It has gone from good to better; let us ensure that, as it reaches its best, it remains untamed, unspoilt, natural. Who knows? In fifty years' time it might be a twelve-mile ribbon of greenery set amidst brick and concrete.

Eastham Ferry Country Park

As we have seen, the Wirral Country Park is based on a redundant transport system – a railway line. The Eastham Ferry Country Park is also based on a redundant transport system – the Eastham Ferry. But any similarity ends there, for whereas the Wirral Way is a park predominantly in the country, the Eastham Park is almost the only piece of "country" left on the commercialized Mersey bank of the peninsula. Its 76 acres of woodland and open space are a buffer between the docks, factories and power stations stretching northwards to Wallasey, and the oil and petro-chemical installations lining the river bank southwards to Ellesmere Port and beyond.

The Eastham Park is a strange place, an area of vivid contrasts. The approach by road from Eastham village is unenticing, the predominant feature being oil storage tanks. Even in the park itself, glimpses of the nearby power station and oil tankers entering the Manchester Ship Canal remind us of the age in which we live. And yet, in spring when the soft light filters through the delicate green foliage of the beeches, when bluebells carpet the woodland floor, industry and commerce are a world away. A fox slinks through the undergrowth showing little concern for the planes flying low to land at nearby Speke Airport. The ceaseless chattering of the woodland birds overshadows the hum of the power station. And it needs little imagination to picture the ferry as it was nearly 500 years ago. . . .

It is thought that there was a ferry service of some kind here as long ago as 1509. It was called Job's Ferry, and was some 300 yards north of the present jetty; the steps used by the passengers still exist in the cliffside, but are hidden from view. The monks of St Werburgh's Abbey were responsible for the ferry from early times, and for many years it was an important service for passengers travelling to Liverpool from Chester and further afield. At the height of its operation, some thirty to forty coaches a day brought passengers and goods to meet the boats going to Liverpool; and three boathouses were needed at Liverpool to house the Eastham boats.

Job's Ferry became known as Carlett Ferry about the end of the eighteenth century, and Eastham Ferry a short time after. About this time the first steam vessel was introduced, cutting the journey time down from eight hours or so to about an hour. Even so, the journey must have been a terrifying ordeal for travellers not used to the sea, as shown by the following account written in 1829 by a traveller from Chester:

> We were now within a few yards of Eastham, from which place we were to proceed to Liverpool by steam-boat. I was much terrified at the appearance of the water, which coming to the coachman's ears, he assured me that there was not the least danger, and promised to lend me a cork collar which, in case of accident, would carry me safely to the destined port. I was much pleased at this instance of kindness in the coachman, and determined to reward him with an extra shilling, but when we were about to embark, I found he had been hoaxing me, and not wishing to encourage the im-

pertinence of coachmen at the inn, determined to proceed no further till tomorrow.

By the middle years of the nineteenth century the number of travellers had declined, with the introduction in 1840 of the Chester-Birkenhead railway. The ferry service continued, however, as day trippers discovered the delights of the extensive woods, fields and beaches in the ferry's vicinity. Three new paddle steamers – *Ruby*, *Pearl* and *Sapphire* – were commissioned in 1897 and ran until the service ended in 1929. People came to Eastham in their thousands on Sundays and holidays. The Eastham Ferry Hotel was built in 1846 by Sir Thomas Stanley, and with it zoological gardens containing lions and tigers, monkeys and bears. Side-shows provided amusements of every kind – Blondin, the French acrobat and tightrope walker performed here – and the place became known as "the Richmond of the Mersey". Alas, by the end of the First World War weekend drunks and rowdies had given the place a bad name and its popularity waned. When the ferry service ended in 1929 the area was left to deteriorate.

The ferry stood derelict until the coming of the petro-chemical industries after the Second World War. Storage tanks took over green fields. Woods were chopped down. In 1970, as a contribution to European Conservation Year, the ferry and remaining woods were designated a Country Park. The ferry area was rebuilt and smartened up; car-parking facilities were provided; picnic areas created; a nature trail established. The park is now a much-valued and greatly used amenity for the people of Wirral. There is much to see. Let us take a look around.

The focal point of the park is the old ferry area itself in front of the Ferry Hotel, a large three-storey house. The small building on the green in front of the hotel is the old ticket office of 1857. The jetty which formed part of the old iron pier now makes an excellent viewing area. Note especially the "end-on" view of Liverpool Cathedral; the brightly painted houses across the Mersey at Cressington and Grassendale, once the homes of wealthy Liverpool merchants; the planes and runways of Speke Airport; and the wide sweep of the Mersey as it swings round towards Runcorn, the top of the arched bridge just being visible on a clear day.

A cliff-top path leads to Job's Ferry. The nature-lover will be quick to spot dunlin, redshank, oyster-catcher and curlew on the rocky shore at low tide; mudflats are the feeding ground of a large variety of bird life, including shelduck, mallard and heron.

In a neat courtyard by the Visitor Centre an old forge has been re-created, using original equipment from the forge at Flaybrick, Bidston.

Many paths criss-cross the woods behind the ferry area. Whichever path we choose, we will find something of interest. Note the fine trees; mainly beech, oak, birch and chestnut, but with one or two less common specimens here and there. I understand there are thirty kinds of tree in all. Wild flowers – wood sorrel, wood anemone, violet, lesser celandine, bluebell and foxglove – thrive on the damp, shady woodland floor; and in the autumn many kinds of fungi are to be found pushing up through the carpet of decaying leaves. Of the 200 different kinds of birds seen here, we will undoubtedly see the more common ones – jay, tree-creeper and wren; we may, if we are lucky, see an owl, woodpecker or partridge. Of the animals, foxes, rabbits, hares, weasels and voles have all been seen hereabouts, but exceptional care and patience is required to see any of these elusive creatures.

Before we go, we must visit the Rhododendron and Azalea Dell, near the Ferry Hotel. These were originally part of the zoological gardens, and the old deep bear pit and monkey cages can still be seen, together with some decorative fountains.

Eastham Park is, perhaps, an appropriate place in which to end this book; like the peninsula itself, it has its history, its maritime connections, its open spaces and woodland, its wild-life; and a future. A future which is dependent not only on those who manage and administer the place, but equally on those who live, work and play here.

BIBLIOGRAPHY

Although by no means comprehensive, this list of works may be of some help to those who wish to undertake further study of specific aspects of Wirral.

General Works

Portrait of Cheshire, David Bethell, 1979
Across the Fields of Wirral, Andrew Blair, 1932
Wirral Fieldpaths and Byways, Andrew Blair, 1945
The Beauty and Interest of Wirral, C. W. Budden, 1921
Romance of Wirral, A. G. Caton, 1946
A Tour Through England and Wales, D. Defoe, 1724
The Place Names of Cheshire, J. Mc.N. Dodgson, 1970
Cheshire, R. N. Dore, 1977
The Wirral Peninsula, Norman F. Ellison, 1955
'Twixt Mersey and Dee, Mrs Hilda Gamlin, 1897
Companion into Cheshire, J. H. Ingram, 1947
Notes on the Old Halls of Wirral, W. Fergusson Irvine, 1903
Merseyside: Facts and Figures, Audrey Lees, 1974
Legends and Ballads of Cheshire, Egerton Leigh, 1867
The Rambler, M. O'Mahony
History of the Hundred of Wirral, W. Mortimer, 1847
History of the County of Cheshire, G. Ormerod, 1819
The Verge of Wales, W. T. Palmer
The Buildings of England – Cheshire, N. Pevsner and E. Hubbard, 1971
The Old Wirral Railway – Some Recollections, John Reney-Smith
The Hundred of Wirral, P. Sulley, 1889
Roman Cheshire, F. H. Thompson, 1965
King's Vale Royal, William Webb, 1616

Geography of Merseyside, H. E. Wilkinson, 1948
A Perambulation of the Hundred of Wirral, H. E. Young, 1909
Anglo-Saxon Chronicle
The Cheshire Sheaf, 1878–96
Transactions of the Historic Society of Lancashire and Cheshire, 1849–1950
Wirral Local Studies Group Publications
Wirral Notes and Queries, 1892–3

Local Works

The World Jamboree 1929 (at Arrowe), The Scout Association, 1929
Birkenhead and its Surroundings, H. K. Aspinall, 1903
Birkenhead 1877–1974, County Borough of Birkenhead, 1974
Auld Lang Syne, H. Neilson, 1935
Birkenhead Official Handbook, Birkenhead Corporation, 1971
Outline Plan for Birkenhead, C. Reilly and N. J. Aslan, 1947
Birkenhead Priory and After, W. F. Bushell, 1950
A Ramble Round Burton, R. Norman Jones, 1978
The Dee Estuary – A Surviving Wilderness, Dee Estuary Conservation Group, 1976
Wings Across a Wilderness, V. McFarland and B. Barnacal, 1978
Eastham Woods Trail, Borough of Bebington
A Guide to the Parish Church of St Mary, Eastham
Eastham Country Park, Department of Leisure Services, Wirral Borough Council
Ellesmere Port – Canal Town, Adrian Jarvis, 1977
St Peter's Church and Parish, Heswall, Revd Canon Kenneth Lee, 1979
Ancient Meols, A. Hume, 1863
The Mersey Estuary, J. E. Allison, 1949
Fort Perch Rock, New Brighton, N. Kingham, 1978
North Wirral Coastal Park: the Old Gun Site Picnic Area, 1979
This is Parkgate, G. Place
Emma, Lady Hamilton, Mollie Hardwick, 1969
A Stroll Through Parkgate, Parkgate and District Society
Wilfred Grenfell: His Life and Work, J. Lennox Kerr
The Lady Lever Collection, Port Sunlight, 1974

The Story of Port Sunlight, Lever Brothers, 1953
The Church at the Ford, Shotwick, Lavinia Whitfield, 1974
Thurstaston, F. C. Beazley, 1924
Historical Guide, Overchurch Parish and Upton Township, W. G. H. Jones, rev. Dr R. A. Pullan, 1979
The Rise and Progress of Wallasey, E. Cuthbert Woods and P. Culverwell Brown, 1929
The History of Wallasey Grammar School, Maurice Eggleshaw
West Kirby and Hilbre, J. Brownbill, 1928
The Story of the Churches of West Kirby Parish, A. R. Myers, 1973
Willaston's Heritage, E. C. Bryan
Wirral Country Park Walker's Guide, Cheshire County Council
The Wirral Railway, Campbell Highet, 1961
History of Woodchurch, B. H. C. Turvey, 1954

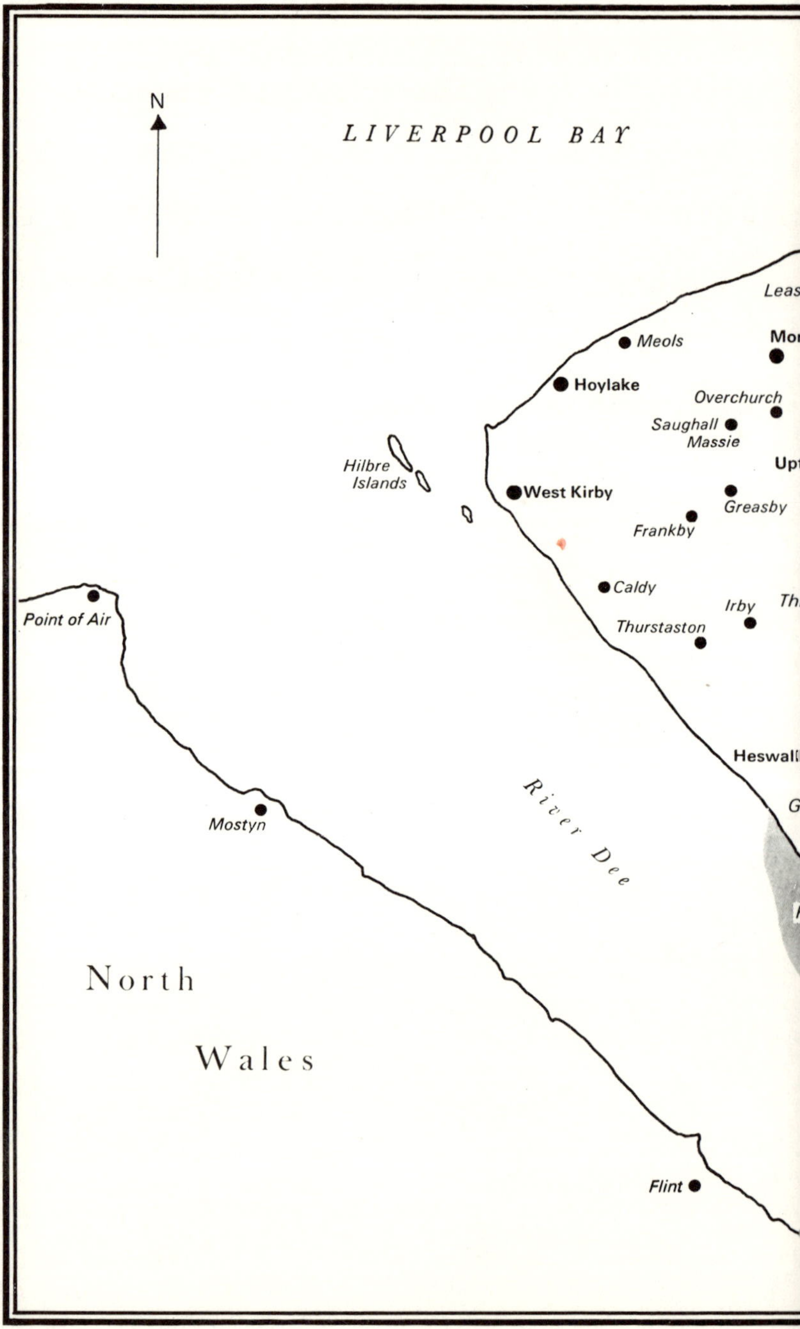
N
LIVERPOOL BAY
Meols
Hoylake
Overchurch
Saughall Massie
Hilbre Islands
West Kirby
Greasby
Frankby
Caldy
Irby
Thurstaston
Point of Air
Heswall
Mostyn
River Dee
North Wales
Flint

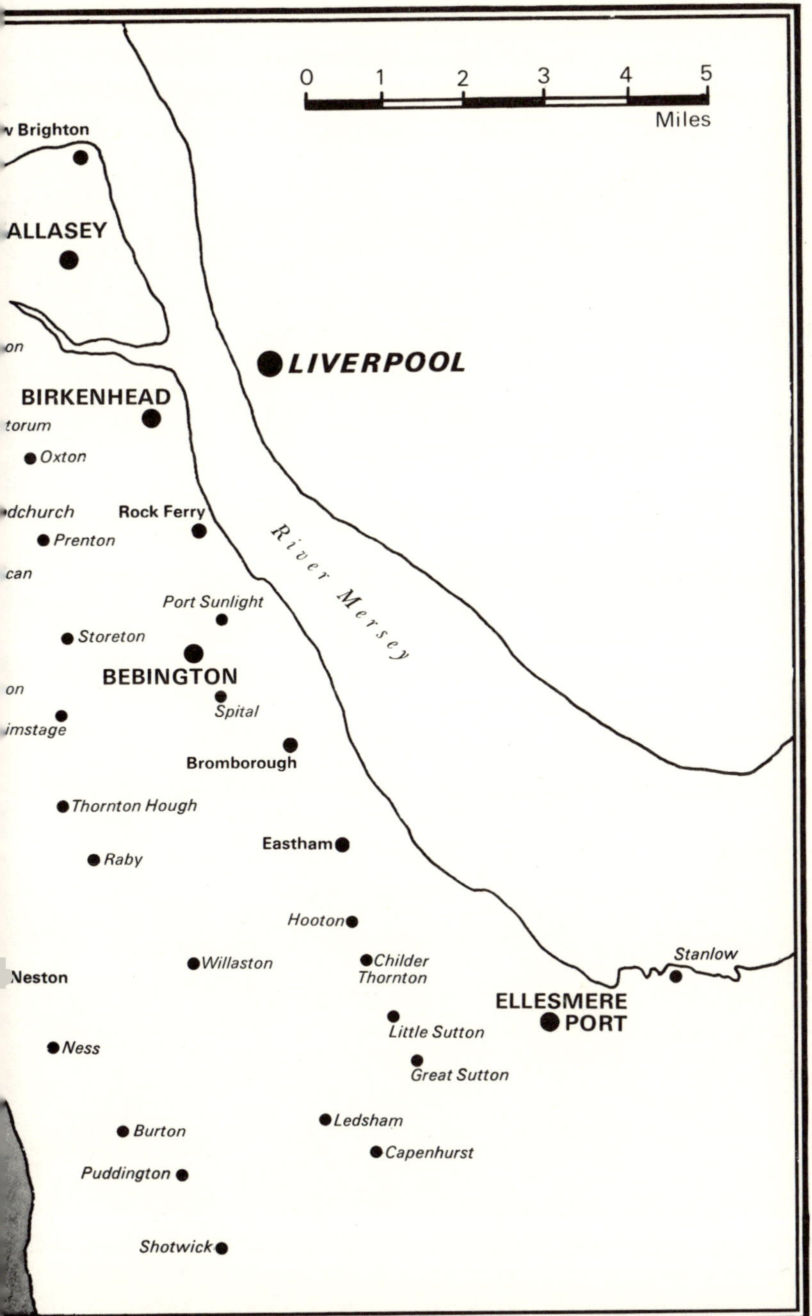

0 1 2 3 4 5
Miles
v Brighton
ALLASEY
on
BIRKENHEAD
torum
Oxton
dchurch
Rock Ferry
Prenton
can
LIVERPOOL
River Mersey
Port Sunlight
Storeton
BEBINGTON
on
Spital
imstage
Bromborough
Thornton Hough
Eastham
Raby
Hooton
Willaston
Childer
Thornton
Stanlow
Neston
ELLESMERE
PORT
Little Sutton
Ness
Great Sutton
Ledsham
Burton
Capenhurst
Puddington
Shotwick

INDEX